'Beautifully written, full of enthusiasm and passion, packed with information, with an overview on how to run ecotherapy sessions and including detailed descriptions of lots of activities. If you are not already interested in the subject you soon will be.'

Jochen Encke, worked for many years with torture survivors on allotments

'[This book] highlights the huge benefits to mental well-being from engaging with green environments and taking part in ecotherapy activities. Havering Mind have seen over many years the positive effects of nature on mental health distress via our green walks, horticulture project and restorative garden. Spending time in the natural world is good for all of us.'

Vanessa Bennett, CEO, Havering Mind

'Research suggests that modern urban environments can have negative effects on mental health whilst contact with green spaces can have positive effects. This timely book, drawing on wealth of research evidence, is an excellent guide to the theory and practice of ecotherapy. It deserves to be read by researchers, practitioners, trainers and students.'

Dr David Harper, Reader in Clinical Psychology, Programme Director (Academic), Professional Doctorate in Clinical Psychology, University of East London

With
Nature
in Mind

THE ECOTHERAPY MANUAL FOR
MENTAL HEALTH PROFESSIONALS

Andy McGeeney
Foreword by Lindsay Royan

With grateful thanks to the following for permission to use their work:
- White Pine Press (www.whitepine.org) for permission to use the Seng T'san poem translated by Richard Clarke
- Mind for permission to use Table 4.1

First published in 2016
by Jessica Kingsley Publishers
73 Collier Street
London N1 9BE, UK
and
400 Market Street, Suite 400
Philadelphia, PA 19106, USA

www.jkp.com

Library of Congress Cataloging in Publication Data
Names: McGeeney, Andy, author.
Title: With nature in mind : the ecotherapy manual for mental health professionals / Andy McGeeney ; foreword by Lindsay Royan.
Description: London ; Philadelphia : Jessica Kingsley Publishers, 2016. | Includes bibliographical references and index.
Identifiers: LCCN 2015043012 | ISBN 9781785920240 (alk. paper)
Subjects: LCSH: Environmental psychology. | Nature, Healing power of. | Nature--Psychological aspects. | Mental health.
Classification: LCC BF353.5.N37 M345 2016 | DDC 615.8/515--dc23 LC record available at http://lccn.loc.gov/2015043012

British Library Cataloguing in Publication Data
A CIP catalogue record for this book is available from the British Library

ISBN 978 1 78592 024 0
eISBN 978 1 78450 270 6

Printed and bound in Great Britain

FSC
MIX
Paper from responsible sources
www.fsc.org   FSC® C013056

To Rowan and future generations, in the hope they all gain a deeper connection to nature.

Wood Rides

Who hath not felt the influence that so calms
The weary mind in summers sultry hours
When wandering thickest woods beneath the arms
Of ancient oaks and brushing nameless flowers
That verge the little ride who hath not made
A minutes waste of time and sat him down
Upon a pleasant swell to gaze awhile…
Who hath not met that mood from turmoil free
And felt a placid joy refreshed at heart

John Clare (1793–1864)

Clare, England's greatest nature poet, experienced prolonged periods of emotional distress in his troubled life. One quality he is admired for is his acute observation of the natural world.

Contents

Part 2 Evidence: A review of the effectiveness of nature on our health and well-being

Part 3 Activities

Foreword

In a world that seemingly embraces ever-increasing noise and haste and is enamoured with technological advances that promote virtual worlds, there is a counter-movement: one that recognises our essential quality as a part of nature. This movement invites us to reclaim our place in the universe, to remind us that we are organic relational beings who influence, and are profoundly influenced by, the natural world. 'No man is an island, entire of itself... Any man's death diminishes me, because I am involved in mankind,' wrote John Donne in the seventeenth century. We forget this at our peril. Our separation from nature is no less than a separation from ourselves, leading to a sense of disconnection, loss and loneliness. This dis-ease with ourselves and our surroundings can provide the foundations for mental distress and disorder. Ecotherapy, which can be considered to be part of the counter-movement, does not claim to 'cure' mental disorder but it can provide the route back to greater connection, sense of self and peace of mind.

I first encountered ecotherapy some 11 years ago when I met Andy on a working group setting up ecotherapy projects in local green spaces. I had previously worked with horticultural therapists and had witnessed the benefits to people with mental health problems of working with plants and soil. However, it was soon clear that ecotherapy could incorporate but also go beyond horticultural work in helping to restore well-being. It was acquiring an evidence base that demonstrated positive outcomes for people presenting with a range of mental health issues. Ecotherapy is a defined intervention that is able to integrated other evidence-based methods, such as mindfulness, acceptance and commitment therapy (ACT) and cognitive behavioural therapy (CBT). Using nature as the core medium in the restorative process allows the practitioner to develop a range of activities to suit all needs, including different levels of mobility and access to green space. We were so impressed by the advantages and possibilities of ecotherapy that we were able to employ Andy for three days a week in the NHS as an ecotherapist, perhaps the first in the country. During this time he worked on projects for people recovering from episodes of psychosis, people with dementia, young people in an in-patient unit and women in acute psychiatric care, to name a few. The people recovering from psychosis often remarked how much they appreciated being able to be in a group yet some distance from it if they felt the need, without any pressure to talk. People with dementia loved the fact that a walk though a country park observing the wildlife helped them feel equal to others with them, as the activity did not rely on the cognitive abilities that were increasingly letting them down. The young people designed, purchased and created their own 'secret garden' in the grounds of the unit they were staying in. The vulnerable women on the in-patient unit created a secure garden for themselves that they could tend and spend time in as a place of safety and sanctuary. Other projects demonstrated a marked reduction in violence and aggression among men on in-patient units. Although the funding, sadly, could not be sustained, Andy still provides ecotherapy sessions on a voluntary basis. He had also trained other staff, including trainee clinical psychologists who worked with him on six-month placements, and they are continuing to use and develop the work. Our next project is to develop sessions for people with long-term physical health conditions, including those with respiratory disease and heart conditions, those recovering from cancer, and people tackling obesity who do not engage with conventional exercise.

In this book Andy McGeeney provides a rationale for connecting to nature and feeling better for it. His profound understanding of the natural world and psychological well-being has enabled him to develop many different activities and opportunities for improving well-being to suit a wide range of needs, interests and abilities. As he points out, ecotherapy can start with simply tending a plant in a therapy room or providing views of the countryside for housebound people. There is something for everyone and you do not have to be fit or know anything about the natural world to gain from his tried and tested methods.

The book draws on material from both the ancient past and the present, including Andy's own extensive experience of ecotherapy with people in mental health services. He has also conducted ecotherapy days for mental health staff. They have all generously provided him with feedback and ideas that have helped him develop further a wide repertoire of activities. Whether it is conservation work, gardening, a walk in the woods or lying on soft grass in the sun, each has had a significant impact on participants. Several have been inspired to write about their experiences and discoveries through letters and creative verse, leaving a lasting account. Others take photographs and many treasure their memories of the experience.

The ancient Greeks understood the importance of nature in the process of recovery. They built their healing centres in beautiful locations knowing that this would help restore their patients in mind, body and spirit. Early medicine, based on the theory of the four humours, believed that an imbalance in a humour was the basis for disease and illness. Even though such ideas have long since been replaced by a more scientific understanding of the body and disease processes, the notion of imbalance still lies at the core of our thinking. The early Victorian designers of psychiatric hospitals knew that green space was important for mental well-being. The formal gardens they created and that were tended by patients were designed to maintain a sense of order that would be mirrored in the minds of those in mental distress. These hospitals were generally on the outskirts of towns and cities so had land for farming and wild spaces for walking in to encourage healthy exercise and the benefits of being in the open air.

Our modern response is to turn to medicine as an easy fix. What we can all do is take more responsibility for our own health and well-being by making adjustments to lifestyles that are out of balance. When we do this we feel in greater harmony with ourselves, those around us and the environment. Ecotherapy has a role to play here and its holistic approach means that it can benefit people with the psychological distress of physical illness as well as those with mental health problems. Many long-term health conditions that increasingly feature in the modern world such as stress, diabetes and obesity are the result of an imbalance in lifestyles.

It is not enough to believe that being in nature can improve well-being. Andy also provides evidence from many independent studies that demonstrate the benefits of engaging in ecotherapy. Being in the outdoors, walking down a tree-lined street, having views of nature from a residential care window or walking slowly through a meadow have all been shown to lower the stress response in healthy people as well as those with problems. He also provides helpful advice on how to present this work to others who may be sceptical about the benefits of something so seemingly simple. He explains how ecotherapy is derived from both Western and Eastern practices, especially citing mindfulness practices. Mindfulness is increasingly recognised as being a key component in health and well-being, both as a stand-alone approach or as part of other therapeutic interventions. Numerous research studies in support of the benefits of mindfulness are helpfully summarised.

This is a book that can be read from cover to cover to gain a real understanding of ecotherapy and its place in healthcare. It is also a great resource to dip into for practical suggestions and ideas to keep sessions fresh, enjoyable and appropriate to the group. The reader is encouraged to develop their own ideas and to keep notes of sessions with suggestions for future activities. As Andy says, many sessions can be run for free or at low cost. Repeating activities at different times of the year can make a profound difference to the experience. Another possibility is that participants may be encouraged to go out in between sessions to increase the benefits for themselves.

You may even do the same yourself and enjoy greater well-being by being in nature and feeling better for it!

Lindsay Royan, Consultant Clinical Psychologist, Head of Barking and Dagenham
Psychological Services and Trust Clinical Health Psychological Services

Acknowledgements

A book like this comes out of a vast ecosystem of experiences, influences and conversations. I want to take this opportunity to acknowledge some of the people who have supported and influenced me along the way in writing the book. I apologise to those I have not named.

I begin with my grandfather Robert Duxbury who regularly took me as a toddler out into the parks and woods of Sheffield and fed my fascination for other living things. I cannot remember a time when I was not spellbound by nature. My parents watched my obsession grow and gave me books and took me on trips to the countryside. I went on to study psychology and biology at university and I quickly became disillusioned with the latter and swapped it for sociology. I very soon realised, from my early forays into encounter groups, phenomenology and Zen Buddhism, that there were more grounded ways of understanding, from the inside, what it is to be human. After leaving university I had some of my most significant and life-changing experiences ever as a result of working with John Crook. He was an ethologist as well as a Zen, later a Chan, Buddhist master who led retreats in deepest Wales. Although I had learnt meditation many years before, my time with John in Bristol and Wales opened my mind to what is *really* going on. My understanding of the ecological self, as Joanna Macy calls it, was revealed in all its loving power.

During a period in my life while I was training and developing my skills as a counsellor and group facilitator I went on a group dynamics course. It was there as a result of a chance conversation on the London Underground with Chris Johnstone that I was introduced to deep ecology and the work of Joanna Macy. A subsequent workshop with Joanna became a major turning point in my life. Her first workshop gave me something I had missed until then. It gave me the coherence and confidence to express what I felt about my place in the natural world. I have the utmost respect and gratitude for Joanna's passion, clarity and compassion for the world.

I want to give warm thanks to Liz Staveley for understanding immediately what I was exploring and enthusiastically agreeing to co-lead workshops in deep ecology. We have shared more than two decades of mutual supervision and conversations that have enriched our friendship and my work in nature. Those first workshops in deep ecology revealed the power that was there when we connected people to nature.

I also want to thank the team of people in the Terma Foundation who created *The Box.** There is an even greater need now for a beautiful, soulful and informative resource like *The Box* to help people explore our intimate involvement in nature at a deep level.

In 2004 I chose a career change that took me outdoors more often. I managed 11 projects to do with health and the green environment collectively called THERAPI. I wish to thank the Director of Thames Chase Community Forest at the time, John Meehan, for giving me his wholehearted trust, support and the freedom to develop projects in my own way.

On my steering group was Lindsay Royan, Head of Barking and Dagenham Psychological Services. Lindsay not only supported my Thames Chase work but fought for a long time to get funding and persuade the mental health trust to create a new post for me. We think I was the first ecotherapist to be employed by the NHS. Thank you, Lindsay, for all the work in promoting ecotherapy and for protecting me from bureaucracy. I am delighted and very grateful you agreed to write the foreword.

In those two years I was able to offer ecotherapy to a wide range of people within the health service. Thank you to Michael Inns and all the other service users who campaigned to try to keep the service going despite funding cuts. HUBB and Havering Mind were also important allies in keeping ecotherapy going in East London. I am grateful to the support staff, psychologists and occupational therapists, too many to name, who understood what we were doing. I am extremely grateful to all the people who have turned out over the years in all weathers to take part in my regular 'Well-being in Nature' sessions each week. The benefits have been reciprocal.

During my time at the NHS Trust I had the fortunate opportunity to take part in training workshops with both Ronen Berger and Joseph Cornell. Both are known for their work with children and nature. They were, in different ways, important confirmation that the work I was doing was valid. I also saw more clearly in what direction my own individual style was taking me. I can highly recommend their inspirational books and work.

While I worked for Lindsay at the NHS Trust we had two doctoral students on six-month placements from the University of East London, Sophie Jeffery and Katie Allan. Both students brought tremendous enthusiasm and commitment to their placements. In that time, as a result of dialogues and their questioning, I further developed my ideas on ecotherapy. I am very grateful to Nicky Tann, an

---

*   *The Box: Remembering the Gift* was created by a collective as a box of resources for individuals and groups to explore their deep connection to nature in a holistic way. It contains literature, artworks, artefacts and instructions for activities.

occupational therapist, who has developed ecotherapy for clients with memory problems and shared her knowledge and experiments with activities.

While writing the book I have had support from many of the people I have already mentioned; I give thanks to them all. I want to reiterate my special thanks to Sophie Jeffery for devoting so much of her valuable time to reviewing draft texts and encouraging me to keep going. I am grateful beyond words for the companionship and critical thinking of my dear friend Jochen Encke. His lifetime's work in psychotherapy and personal change includes working with clients on an allotment project in London. Our conversations over many years have been a powerful influence on how I work in ecotherapy and on my thinking for the book.

Lastly I wish to thank all those people who have attended my ecotherapy workshops over the years. I recall the many times at the end of a wonderful day when participants concluded by thanking me, while I felt such deep gratitude for their willingness to open their minds and to follow me into the woods.

Andy McGeeney
www.andymcgeeney.com

Disclaimer

Before implementing any of the activities outlined in this book, readers should seek legal advice to ensure compliance with the health and safety regulations and risk assessment that govern outdoor activities. Neither the author nor the publisher take any responsibility for any consequences of any action taken as a result of the information contained in this book.

Please see page 62 for a more detailed discussion of the potential risks involved with ecotherapy.

Preface

This book is a manual of ecotherapy for those wanting to give others a deeper connection to nature in order to improve their well-being. It is particularly useful if you are working with people experiencing emotional distress but is useful for working with anyone. The book examines the latest psychological research evidence into how and why the natural world has such a positive effect on us. It also offers detailed guidance on how to run successful ecotherapy sessions, including instructions for doing over 100 activities.

There is good scientific research into ecotherapy supporting the claim that nature has a positive effect on the human condition. In this book you will discover the evidence that: we are intimately and inseparably a part of nature; we have evolved to be adapted to nature; our physical health improves faster and exercise seems easier to do in nature; our thinking, mood and spiritual sense are enhanced in nature; and we live in more satisfying and harmonious communities when nature surrounds us. When seen like this the huge benefits for us all to be more connected to the natural world become self-evident.

Much of our beneficial contact with nature is done without conscious effort. You and your clients have most likely been doing ecotherapeutic activities without calling them by that name. For example, people will pay more for a house in a good location – good neighbours, near shops, rail and schools. But if the road is tree lined they will pay even more. And if it has a big, colourful garden even more still. Millions of people feed garden birds, keep a pet and go for walks in the park. Hotel foyers and office spaces are usually decorated with green plants. We go on holiday, sometimes for a city break, but longer trips are often to the coast or countryside. Advertisers use nature images and themes to attract our attention, reassuring us that a product is healthy, relaxing, and free of toxins. Wildlife content is among the most popular documentary TV. We say we love someone by giving them flowers. The examples are endless of how we include nature in our lives to make us feel better (references to the above examples appear in Chapter 6).

Mental illness – stress, depression, psychosis – is the scourge of modern life and we are all affected by it, directly or indirectly. The causes of mental distress are in our minds and in the environment, both physical and social. Social causes are not the subject of this book; they demand a change in society. What is offered here are contributions to reducing and healing the other two causes and cures, that is, the mind and the physical environment.

The need for a mindful connection to nature has never been more important. Most of us do not live surrounded by wild nature. Over half the people on the planet live in cities. You are more likely to experience psychosis if you live in a city, although the reasons for this are complex. You are more likely to go mad if you fully embrace the lifestyle offered by the modern industrial world. When we are mindful in nature we are more able to put our urban concerns to one side and to be alive to all that is around us.

> The world is too much with us; late and soon,
> Getting and spending, we lay waste our powers:
> Little we see in nature that is ours;
> We have given our hearts away, a sordid boon!
> This sea that bares her bosom to the moon;
> The winds that will be howling at all hours,
> And are up-gathering now like sleeping flowers;
> For this, for everything, we are out of tune;
>
> *William Wordsworth, Sonnet XXXIII*
> *(1959 [1807])*

Soon after the National Health Service was born our National Parks were created. It was recognised at the time that there was a strong connection between people's health and access to the nature. As Lewis Silkin, Minister of Town and Country Planning 1949, stated:

> The enjoyment of our leisure in the open air and the ability to leave our towns and walk on the moors and in the dales...are, just as much a part of positive health and well being as are the building of hospitals or insurance against sickness. (Silkin 1949)

Unfortunately it is still not fully recognised how important being in wild nature is to our well-being. In part this is a result of mainstream clinical psychology's focus on intra-psychic causes and psychiatry's reliance on pills.

Consider this: 98 per cent of the genes in your body are the same as those of a chimpanzee. The consequences of knowing this information are profound. We are animals. We are as much part of the natural world as any other ape. For 99 per cent of our time on Earth we have lived as hunter-gatherers. No cities, no Internet, no countries – small bands of people, like us, living entirely in nature. Our ancestors lived well only because they had an intimate connection to nature. As we shall see when we examine the evidence, humans can recognise and will feel better when we are in ecologically rich habitats.

What this evidence means is that we can powerfully utilise our deep connection to nature to improve the quality of our lives. This book shows you how to do it. *With Nature in Mind* is a complete manual of ecotherapy, including supporting evidence, therapeutic models and clear instructions for practising all the activities.

This book offers more. In order to enhance and intensify the therapeutic connections to nature the third cause and cure of all our woes is also addressed: that of the mind. The human mind seeks stimulation, it makes imaginative predictions and can draw upon a vast memory store of past experience. These are great capabilities but they can also create distress. We can become distressed when we allow unpleasant memories to become the focus of our attention. Or we worry about possible events that have not even happened.

When we are mindful we can disengage from our busy mind and be in the moment. The consequences of mindfulness are numerous. We become more sensitive and aware of what is going on. An acknowledgement, an acceptance of how things are can come over us. In turn this can lead to a letting go of anxieties and worrisome moods. The emotional state of the moment no longer has the mind feeding on past memories or imagined future concerns.

The philosophy of this book is to step aside from seeing human experience as problems or happiness states. This is not to ignore the fact that we all can spend a lot of our time assessing and evaluating ourselves, things and other people. We just don't have to take the mind games seriously. Mindfulness is the way to let go of the mind games.

Regardless of whether one has been labelled/diagnosed with a mental condition the key intention advocated here is to increase awareness of the moment as it changes, and to do that out in nature.

Ecotherapy is relatively new in the field of mental health, and is growing year by year. It comes in a variety of forms but as Arnie Naess said, 'the frontier is long' (Naess, p.114). In other words there are many ways to connect positively with nature. The particular style of ecotherapy offered here is effective because it draws on the two powerful therapeutic influences: wild nature and mindfulness. Ecotherapy, what its roots are and the different approaches to its practice are explained in detail. The latest research evidence on the effects of the natural environment on improving mental states for different groups of people is critically examined. The possible theories and explanation as to why nature is therapeutic are thoroughly explored. Finally there is an extensive collection of easy activities designed to enable people to get closer to nature. Everything a person needs to run ecotherapy sessions is here in an easily accessible format.

If you work in mental health, mindfulness training or wildlife education you will find this book invaluable. It is the complete resource for you to engage people with the wild outdoors, and for the people you take out to have a deeper connection to nature.

I hope you enjoy leading groups in nature as much as I have, and that by getting closer to nature you all feel better for it.

Part 1

Ecotherapy
What it is and how to do it

Chapter 1

Introduction
Entering the forest

I only went out for a walk, and finally concluded to stay out till sundown, for going out, I found, was really going in.

John Muir (2001 [1938])

In this chapter I will explore these questions:

» What is ecotherapy?

» What is the relevance of ecotherapy to mental health?

A group out on an ecotherapy walk in Essex

Putting 'eco' into recovery

What is ecotherapy and how does it help people's recovery from mental illness and emotional distress?

Imagine a scene: you are on your own or with a friend and you are lying in a flower-filled meadow in summer, birds are singing and you can smell wild roses nearby. Up above the sky is a deep blue and bright clouds drift across your field of view. You let out a deep sigh, letting go. And when you let go you notice more of the sensations around you. Thoughts and emotions subside and you are content to be in the right place. Do you know what I'm talking about?

Ecotherapy is about creating a deeper connection to nature and feeling better for it. It has affinities with other nature-based activities such as green exercise, conservation work, pet ownership, mountaineering and gardening. But what is special about ecotherapy and how did I begin to do this work?

When I was quite young I realised I had a way of introducing others to nature and infecting them with my fascination and excitement. I have managed to retain that openness to nature and an ability to enable others to feel relaxed and uplifted by spending time outdoors. Once I realised I had this ability when working with people outdoors I wondered if it was possible to increase these positive experiences of lifted mood and clearer mind. I drew on other skills and experiences in my life to develop a way of working that I now call, for want of a better word, ecotherapy.

Exploring how to do nature-based ecotherapy with people recovering from mental distress, and to evaluate it so others can do ecotherapy themselves, has now become my passion.

How do we do ecotherapy? I usually work with a group. It is important at the start to get us all physically relaxed, releasing tensions but more importantly getting people in touch with their bodies. Our bodies are part of nature and so it is a way of beginning the process of connecting. I remind people that we are made of the same stuff as the rest of nature. Our bodies are up to 70 per cent water and the clean water we drink has been circulating through life forms for millions of years, likewise the food we eat, and our breath comes courtesy of all the plants around us. Being in touch with our physical self also brings us into the present. It is from the full experience of the present that we can open up our senses and increase our contact with nature around us.

To further increase that sense of being in the now I do breathing exercises based on meditation. Mindfulness is a core part of the approach I am advocating here. I also encourage people to let go of memories of what has happened that day and what they imagine might occur later: to let go and enjoy being wherever they are.

I am guiding people away from ego to eco, the bigger world that is alive around them. In this process some people can have a profound sense of being connected to nature at a deep level. The healing thoughts can come from a realisation that we, humans and animals and plants, share the same fundamental qualities: we are born and we will one day die, we live and deal with good and bad times, we are wounded and we heal. It is possible to break out of our isolated self and recognise we participate in a wider ecological self where matter, air and social connections pass through us continuously.

I remind everyone to stay with the open relaxed state we are in as we move off on a leisurely walk through grassland and woods, open and intimate greenery. In winter maybe we go and feed the ducks, in summer we listen to birdsong. I encourage sensory 'openness' to smells and sounds which further takes people away from their possible preoccupation with self.

At the core of ecotherapy is the combination of increased awareness of the present and an immersion in wild nature. Recovery is often spoken of in terms of changing thoughts and feelings in order to live a happier more positive life. Cognitive behavioural therapy (CBT) and counselling are two of the methods used for achieving this. I think this is fine and yet I'm interested in something different. If a person can put aside for a moment their internal dialogue and imaginings of what *might* happen and begin to pay full attention to what *is* happening in the present then they can open up to a different way of seeing. If this different way of seeing, attending to the world, is done in nature then the work of ecotherapy can begin. There is a quality of experience that is different when people connect to nature as opposed to human-made environments. In wild nature we are surrounded by other living things which grow of their own volition according to their own character; they face similar challenges of survival, and have a beauty we are drawn to.

Imagine an experience that:

- improves your mood and Clarity of thinking

- has no known side-effects

- is backed by research

- and is free.

WELCOME TO ECOTHERAPY!

Participating in a group enlarges the experience. We can chat, get to know other people and share our wonderment. If you just want to be on your own in nature that's fine too: the permissive atmosphere allows for many choices. And for those who are uncertain of others a group walk allows you to choose your distance in relaton to others and how much you want to get involved or not.

My invitation to everyone is to put a little eco into your recovery (and prevention of stress) by shaking off city life for a while, reconnecting with life around you and listening to the woods singing.

Bench at Minister's Pool near Nairn, Scotland

The particular relevance of ecotherapy to current issues in mental health

The UN has identified depression, along with cancer and heart disease, as one of the major global health challenges of the twenty-first century.

To emphasise the significance of mental illness a handy statistic is often quoted: one in four of us will experience mental illness sometime in our lives. I can see why campaigners use this ratio to get a simple message across but I don't think it helps the cause. The one in four statistic divides the ill from the well in a simplistic way; you either are or are not mentally ill. In turn it elicits a schadenfreude response among the majority who see themselves as 'stressed yes, but certainly not mental'.

In fact, who among us will live a life of complete sanity at all times? Consider the number of people just coping and not entering the health system, plus everyone who goes to their GP with a stress-related physical illness. Nearly half of us report feeling stressed, and over a quarter say they have been stressed for over a year.

Mental illness is a socially defined category in which psychological and biological notions are drawn in to legitimise the labelling. However, this is not the place to discuss the causes of mental distress. I want to make a point because

I believe ecotherapy is for all of us not just the diagnosed. I hope everyone can agree that there is a problem in our society: too many of us are too often mentally distressed, and we need to do more to improve lives.

The sheer numbers of stressed and depressed are a challenge to us all to change the way we live our lives and the life choices we make. More and more people are now realising that the way the world is run needs to change but also they as individuals can take more control over their health and well-being. Spending time in nature is one important way we can all look after ourselves.

Approaches to improving the mental health of the nation are changing, whether it is people with mild stress and depression or more severe and enduring conditions. The trend is towards greater integration of those affected by mental illness into mainstream activities. In turn this approach presupposes offering much less medicalised forms of treatment. How can we enrich people's lives, reduce social exclusion and provide a greater choice of activities that will help individuals more successfully overcome their difficulties?

The work we do in ecotherapy is congruent with the the NHS National Service Frameworks (NHS 1999). Ecotherapy is not intended as a replacement of existing treatments but as a complementary approach based on evidence-based research. It encourages a non-medicalised and non-drug-related approach to self-development and recovery. It is cost effective compared to conventional therapies and drug treatments.

The following list of characteristics of ecotherapy uses the same terms the government used (bold text) when giving advice on what it expected of mental health treatment.

- Ecotherapy activities are almost entirely **outdoor based not confined to a specialist building base**.

- They enable those who feel excluded to be involved in **mainstream** activities as much as segregated provision. Ecotherapy is open to all and is not seen as specifically for people who have experienced mental ill health; in that sense it is socially inclusive. Excluded groups are targeted.

- **Participant involvement:** it is essential to have service-user involvement in the decision making and planning of services such as ecotherapy.

- Most of our work is carried out in diverse **partnerships** with other agencies. This ensures greater opportunities for funding and increased take-up by service users.

- **Joined-up working** is evident, for example in the links we have made between people's health and well-being and the appreciation and protection of the local countryside.

- Many of our activities have been shown to **increase self-confidence**.

- All our **work is monitored and evaluated** and the results are shared so that the learning can be used by others.

- Working with trees inevitably creates a mindset that is looking to the long-term future. Our work is designed to be **sustainable and enduring**. Ecotherapy builds resilience.

- In addition the government is emphasising **a holistic view** of treatment for mental health users that goes **beyond medical interventions**.

- **Good practice** is shared with others about what works, after the work is monitored and evaluated.

Since the National Service Frameworks were published in 1999 there have been two changes of government and I expect that by the time this book is published there could well be further changes. The Conservative and Liberal Democrat Coalition produced a strategy document for mental health (NHS 2011). It talked about a strategy that would 'ensure that the population as a whole knows what it can do to improve their own mental health: for example experiencing the natural environment'. The natural environment is defined as the 'green open spaces in and around towns and cities as well as the wider countryside and coastline'. That sounds like a promising intention, even if it is only a commitment to pass on knowledge, not to treat people. So far I haven't seen any actions taken on that statement.

The latest Chief Medical Officer's report (Chief Medical Officer 2013) when referring to mental health appears to be working to a different set of assumptions! It distances well-being from mental health and dismisses evidence criteria used by the government. While this confusion at the highest levels is taking place the government's own statistics show the situation is deteriorating. Seventy million days are lost to work, costing £100 billion per annum in England alone. Depression and anxiety have increased since 2009 by 24 per cent and 75 per cent of sufferers receive no mental health treatment at all (Chief Medical Officer 2013).

The conclusion is that waiting for government initiatives to promote evidence-based ecotherapy is fruitless. As part of client empowerment mental health professionals could encourage people to use the natural world to improve their mental health and well-being. People who are experiencing mental distress themselves could do similarly and take heart from Mind, the leading mental health charity. Mind has raised millions of pounds to fund projects on ecotherapy and the evaluative research that went with them (Bragg, Wood and Barton 2013). There is much that can be done without waiting for initiatives from above.

Chapter 2

Deeper into the Forest

It is eternity now. I am in the midst of it. It is about me and in the sunshine; I am in it, as the butterfly floats in the light laden air. Nothing has to come, it is now. Now is eternity; now is immortal life. Here at this moment, by this tumulus, on the earth now: I exist in it. The years, the centuries, the cycles are absolutely nothing; it is only a moment since this tumulus was raised; in a thousand years more it will still be only a moment... There may be time for the clock, the clock may make time for itself; but there is none for me.

Richard Jefferies (1883)

> In this chapter I place ecotherapy in a wider context. The chapter explores the different meanings given to ecotherapy and defines related areas and influences. It also discusses the different forms of ecotherapy and the distinctive features of the approach used in this book.

Defining and distinguishing ecotherapy

Defining ecotherapy is not straightforward. This is because of its origins and because different groups use the term in different ways. I will take the reader through the commonly used meanings and offer a working definition as a benchmark for this book.

The ecotherapy I work with is about 'creating a closer connection to nature and feeling better for it'. The 'how' of this particular approach will become clearer through the book. For the moment I want to discuss ecotherapy in general terms before distinguishing the approach taken by this book. I want to also emphasise, as will become clear fairly soon, that 'ecotherapy' and the various subcategories are not fixed entities. Groupings overlap and terms are sometimes used interchangeably. My intention is to help clarify such terms. I hope I have done so in a way that is acceptable to others in the field.

Some of the activities included in this section do not have therapeutic intentions: deep ecology and ecopsychology, for example. There are two reasons why they are here. One reason is that they often have positive outcomes of self-discovery and personal change. Second, they overlap and have had a positive influence on the development of ecotherapy.

The Mind evaluation report on ecotherapy written by the University of Essex offers a clear definition of the domain. 'Ecotherapy' (sometimes called green care) comprises nature-based interventions in a variety of natural settings. Ecotherapy initiatives usually consist of a facilitated, specific intervention, for a particular participant, rather than simply 'an experience in nature' for the general public. Ecotherapy approaches are 'therapeutic' in nature although some ecotherapy initiatives also include formal therapy (e.g. counselling sessions, CBT, psychotherapy, etc.) as an integral part of the programme. Although the area of ecotherapy is very diverse, the common linking ethos is the contact with nature in a facilitated, structured and safe way, where many vulnerable groups gain therapeutic benefits (Bragg *et al.* 2013; Bragg and Atkins 2016).

Rachel Bragg (Bragg *et al.* 2013) also discusses the ambiguities around the term 'ecotherapy'. She points out that Jules Pretty (Pretty, Hine and Peacock 2006) proposed the term 'green care' to be used as an overarching word for all types of therapeutic activity related to nature, animals and plants. Rachel Bragg acknowledges that 'ecotherapy' is also a broad term for a range of activities and is more commonly used than green care. The Ecominds project supported by Mind and evaluated by Rachel Bragg is a case in point. Under ecotherapy the report had a range of activities from gardening to farming and country walks. In this instance the generic use of the term applies to any facilitated activity that relates to nature (plants, animals and landscape) and that has therapeutic benefits. Many activities in nature, such as conservation work, mountaineering and rambling, will have positive effects such as are observed in ecotherapy but these are secondary consequences and not part of the original intention.

There is still some confusion because 'ecotherapy' is used as a general and a specific term. It is as if 'running' became adopted as the general term for 'athletics'. The Mind report clarifies the situation to some extent by using 'green care' as the umbrella term covering all forms of therapeutic contact with living plants and animals. It then admits that 'ecotherapy' is used by many people, including Mind and the media, to refer to the whole field and that it will use 'ecotherapy' in the general sense in the report.

The situation has recently become more complex in an attempt to bring order into the terminology. The Natural England Review of nature based interventions for mental health care (Bragg and Atkins 2016) proposes using the title 'Green care: Nature-based interventions for vulnerable groups' for ecotherapy activities for individuals with what they call 'a defined need' (pvi). The report proposes that providers and commissioners separate out people experiencing mental illness from the general population. This runs counter to the prevailing move in mental health to blur the distinctions between those with a diagnosis and the general population. The report is also limited to reviewing care farming, conservation and horticulture with regards to ecotherapy.

Because the definitions have not settled down yet I am going to offer explanations of the subcategories based on the green care model but with some slight modifications (see Table 2.1 for an overview of activities related to green care). Doubtless in a few years the situation will have stabilised and we can all be clearer about what we mean by the word 'ecotherapy'. All of these activities may work with a variety of people – not only those who have experienced mental distress – for example, young offenders, people with learning difficulties, school children and the general public.

Table 2.1 The green care umbrella

Green care sub group	Key features
Social and therapeutic horticulture	Gardening
Animal-assisted interventions	Pets, horses and other domesticated animals
Care farming	Farm work
Environmental conservation	Conservation work
Green exercise	Walking and other physical exercise
Nature, arts and crafts	Art therapy
Wilderness Therapy	Individual/group work in remote locations
Ecotherapy	Therapy outdoors/contact with wild nature
Nature therapy including wilderness therapy	Contact with wild nature

(modified from Bragg et al. 2013)

Social and therapeutic horticulture

Social and therapeutic horticulture (STH) is the most popular therapeutic interaction between people and plants. It can be the passive appreciation of a garden, active gardening or growing vegetables. It is the term most often conflated with ecotherapy and yet it has many distinctive features that distinguish it from other forms of ecotherapy. Mind has widely and consistently promoted ecotherapy more than any other mental health organisation in the UK. However, the majority of the projects in their Ecominds were horticultural rather than connecting to wild nature.

Thrive is the major UK organisation supporting and promoting therapeutic horticulture. Their definition is 'Social and therapeutic horticulture is the formal name given to the process of using gardening, plants and horticulture to help individuals develop' (Thrive n.d.). Emphasis is not only placed on the positive benefits of growing plants but other factors such as physical fitness, social skills, employment skills, and basic skills such as numeracy and literacy. Thrive work with a range of client groups including people who have physical disabilities, learning difficulties, older people and people who have experienced mental illness. A good place to review the underpinning evidence for STH is a collaborative work by Thrive and the University of Loughborough – *Health, Well-being and Social Inclusion: Therapeutic Horticulture in the UK* (Sempik, Aldridge and Becker 2005).

Animal-assisted interventions

Animals have been used for a variety of therapeutic interventions to improve well-being and self-esteem in many client groups. Examples include bringing a friendly dog onto a mental health hospital ward that in-patients can stroke, and caring for animals on a farm. An important aspect of animal-assisted interventions (AAI) is the fact that a pet animal such as a dog is likely to be friendly and affectionate to anyone. It does not approach a human being with all the prejudices that many of us have regarding people with a mental illness.

Some activities are more formalised in animal-assisted therapy (AAT). In these cases the process is focused and task oriented with evaluated outcomes. Dolphins and horses have been used in this way. Anecdotal evidence of the effectiveness of AAT is easy to come by but more rigorous research is harder to find. It is to be hoped that it won't be long before this situation is remedied.

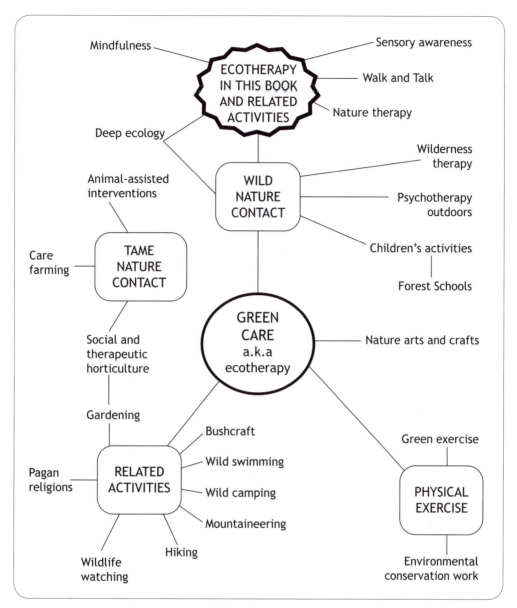

Figure 2.1 Mindful ecotherapy and related activities

Care farming

Care farming is 'the therapeutic use of agricultural landscapes and farming practices' (Bragg *et al.* 2013, p.14). It covers a variety of contexts and farm-related activities such as looking after animals, vegetable growing and crop management. Research has identified benefits similar to other forms of green care such as improved self-esteem and mood (e.g. Hine 2008). Care farming offers a positive combination of outdoor activities, access to nature, physical exercise and opportunities to socialise in a context which is akin to the world of work.

Environmental conservation

Dr William Bird, an English GP, came up with the idea of encouraging his cardiac patients to go for walks as a way of maintaining fitness (the seed which led to Walking for Health groups; see the following section). He then suggested patients join a conservation group as another way of getting active. In 1998 he set up the first green gym in Sonning Common as a conservation group for health improvement. At an early stage Dr Bird saw the dual benefits of physical activity outdoors as being good for body and mind. The Conservation Volunteers (formerly the BTCV) along with many other groups run green gyms for anyone wanting to improve their health and well-being. Green gyms manage to combine the joint effects of physical activity and being out in nature for which there is now ample research demonstrating their mutual benefits (Yerrell 2008).

Green exercise

Green exercise is what is says, exercise outdoors. Typically it involves going for a walk in parks and the countryside. It has been the subject of much research by the team at the University of Essex (Barton and Pretty 2010) who found multiple mental and physical health benefits from green exercise. After a government initiative led by English Nature, 'Walking for Health' groups are now found all over the country.

Guy Holmes and colleagues developed 'Walk and Talk' around 2007. From what I have read the approach has many similarities with some of the walks I lead. The focus is on socialising, talking about anything and not just mental health, appreciating the natural world, not walking for fitness alone, and no requirement to mix. There is tremendous freedom of thought and conversation when out on a walk which is not found indoors (Holmes and Evans 2011).

Nature, arts and crafts

Many people who take groups outdoors into parks or the countryside use the natural settings for creative work. Drawing, painting and photography as well as writing poetry are common media, but often natural materials themselves are employed creatively. Variations on art therapy have been used, and inspiration taken from land artists such as Andy Goldsworthy (1988; Goldsworthy and Friedman 1993) and Chris Drury (1998). Children of course take very easily to the suggestion of playing outdoors with natural elements. Jo Schofield and Fiona Danks have written many books packed with ideas and beautiful photographs of kids having fun with sticks, leaves, feathers and stones (Schofield and Danks 2005, 2012).

Wilderness therapy

Wilderness therapy is the use of wild remote areas, such as the Scottish Highlands, to provide a context for individual and group therapy. One of the benefits of working in remote areas in nature is that the clients are removed from their familiar environment which may have stimulated negative thinking and stress. The client is professionally facilitated in a way that uses the learning potential provided by interaction with nature. In a very real sense, however, the natural world is more than an escape or a context. It is seen as a participant in the process of self-discovery and change.

Wilderness therapy can be placed in a wider context of self-development and leadership training where the intention is not explicitly therapeutic (see Wilderness Foundation n.d.).

Ecotherapy

Ecotherapy as a subcategory of green care and the wider definition of the word acknowledges the research evidence and experience of practitioners who have seen the benefits of people spending time in nature. It is the approach most closely associated with this book. The specific features of ecotherapy include interaction with wild or semi-natural areas of nature. This is in contrast to working with cultivated plants and tame animals, which come under the respective categories of horticultural therapy and AAT.

A distinctive feature of the approach taken in this book is the central assumption that nature itself is the primary therapeutic source. Just being in natural surroundings, as we shall see when we examine the evidence, has a positive effect on affect and cognition. We can enhance the process through increasing sensory contact and mindfulness.

Many other practitioners who call themselves ecotherapists are actually doing counselling or therapy outdoors. They acknowledge the benefits of being in natural surroundings and the triangular relationship between therapist, client and the natural world. Jordan (2015) discusses the issues involved in taking counselling outdoors into nature. The outdoor therapists come from a variety of psychological perspectives. They could be Jungian, psychoanalytic, rogerian, using CBT or any other style of working. Siddons-Hegginworth (2009), for example, works from a Jungian perspective and includes ritual and symbolism in his work.

Nature Therapy

Nature Therapy is occasionally used as a synonym for ecotherapy as a sub-category of green care. Its wider use is limited now that it is trademarked by an Israeli organisation (the Nature Therapy Center). It is also used by commercial organisations to sell health products that have nothing to do with the green outdoors or nature!

The distinctive features of the ecotherapy advocated in this book are discussed later. The approach shares a great deal with other styles of ecotherapy, and the activities in this book can be adapted to a variety of styles. In essence the approach advocated here includes mindfulness, sensory awareness and connecting to wild nature.

Nature Therapy of Ronen Berger

Ronen Berger has proposed a way of working with clients in nature and a theoretical context for working in this way which he calls 'Nature Therapy'. 'Nature Therapy is a postmodern experiential approach based on the integration of elements from art and drama therapy, Gestalt, narrative, ecopsychology, transpersonal psychology, adventure therapy, shamanism, and body-mind practices' (Berger and McLeod 2006). He has defined what he considers to be the differences and advantages of Nature Therapy over conventional indoors therapy as used by the majority of practitioners.

Working indoors means that the therapeutic process happens in a place designed for doing therapy, under the control and official ownership of the therapist. The location is permanent, unchanging and remote from the rest of the world. In contrast the setting for therapy in nature is alive and dynamic, ever changing with seasons and life forms. It exists in its own right and continues once the clients and therapist have left.

A case study of working with a young boy 'building a home in nature' illustrates many of Berger's themes. The boy is initially very quiet and hesitant. Through the joint exploration of a riverbank tree area he finds ways to express his predicament and to explore possible meanings and changes that could occur in his life. A home is created under the tree where the boy and Berger can boil tea over a fire. Berger emphasises the importance of allowing the client to make more choices and take some control of the place and activities. He also makes comparisons between his approach and traditional culture's creation of sacred space to perform transformative rituals. Berger and a colleague have written a brief account of his way of working with war-traumatised children in Israel, with guidelines for practitioners on how to use Nature Therapy with children and adolescents (Berger and Lahad 2013).

Berger draws upon his training in drama therapy to use constructs such as the 'as if reality' assumption: to allow an imaginative distancing between current reality and new fantasies, experimental roles and situations. The creation of a home in nature allows the client to reflect on their current real home and what is needed. Working with nature empowers the client to take shared responsibility for the direction of the therapeutic process, always assuming the therapist is willing to relinquish positions of hierarchy and power.

The creation of rituals is an important principle in Berger's Nature Therapy. He makes direct comparisons with the traditional role of shaman and modern nature therapist. The shaman facilitated individuals and groups through change, held specific values and beliefs, and guided ritual processes. Berger suggests the nature therapist could do the same.

Berger acknowledges so much of what has been lost in our individualistic technical secular world and reminds us that we face the same fundamental issues as our ancient ancestors. There are universal truths, as he calls them, such as the cycle of life and death: transitions which are mirrored more clearly when we are in nature and away from the city.

The physical journey in nature – walking, creating a home or whatever is explored in nature – can stimulate a psychological and spiritual journey within. The elements in nature, such as animals, plants, weather and landscape, can be a prompt to the client as they explore their inner landscape.

Berger describes a triangular relationship between the therapist, client and nature. The therapist can act as a shamanic guide or take a minor role, allowing greater dialogue between nature and client. The direct sensory contact with natural elements by a client can be a powerful stimulus to deeper thoughts and feelings. It readily allows access to non-verbal expression, particularly for clients who are reluctant or unable to express themselves verbally (Berger 2009).

Deep ecology

Some understanding of the thinking within deep ecology is essential in order to understand the approach taken in the practice of ecotherapy. The term deep ecology (DE) was devised by the Norwegian philosopher Arnie Naess (Naess 1973; Seed *et al.* 1988) to refer to a deep awareness of our interconnectedness to nature. Naess (2008, p.93) says that:

> Unhappily, the extensive moralising within the environmental movement has given the public the false impression that we primarily ask them to sacrifice, to show more responsibility, more concern, better morals. As I see it, we need the immense variety of joy opened through sensitivity towards the richness and diversity of life and the landscapes of free nature. We can all contribute but it is also a question of politics, local and global. Part of the joy comes from the consciousness of our intimate relation to something bigger than our ego… The requisite care flows naturally if the self is widened and deepened so that the protection of free nature is felt and conceived as protection of ourselves.

Fritjof Capra has written a very clear exposition of the theory of DE, including Naess's ideas, and how it connects to other frontiers of science (Capra 1997). The practice of DE is most associated with people such as Joanna Macy and Dolores LaChapelle in the USA and John Seed in Australia. There is a strong spiritual aspect to their approach. A third strand is the call to political action found in some of today's ecopsychology (see below) and the work of people like Bill Devall (Devall 1990; Devall and Sessions 1985). Gary Snyder and Paul Shepard are also names closely associated with the formulation of the underpinning ideas in this area (Shepard 1998; Shepard and McKinley 1969; Snyder 1993). More radical environmental movements like Earth First! (Earth First n.d.) have co-opted aspects of DE into their thinking but tend to be weak on the economic and political aspects of the environmental crisis.

There is only space to give an outline of the ideas and some pointers for further reading. I suggest beginning with these authors if you want to understand more about the philosophy and ideas underpinning DE: Capra (1997) Devall (1990) Devall and Sessions (1985).

Naess was a philosopher and a mountaineer. He enjoyed spending time in a mountain retreat reflecting on the wild Norwegian landscape around him. From these reflections he developed his ideas on DE. He contrasts the belief that we are separate observers of our environment with the systemic perspective. The latter sees ourselves as an embedded component of wider processes in which we are interdependent for our existence.

Arnie Naess's thinking offers a new paradigm for sustainability (see Table 2.2).

Table 2.2 Shallow and deep ecology

Shallow ecology	Deep ecology
• Mechanistic	• Holistic, systemic. The world as a network of phenomena that are interconnected and interdependent
• Sees the world as separate isolated objects	• World as a living system
• *Anthropocentric*. Nature seen solely in terms of human use value. We are above or outside nature	• *Biocentric*. Intrinsic value of all living beings, humans a strand in the web of life
• Environmental problems seen as they affect humans	• Ecological ethic, concern for future generations as well
• Ideology of economic growth and damage limitation. Environmental concerns secondary to economic ones	• Ecological sustainability. Accepting economy depends on ecology. A paradigm shift
• Ask how to save energy or recycle better	• Ask deeper questions of ourselves and our place in the world

Joanna Macy

Another characteristic of most DE workers, illustrated most clearly by Joanna Macy, is the acknowledgment that an awareness of global environmental destruction has psychological, some would say spiritual, consequences. Anyone with an open mind who informs themselves about the depth and extent of global environmental destruction cannot remain untouched for long. Is the response one of despair, or empowerment to change the way things are? Is the comment of others, 'Well of course you are upset,' or is it 'You should see a therapist?'

For a deep ecologist the distress is 'a normal reaction' in the sense that it does not require treatment as a symptom of some deeper personal projection (although that can occur as well). Coming from a Buddhist perspective, Macy has worked with the emotional distress that many people feel when they become fully aware of what humanity is doing to life on earth.

When a person becomes fully aware of environmental destruction they can experience painful emotions. In Western societies this usually generates fear. Fear of guilt, despair, hopelessness, pain and so on. The mass media sell content by reinforcing the fear response and at the same time offering distractions. One response to fear is to repress it: to ignore, distract oneself, criticise others and more. But this comes at a heavy price. By shutting off our true feelings we become insensitive and lose authenticity. We eventually become apathetic, disempowered and burnt out (Macy and Young Brown 1998). In such a state we are open to further manipulation by powerful forces in the media.

What is the way out of this depressing trap? Macy directs you to get in touch with the repressed emotions and acknowledge them as a sign you are alive. From this place a person feels in contact with their deepest being and can act with empowerment through collective work. Second, there comes the reassurance that the individual self is an illusion. We have no need to defend ourselves. We are already interconnected with everything else.

> The crisis that threatens the planet, whether seen from its military, ecological or social aspect, derives from a dysfunctional and pathological notion of the self. It derives from a mistake about our place in the order of things. It is a delusion that the self is so separate and fragile that we must delineate and defend its boundaries, so that it is so small and so needy that we must endlessly acquire and endlessly consume, and that it is so aloof that as individuals, corporations, nation states, or species, we can be immune to what we do to other beings. (Macy 1991, p.187)

> The self is a metaphor. We can decide to limit it to our skin, our person, our family, our organisation, or our species. We can select the boundaries in objective reality. As the systems theorists see it, our consciousness illuminates a small arc in the wider currents and loops of knowing that interconnect us. It is just as plausible

to conceive of mind as coexistent with these larger circuits, the entire 'pattern that connects' as Bateson said. (Macy 1991, p.189)

The obvious choice is to extend the notions of self interest. For example, it would not occur to me to plead with you, 'Oh, don't saw your leg off! That would be an act of violence.' It wouldn't occur to me because your leg is a part of your body. Well so are the trees in the Amazon basin. They are our external lungs. And we are beginning to realise that the world is our body. (Macy 1991, p.192)

I have only touched upon the work of Joanna Macy. If you want to know more I can highly recommend her books. They interweave science, Buddhist philosophy, group processes, cultural explanations and empowered writing (Macy 1991; Macy and Young Brown 1998). Another founding pillar of DE who I don't have space to discuss here is Dolores LaChapelle. Her *Sacred Land, Sacred Sex: Rapture of the Deep* (LaChappelle 1988) is an incredible tour de force exploring our relationship with nature from multiple perspectives.

Political activist deep ecology

I wrote earlier that from my understanding there are at least three different overlapping strands to the use of the term 'deep ecology'. There is the philosophical deep ecology exemplified by Naess, the more spiritual and psychological approach of Macy and LaChapelle and a political activist side such as Earth First!

I will outline the arguments of the political activist strand, and then offer a critique of their position by Bron Taylor (Taylor 1995, 2000). I will refer to them as the deep ecology movement or DEM Activists for short.

They argue that anthropocentric thinking – that humans always come first in moral issues regarding the environment – is the cause of environmental destruction. We need ecocentric attitudes which see humans as equal to other species on the planet. If we don't then we won't survive and neither will most other living things. How do two of their key protagonists, Shepard and Snyder, say this has come about?

Paul Shepard saw the move to farming as the leaving of the Garden of Eden and the separation between humanity and nature. Hunter-gatherer societies have earth-based religions and see themselves as part of nature and not owning the land they live from. The pastoral and agrarian societies that followed had a sense of land ownership because they invested time and effort in looking after its crops and animals. The farming societies of Neolithic times were vulnerable to marauders stealing their livelihood and so a warrior class developed to protect them. This in turn, they argue, made warfare and increasing centralisation of political power come about. The Mother Earth religions diminished as new belief systems reflected the changing male warrior-farmer societies. They created sky gods who stood outside of nature. Shepard saw the move to farming as the leaving of the Garden of Eden and the crucial separation between humanity and nature.

The DEM Activists go on to say that in the Middle East, where the agricultural revolution began and spread across Europe and North Africa, the monotheistic religions emphasised the heaven of the sky gods. The holy is above and beyond the world, our life on earth was secondary and temporary. The religious beliefs dictated people's behaviour, which was to have little regard for nature. Western religions desacralised nature and became anthropocentric. They give permission to humanity to exploit natural resources for themselves with no regard for the consequences.

Certainly if we look around the world today we see environmental destruction on a grand scale fuelled by large corporations intent on making money regardless of moral rectitude. The globalised political systems are unwilling to grasp the significance of what is required. At the same time governments have become more and more remote from local democratic concerns. The religions of the capitalist countries who control the economic order are predominantly Abrahamic: Christian, Jewish, Muslim.

Shepard's solution is a new consciousness to match the environmental destruction of our home planet, beginning with a rejection of Western monotheism and a support for indigenous religious cultures and mystical beliefs that emphasise humanity's harmony with nature. Examples are earth goddess worship, witchcraft, pantheism and animism. New earth rituals have been created to enable people to bond with nature.

Shepard argues that it is in our genes to live in harmony with nature; we evolved over millennia to live well in nature. We need to live as people in the Pleistocene did and then we will be healthier, emotionally stronger, less warlike and closer to nature. Inspiration within DEM Activists (who are strongest in the USA) comes from earlier American thinkers like Thoreau and Muir.

The political and economic way forward for Shepard is to embrace bioregionalism. The idea is for cultures to be self-organised, based on bioregions such as a river catchment area or similar habitat zone. In the process of deepening themselves with the land people will develop distinctive cultures. The argument runs that if people identify with the land around them they will want to care for it more. Environmental protection will seem obvious. Much of the inspiration for these ideas comes from observations of the indigenous North American cultures. Plains indians followed the buffalo over the grasslands and had a different connection to nature and culture compared to the forest people of North West USA. They both had rituals and beliefs affirming their connection to the rest of nature.

Critique of the DEM in North America by Taylor

Bron Taylor offers a cogent critique of the DEM. She argues that the analysis put forward by the DEM is simplistic, mono-causal and binary about a complex situation and set of solutions. This is somewhat paradoxical for a movement acknowledging the importance of ecological systems thinking and a tolerance for other living beings. Their analysis does not match the sophistication found in historical and anthropological evidence. It also suggests that the humility combined with analytic thinking so skilfully applied to global ecosystems and sustainability is not seen to be readily transferred when thinking about social and political issues. It does not help a movement to see those that oppose you as being completely unlike you.

Research indicates that at a global level opposition to environmental degradation is not driven by spiritual and DE values but more by a recognition that environmental degradation directly threatens human livelihood, health and the survival of children (Taylor 1995, 2000). The work of Vanada Shiva and Wangari Maathai comes to mind in this respect. Both women are known for their campaigning on the environment and people's rights. There is only space to signpost a couple of examples of their work. Vanada Shiva began her work in agriculture in 1984 after the Bhopal gas leak disaster in which many people died at a Union Carbide pesticide manufacturing plant in India. She has drawn links between the use of chemicals and soil destruction, rural poverty and bio-piracy. She has championed the role of women farmers in retaining biodiversity through small-scale farming. In other words it is not an understanding of early agrarian societies and monotheism which informs and motivates environmental activists in developing countries. It is a *social analysis* by local people of how outsiders in multinationals or corrupt governments have stolen our land and resources for quick profit rather than sustainable land use. It is not farming that is destructive but the economic system that dominates local cultures. Many people in developing countries understand sustainability and environmental justice only too well. In advanced industrial societies there has also been a shift in radical thinking to embrace environmental issues within a wider critique of capitalism (Klein 2015). It is not necessary to have an ecocentric view in order to make the connections between environmental destruction, economic oppression and a lack of true democracy.

With regard to the necessity to abandon monotheistic religions in favour of indigenous and Eastern religions the evidence is complex and not straightforward. In situations of change and crisis people usually turn initially to their indigenous belief systems. These are often adapted to take into account changing circumstances. They may also form coalitions with other groups, some of which may have more explicit and thought-through environmental agendas. There are advocates for environmental spirituality coming from a Christian perspective, such as Thomas Merton, Matthew Fox and Thomas Berry. Jewish and Muslim environmentalists have found interpretations within their own sacred texts to support environmental protection. Also the evidence shows that not all indigenous societies have shown respect for the environment. Many large mammals were lost in America soon after the arrival of people from across the Bering Straits, for example. What we are faced with is a complex world in which people can change their attitudes in the face of evidence from their circumstances for a variety of reasons.

Although the contribution of bioregional thinking and a spiritual link to nature are an important contribution by DE, the concept comes with its own difficulties. It fails to take into account existing linguistic and cultural ties that people have. It also presupposes that the new bioregional states will not indulge in conflict and result in a Balkanised world that does not engage in regional and global issues. Failure to tackle globalisation and global environmental issues such as the ozone layer, climate change and overfishing from a localised view in bioregionalism is not sufficient. The problems come from a utopian thinking which is naïve about power relations. The paradox is that while local regional democracy is beneficial, some account has to be made of power relations. Some bioregions are bigger than others. There would need to be constraints in place to prevent interstate violent domination.

Dan Deudney (Deudney 1995) appreciates much of the DEM's ideas but is most critical of its failure to address power relations. He also has serious limitations to a purely local perspective. He proposes a 'terrapolitan' view that sees the earth as a unity to which all cultures need to commit. He also argues that unlike previous monotheistic religions a deep ecology spiritual belief system could be the first to be compatible with modern science through ecology. However, history tells us that people do not switch religions readily and that adaptation of existing belief systems is more likely under collective statements such as the Earth Charter.

> At their best, bioregional deep ecology movements represent a morally laudatory humility and compassion. Their activists are among the most passionate defenders of life on Earth. Stripped of overbroad critiques and simplistic prescriptions, their insights can be a bedrock for the construction of Green social philosophy. They should be welcomed into the sustainability debate, along with the raucous chorus of new and old environmental philosophies, traditional religions, diverse political theories, and nature religions. Perhaps in this stew of rapidly mutating and cross-fertilizing political life and thought, we can find hope and take heart. (Taylor 2000)

Ecopsychology is that branch of psychology concerned with the relationship between the mind and our environment. The book edited in 1995 by Roszak, Gomes and Kanner – *Ecopsychology: Restoring the Earth and Healing the Mind* – was a significant milestone in defining the subject area and is still a good starting point to explore the subject. Buzzell and Chalquist talk of ecotherapy as being applied ecopsychology (Buzzell and Chalquist 2009). Ecopsychology, like ecotherapy, is different things to different people. For some it is the psychological study of how we make sense of the natural environment. Many focus on why we as a species feel psychologically nourished by nature and at the same time display a dark side of environmental destruction in the face of mounting evidence of how much we trash our natural life support systems. Ecopsychology includes social and political strands (overlapping with some deep ecologists). This branch of ecopsychology challenges our contradictory relationship with nature and attempts to change people's beliefs and behaviour in a positive direction. A major focus is the distress people feel at what is happening to the global environment and how to respond to it. It is not primarily concerned with the key issues in this book, that is to say the positive role that wild nature can play in coping with mental distress of a non-environmental origin. The wider field of ecopsychology has much in common with the practical ecotherapy advocated here.

Mindfulness and ecotherapy

Mindfulness is a psychological state of increased awareness and attention in the present moment. One of the distinctive characteristics of the approach to ecotherapy advocated in this book is the central place of mindfulness. I go into mindfulness in more detail in the section 'The evidence for mindfulness in nature' in Chapter 5. Here I want to highlight the significance of mindfulness to this particular style of ecotherapy. I will do this by describing my own process of developing a distinctive style of ecotherapy.

I have professional training and experience in psychology, counselling and group work going back over 45 years. Since childhood I have been fascinated by the natural world. These two threads in my life remained relatively separate until about 25 years ago.

All my adult life I have been curious as to why I was attracted to being in nature. This curiosity grew over time until it came to a head. Without going into too much detail here, I realised that for me, connecting to nature was central to my own psychology, my sense of self. The self-revelation blended the division I had had between mind and nature. All this was enhanced by many years of practising mindfulness through meditation and other personal development practices. I had taken people on informative nature walks and now I wanted to do more. I had worked with people on their personal development and wanted to take them into nature. The blending continued until I realised my place in all of it.

I began experimenting. I didn't have a name for what I was doing initially. I adopted 'ecotherapy' at some stage because it ended in '-therapy' and I thought it would be acceptable to health professionals. I am still not content with the term but use it for its familiarity and because I can't come up with a better one.

I knew that taking people on country walks had a positive effect on them but I didn't know why it worked or how I could enhance the experience. I wanted to increase the depth of contact with nature and so I drew on my own positive experiences. I continued to experiment. I introduced meditation outdoors and used sensory awareness, visualisations and stress reduction exercises from my professional work. They all had the desired effect of enhancing a deeper contact with nature in my clients. This is why I say ecotherapy is more than a walk in the woods.

In the early stages I worked in isolation but felt I was onto something useful. Later I discovered others were doing things like mindfulness-based stress reduction, outdoor games with children and such like, which gave me the confidence my work would be understood and accepted.

Over time I came to realise that for me, mindfulness was central to the way I wanted to work. If I could encourage people to be mindful while outdoors then all the other processes of gaining a deeper connection to wild nature would follow more easily. Many outdoor activities come under the umbrella of 'ecotherapy' but for me the key ingredient is mindfulness.

Multiple effects of ecotherapy

Ecotherapy sessions commonly have multiple components to them which in turn offer multiple benefits to participants. This is a strong argument to present to sceptics and financially hard-pressed health managers. As well as the positive effects of contact with nature the most obvious benefits are the opportunity to socialise, to be mindful, to be in fresh air and to get exercise. Exercise and mindfulness are both approved by NICE (the National Institute for Health and Care Excellence).

Our own web-published research (McGeeney and Jeffery 2011) shows that these multiple effects are recognised by almost everyone who takes part. We used both quantitative and qualitative methods. There were seven themes identified in the interviews: 'Getting out of the house', 'Stopping thinking about problems and negative thinking patterns', 'Relaxing and physical effects', 'Ecotherapy as separate from daily life', 'Anticipating and remembering sessions', 'Appreciating being in a natural environment' and 'Safe, trusted and valued social group'. Walking was also often mentioned as an important aspect. This was rarely elaborated on, but may have been used as a shorthand for the whole session. What we also found was that different elements are of primary importance to different individuals. Underpinning all of them are the positive benefits of being in nature. Someone might initially come along to overcome isolation and make new friends. They may not be particularly interested in the details of watching how a butterfly feeds but they may later play an important role in the group's cohesion. I can think of others who really appreciate the mindfulness activities and then take the practice home with them to do on their own during the week. The diversity of positive benefits has implications for the evaluation and marketing of ecotherapy sessions.

The overlapping attractions and positive outcomes for people are a real strength of ecotherapy. Entry into one mode may lead to connections with other relationships to nature. A sensory pleasure from being in a wood may lead to artistic creative work. Or a deeper connection to nature from realising the ecological self may lead a person to carry out conservation work or join a campaigning organisation to protect life on earth. For others it may strengthen their beliefs about religion and the meaning of life.

The most important benefits for mental health professions to recognise are those which improve a person's sense of well-being and enable them to feel more relaxed and less depressed. These outcomes are well documented in the rapidly increasing body of good-quality research.

From my experience of taking groups out over many years I have noticed a positive secondary advantage of ecotherapy for people trying to overcome social phobia. If someone has a social phobia then they will want to control social interactions with others. If they are in a group, or an even more threatening one-to-one situation, it can become stressful and difficult for them to quickly cut off interaction without appearing antisocial. On an ecotherapy walk, someone who is socially phobic will have a great deal of control over their interaction with others. They can hover around the periphery and still take part in the activities and choose when to get more socially involved. Unlike the cocktail party situation, where one can feel trapped with one other person and feel obliged to make conversation, on a walk it is socially acceptable to walk alongside someone else and not talk. It is assumed if you are silent that you are appreciating the view or just looking ahead. I have noticed individuals, who have told me they are social phobics, move in and out of social interactions in this way. One week they may be 25 metres from the main group and at other times chatting with someone about the wildlife.

Is ecotherapy an escape or a return?

Ecotherapy can be seen as an escape from the pressures of one's life, a time to relax in nature away from busy life in the city. However beneficial respite can be, is that all ecotherapy is? The answer is no. Ecotherapy can feel like an escape because it is an unfamiliar way of being for many people, but it is actually a way of being more alive. The processes advocated in this book are designed to bring a person more closely in touch with the natural world around them and by doing so more in touch with themselves in the present moment. In this very real sense it is not an escape from anything, rather a return to being more at home in the world.

One way in which people know they are shifting how they experience things is the loss of 'clock time' when doing ecotherapy. I call the alternative experience 'soul time' because we drop all sense of time passing, even though the clock is moving forwards. We are more aware of events unfolding and concerns about the past and future fall away.

Related activities

In the definition of ecotherapy used here – 'creating a deeper connection to nature and feeling better for it' – there is the positive intention to 'connect and feel better' and it is this which possibly makes it a therapy. There are other activities which people have been doing since long before the invention of the term 'ecotherapy' that have similar outcomes even if the intention is not 'therapeutic'. Sometimes when I meet people and explain what I do their response is to tell me how they do ecotherapy. For example: 'I go for a walk and find that it clears my head and lifts my mood.' If you talk to mountaineers, ramblers, people interested in wildlife (who used to be called *nature lovers* interestingly), wild campers and holidaymakers who choose to stay in remote places with wild scenery, they all talk the same language that people use after an ecotherapy session. Henry Thoreau, the nineteenth-century thinker and writer, wrote in 'Walking' in *Nature and Walking*:

> Life consists of wildness. The most alive is the wildest. Not yet subdued to man, its presence…refreshes him… When I recreate myself, I seek the darkest wood, the thickest and most interminable swamp. I enter a sacred place, Sanctum Sanctorum. (Thoreau 1991, p.100)

I am happy to maintain a blurring of boundaries between therapeutic and non-therapeutic activities in any discussion of ecotherapy – just as local ecosystems interpenetrate with others to form the biosphere, no boundary is impermeable. For an activity to be labelled therapeutic there has to be some intention to heal or relieve an unwanted condition. Someone, for example, goes to a psychotherapist because they say they feel depressed and anxious and they want to feel better. In order to improve their state of mind the person will embark upon a course of self discovery which may lead to personal change. They do this with someone who has adopted the role of therapist.

Overlapping this kind of therapeutic process are many activities which are not labelled therapeutic but which nevertheless involve self-discovery and personal change. In these situations the participants do not usually define themselves as having something wrong with themselves. Something which needs fixing with the help of a therapist is not their main motivation for participating. Life events such as travel, relationships, even trauma, can do this for some people. There are also outdoor activities which people participate in because they feel better for doing them. Examples include hiking in remote areas, mountaineering and meditation. The intention is not therapeutic although the outcome may involve self-discovery and a sense of feeling better about life.

Theoretical perspectives

Ecotherapy is not dependent on one particular theoretical perspective. I know ecotherapy practitioners who would call themselves psychodynamic, Jungian, deep ecological or humanistic, for example. The ecotherapy these people use becomes a way of working with the theoretical perspective, giving rise to different activities and different views of the significance of our relationship to Nature.

Art therapy is possibly the nearest comparison to ecotherapy because it also uses different theoretical perspectives and has a body of techniques for using art for therapeutic purposes. This book offers many techniques for practitioners to use as a way of enabling people to gain a deeper connection to nature. However, as I explain below, I see the main intention of my work to be a change in a person's being rather than a curing of symptoms. As time goes on the person develops self-awareness and then the techniques become less important.

In Chapter 4, 'The Evidence from Evolution and Ecological Systems', I discuss some of the theoretical explanations as to why the natural world has a positive effect on our minds.

Shallow and deep ecotherapy

The first stage is to feel connected to nature
The second stage is to feel connected to Nature

(See page 88 for a discussion on the distinction between nature and Nature.)

An important distinction in ecotherapy is made clearer by using Arnie Naess's terms 'shallow' and 'deep'. He applied the terms to the word 'ecology' as a way of distinguishing two approaches to environmentalism. Shallow ecology sees sustainability only in a human-centred, mechanistic form: the environment is something out there, and ecological protection comes second to economic growth. In contrast deep ecology is a systemic perspective acknowledging the interconnectedness of all life including our own.

My use of the terms 'shallow' and 'deep' has a similar quality to it. There is no judgement here about one term signifying a better approach than the other. What is profoundly different is the mindset. The distinction between shallow and deep ecotherapy rests on certain assumptions about why a practitioner is doing ecotherapy. It is in their intentions. In shallow ecotherapy the intention is to relieve stress and improve mood and positive thinking by using the innate positive attraction we have for being in nature along with psychological techniques. The well-known work of Ulrich and the Kaplans, which we will explore later, explains this process very well. In deep ecotherapy the intention is to acknowledge we are already intimately part of nature. Furthermore this view begins with the belief that there are no problems to solve, no illness to fix, no therapy required. Ecotherapy becomes more than a technique to fix things but is a way of being in the world. It is the transpersonal which is sought after: to experience a loss of the individual self and to live in the ecological self. This may seem like a big challenge to work with and it is. The alternative, of working with people's fantasies, irrational anxieties and memory reviews of past events, may bring some form of happiness. However, for some a question still remains. For many people the pursuit of happiness and freedom from stress are all they are asking for when they seek counselling. Another approach is to become aware of experience in a mindful way; to become aware of the ultimately illusory quality of our fantasies, worries and hopes. It is in this place that mindful deep ecotherapy comes in to its own.

William Wordsworth (1959 [1798]) expresses the experience of deep ecotherapy very well in his long poem *Composed a Few Miles Above Tintern Abbey*:

For I have learned
To look upon nature, not as in the hour
Of thoughtless youth, but hearing oftentimes
The still, sad music of humanity,
Not harsh or grating, though of ample power
To chasten and subdue. And I have felt
A presence that disturbs me with the joy
Of elevated thoughts; a sense sublime
Of something far more deeply interfused,
Whose dwelling is the light of setting suns,
And the round ocean, and the living air,
And the blue sky, and in the mind of man,
A motion and a spirit, that impels
All thinking things, all objects of all thought,
And rolls through all things. Therefore am I still
A lover of the meadows and the woods,
And mountains; and of all that we behold
From this green earth; of all the mighty world
Of eye and ear, both what they half create,
And what perceive; well pleased to recognise
In nature and the language of the sense,
The anchor of my purest thoughts, the nurse,
The guide, the guardian of my heart, and soul
Of all my moral being.

Spirituality and psychological states

The term 'spiritual' is frequently used when talking of holistic, less medical perspectives in mental health. My own work in ecotherapy has been described in this way. The word is often used in conjunction with body and mind in this context to acknowledge that all three are interlinked systems; when the body is unhealthy the mind is affected and vice versa.

In the phrase 'body, mind and spirit' I can accept the term 'body' – my body is a physical part of my experiencing world. The mind I equate with my experiencing world, an ongoing shifting matrix of different senses, thoughts and emotions. I understand the mind to be a process of mental activity which is inseparable from the body.

The term 'spirit' is the one I find most confusing in this trio because I have yet to see a definition which matches my experience. I don't see any evidence for a spirit or soul and I believe current definitions blur different things together which adds to the confusion. The Oxford English Dictionary Online (ODO) has these definitions:

> *Spirituality* – 1 relating to or affecting the human spirit or soul as opposed to material or physical things: 2 relating to religion or religious belief.

The ODO gives five definitions of 'spirit' of which only one is relevant here:

> *Spirit* – 1 the non-physical part of a person which is the seat of emotions and character; the soul: the non-physical part of a person regarded as their true self and as capable of surviving physical death or separation: the non-physical part of a person manifested as an apparition after their death; a ghost: a supernatural being.

Research into the theoretical understanding of spirituality in a clinical setting by modern nurses identified five concepts that people frequently use when discussing what is meant by spirituality (Martsolf and Mickley 1998). These aspects have been widely adopted in discussions of spirituality and mental health; see for example Swinton (2001). The five aspects of spirituality are:

Meaning: finding a meaning or purpose in life; making sense of how things are.

Value: a person's fundamental beliefs; those things, ideas, actions we consider important in life; often relating to beauty, truth and worth.

Transcendence: that which is beyond the individual self and its boundaries; experiences and awareness of something more than oneself.

Connecting: the sense of being more connected, whether it is with one's self, other people, nature or a deity.

Becoming: a sense of a developing self; who one is and the acquisition of wisdom from life's experiences.

What we have here is a mix of beliefs and psychological experiences. The belief aspects of the above definition are Meaning, Value and Becoming and I don't see that you need call yourself spiritual to reflect on making sense of life situations or having cherished beliefs and standards, or a sense of who one is. These are really philosophical themes and can be considered without recourse to anything spiritual.

That leaves Transcendence and Connecting in Martsolf and Mickley's definition. The ODO defines 'transcendence' as existence or experience beyond the normal or physical level. I can appreciate Martsolf and Mickley's use of the word transcendence as a psychological state of awareness that goes beyond the individual self. Transcendence may be a quality of the term 'spiritual' but experiencing a transcendent state does not mean one is necessarily being spiritual.

'Connecting' in their definition seems very similar but I need another term which takes out the religious connotations. I prefer the term 'transpersonal', which the ODO defines as: denoting or relating to states or areas of consciousness beyond the limits of personal identity. This definition makes it a psychological experience and it could be nothing more than that. When this dissolving of the sense of individual self takes place other experiences such as connectedness, awe, love and mindfulness come to the fore. Again these are mental phenomena and do not require recourse to the supernatural.

The core of my work in ecotherapy is to foster the transpersonal, devoid of religious or spiritual connotations, allowing the strength of personal experience to be lived directly, with minimal cultural interpretation.

Chapter 3

Doing Ecotherapy in Our Work

Gazing at the flowers
Of the morning glory,
I eat my breakfast.

Basho, trans. Blyth (1942)

In this chapter I will discuss:

» what is required to be an ecotherapist

» how to set up ecotherapy sessions

» how to run successful ecotherapy sessions

» how to bring ecotherapy into other aspects of your work: the therapy room, residential care, gardens, etc.

Am I competent to be an ecotherapist?

This is a common question asked in training: the issue of competence. It needs to be addressed before we go into the details of how to run a session. Maybe you are someone who does not feel expert enough to run an ecotherapy session because you don't know enough about wildlife or therapy. Read on!

It is important to stress that there is no protocol to follow and certainly no requirement to be qualified in ecology, forestry, environmental studies and such like in order to do ecotherapy. As someone who is trained and experienced in counselling and group work *and* is very knowledgeable about wildlife I often get asked how a person can do ecotherapy when they know so little about wildlife. I train people mostly in the mental health professions but I also get asked a similar question by people working in conservation, land management and wildlife guiding – can I do ecotherapy if I'm not a therapist? I will address this second question later on.

With regard to mental health professionals first of all, I want to explore two issues relevant to the question of competence. One is about the changed role of the professional and the other is about the place of wildlife knowledge in ecotherapy.

The triadic relationship in nature

It is in the nature of ecotherapy (or at least the version I work with) to question the client–expert dynamic. Therapists working from a model which is highly dependent on being an interpreter of another's experience may find this approach challenging. Ecotherapy readily creates a challenge because there is a third party in the therapeutic process which is not present in the therapy room – nature itself. By saying that, I'm not ignoring the relationship between therapist and client. I am merely pointing out a significant change of emphasis. I believe the primary focus of ecotherapy should be the relationship between nature and the client. The role of the ecotherapist is to facilitate that relationship.

Even before the client and therapist reach green space there are significant changes taking place. However welcoming a consultation room is, it is implicitly the territory of the professional. It may feel reassuringly safe, predictable and under control for the therapist but it still represents and expresses the professional's place not the client's. Beyond the walls of the counsellor's office or hospital ward there is a dynamics shift between the people involved. Some therapists may find this change in the power dynamics and boundaries unsettling. I would encourage those people to experiment and discover the benefits for themselves.

In my experience reducing the power difference between a client and me is very liberating for both of us. The role of ecotherapist and client is never lost but the opportunity for both parties to gain a deeper connection to nature and themselves is ever present. Outside the hospital it is easier to be two people just walking and talking.

It is also somehow easier to let go of notions of illness and diagnosis when confronted by the immediate experience of being in nature. Nature shows itself in all its forms if one takes the time to look. All human conditions are there. A beetle is unknowingly squashed on the path, a tree recovers from storm damage, and new life returns in spring after so much has died down.

Wildlife knowledge

I now want to turn to the relevance of wildlife knowledge. What is the place of wildlife knowledge when the intention of ecotherapy is to enable people to be aware of themselves and their deep connection to the natural world?

I want to distinguish between what I do in ecotherapy and what I might do on a conventional wildlife walk, although the two styles do overlap. In ecotherapy my intention is to bring people closer to nature, to feel they are right there embedded in the natural world around them. Nothing else matters at that moment except to be engaged with nature. You can see from reading much of the rest of this book that I encourage people to be in the moment and to be fully aware of their senses and emotions. When I slip in factual information I do it lightly and when it seems most appropriate, mixing the sensory pleasure with more information. I do it almost without thinking as you might in a conversation when suddenly coming across something remarkable: 'Ah, look, the swifts have arrived at last, can you see them flying high up in the sky?' Everyone's attention is on the aerobatics of the swifts as they slice through the air at breakneck speeds. At that moment we are with the swifts and not in our self-chattering minds. Seeing the first swifts is a reason for us to celebrate early summer. Ted Hughes expressed this feeling really well in the poem 'Swifts'. Here is an extract:

> They've made it again,
> Which means the globe's still working, the Creation's
> Still waking refreshed, our summer's
> Still all to come –

> *Hughes (1976)*

I might say at some point, 'Do you know that once they leave the nest swifts don't land for two to four years, that is until they are mature enough to have their own nest?' This sort of comment usually provokes wonder and curiosity. I can leave it at that and move on. Or I can develop the conversation by adding, if the question hasn't already come up, that swifts sleep on the wing very high up, in short bursts, and they can end up 50 miles from their home area by morning.

The thoughts, beliefs and information placed in context can affect how people perceive the natural world and that in turn does affect how people feel about life around them. These assumptions are based on the idea of the ecological self: the idea that I am not a separate individual but a participant in a wider drama in which all living things are involved. This is not some wacky idea but basic science: you are breathing oxygen right now which you could only do if plants continuously took in carbon dioxide and let out fresh oxygen. In other words plants and animals, including us humans, are codependent for life. Read some of the visualisations in the Activities section, which combine science with wonder, to get the point I'm making.

Factual knowledge does have a place in this work, but it is a question of balance between expert information and other modes of being, and also the appropriateness of introducing information. When I first began doing this work I made a big effort to distinguish what I was doing in ecotherapy from my other work as a wildlife guide. I wanted to be clear in my mind between therapeutic work which aimed at encouraging a mindful connection to nature and informational walks where my job was to point out wildlife and talk about it.

A distinction has grown up in our culture, which is reflected in how I used to think, between two views of nature. One is the world of wildlife experts, Attenborough programmes, geeky biologists and bird spotting, where the focus is on information. The other is aesthetic, sensory and transpersonal, expressed more often in poetry and art. I think the distinction is false and limiting. Our deep appreciation of nature can be enhanced by knowledge of its workings. And in turn some of the best wildlife programmes convey a sense of awe and wonder. For example, to know that there are more cells in your body that are not genetically you (i.e. benevolent bacteria), is pause for thought, is it not?

I have now softened the distinction between information and emotion in my work, even to the extent of introducing ecotherapy methods on a wildlife walk. And in turn, despite my early cautiousness in giving too much informational knowledge on wildlife during an ecotherapy walk, the feedback has been positive. I often carry a small pair of binoculars and a magnifying glass with me, and maybe a couple of identification guides to show clear pictures of what we are talking about. After workshops, when I've asked for feedback, many people say they enjoyed hearing about wildlife and learning how to identify things like birdsong or the names of wild flowers, and so I have continued to include these snippets of information.

Some people who are beginning training in ecotherapy become concerned that when they come to take a group out they won't have the knowledge to do the same as me. I have a number of points to make in response to this concern.

First, if you don't know much about wildlife then it is possible to learn over time, and the longer a person spends outdoors with their eyes and ears open the more they will learn. Learning to identify things can be an activity in itself for your group. Make it into detective work. There are many good identification guides and websites on flowers, birds and trees. Usbourne publish excellent books aimed at children. They are also a good starting place for adult beginners because they are concise and basic.

The second point is the one I made earlier. The intention of ecotherapy is to increase human contact with nature, and while that can be done by noticing and naming wildlife this is not the core activity. The core process is to enable all the senses to be open to nature, to be fully present and to respond with the heart. At times I enjoy puzzling over the identification of a new insect I've discovered for myself. But our culture is dominated by the scientific approach to the natural world. I am keen to encourage a different, more fundamental, felt connection between ourselves and the rest of nature. This can be done without any knowledge of the names of things. The ability to really listen to a dawn chorus is more important in ecotherapy than being able to analyse who made what sound, however intriguing that may be.

One last point on this issue. A client may have much more knowledge of the natural world than the ecotherapist. If this is the case the client's expert knowledge is something to be utilised.

Ecotherapy by non-therapists

The answer to the question 'Can I be an ecotherapist if I am not a qualified therapist?' depends on what you are offering to do with participants.

The first point to make is that whoever you work with you will need a sensitivity to people and their feelings. The next issue is the contract you have with the participants. Some ecotherapists effectively do therapy outdoors; they use the time to directly address personal issues a client brings up while they are both in nature. This is a valid form of ecotherapy and there are benefits from having a therapy or counselling session outdoors in nature. This book is not about that approach. The style of working I use recognises that people have other opportunities to focus on their personal problems if they want to and what I am offering is something different.

My contract is to enable people to gain a deeper connection to nature, not to sort out problems. Happiness or problem resolution may follow as a secondary consequence of gaining a deeper connection to nature but that is not my intention. I am more interested in clarity of experience than happiness. The latter can be achieved through many methods which are in denial of reality, hence one of the attractions of drugs, both pharmacological and recreational. It has been suggested to me that my approach to ecotherapy is complementary to CBT which focuses on the thoughts and beliefs a person has. This may be the case because in working with mindfulness and direct experience I am not intending to analyse or change behaviour, but CBT is.

I do not ask people's diagnosis if they are referred from a mental health organisation and I do not invite people to talk about their problems. If someone chooses to talk about themselves to me that is fine and I will do what I can to help them. But if the session is dominated by personal issues I will shift the orientation and bring our attention to the present experience of where we are in nature. Without wishing to dismiss people's mental problems, stress, anxiety and coping strategies, I see that much of what we call mental illness is a problem of the mind. And we are so much more than our minds. When you are mindful of the present then memories about what happened in the past and imaginings about the future (neither of which exist in the material world) can lose their fear. When this is done in nature the power of thought can lose its grip and a person can get a vacation from themselves and their problems, and more importantly gain deep insight.

Are you planning to work with people who have been diagnosed as mentally ill or are you working with the general public? If you are working with people who have experienced mental distress then various options are open to you if you feel inexperienced. One option is to co-lead with someone who does have expertise in working with people experiencing mental distress.

Another consideration is to question your own assumptions about mental illness. Mental illness is still a taboo subject for many in our society and one which many people find fearful to contemplate. It is not helped by distorted and alarming caricatures presented in the mass media. The 2012 Paralympics did a great deal to dispel falsehoods and prejudice about physical disability. We saw people achieve great feats and their disability was only one of many challenges to success. We need a similar change of mindset regarding mental distress. Mind and other organisations run excellent awareness programmes. If you are uncomfortable working with people who have experienced mental distress this is the next professional development step for you to take.

An essential development for anyone wanting to take up the style of ecotherapy expounded in this book is to learn and regularly practise mindfulness. There are specific courses you can attend or you could find a local Buddhist group and take a meditation course with them. You will find that there is no compulsion to take on the beliefs of Buddhism, although you may well find Buddhist ideas helpful in developing mindfulness.

As a first step, and to gain confidence if you are a ranger or conservation officer, you could do what the park rangers of Barking and Dagenham did after a training programme with me. They set up and ran walks in the local parks for local people entitled 'Explore, Discover, Relax'. The walks were not targeted at people who had experienced mental distress but were open to everyone. They used mindfulness combined with some of the activities in this book, as well as their own. They were able to draw upon their wide knowledge of wildlife as well.

As you can see from above if you are a wildlife expert your style of leading the group in ecotherapy will be different from wildlife walks you may have run before, such as fungi forays or birdwatching sessions. Your expert knowledge will be a real bonus at times. People are more engaged when you tell them a wildlife ecological story relevant to the situation. As long as you follow the guidelines presented in this book and give factual information in small doses you should be fine.

One last point which I believe is very important. Everyone has their own style of running sessions and I would encourage everyone to adapt what is in this book to their own talents and interests. When you work from who *you are* and not someone else your work will improve greatly.

Setting up ecotherapy in your work

You are attracted to ecotherapy and are convinced it would be of positive benefit to your clients. The question is how are you going to go about doing it?

This section explains all you need to know to successfully set up an ecotherapy programme. It will focus on taking groups out but the advice can be adapted to suit other formats such as working with individuals. The first thing to say is that ecotherapy is easy. It does not require expensive equipment, or the learning of complex skills, and it is very cheap to run – all positive things your manager will like to hear.

I believe that just being out in nature has a positive effect on most people. Which means that if all you do is take a group of people out for a walk in a country park then you are doing ecotherapy. That is the entry level if you like, but how can you intensify the effect? I have been asking myself these two questions for a long time: what is the positive effect of nature on people's well-being, in other words what is it that makes the difference? And can we intensify these key elements? In order, as an ecotherapist, for you to do that you need to bring more awareness into your work: a sensitivity to the wild world and the effect it has on you and other people.

The two main requirements for a good ecotherapist are: a passion for being out in nature and a sensitivity to people. If you are someone who enjoys going for a walk regardless of the weather, who stops to listen to a bird singing in a tree, and who appreciates the change in the seasons, then you are more than half way there. Knowledge of natural history is not required, a desire to share the pleasure of being in nature is. The other half of being an ecotherapist is the ability to engage with other people. The core counselling skills of genuineness, acceptance and empathy, along with the confidence to lead groups, are all important. Experience of some kind of mindfulness practice is essential for the kind of ecotherapy that is presented in this book.

Once you have decided you want to do ecotherapy then a simple strategy is required. I suggest the following actions need to be carried out.

Decide on a suitable client group

You don't want to begin with the most intractable, reluctant group who will be hard work for you and who won't offer you results that will impress the management of your workplace. You want a group that is going to show benefits early on so that ecotherapy can become established and you can develop your skills. I have had some great successes taking people out from the acute ward of a psychiatric hospital, which might seem like a tough assignment. However, the nurses and ward managers later gave me positive feedback on how improved the participants were. In this situation it was important for the staff to understand what I was attempting to do and to select patients who were most likely to benefit. A less challenging group with a much greater chance of initial success would be one made up of people in recovery, individuals living in the community who volunteer to come along to the session and who are referred by their care coordinator or similar. You may want to start with the general public as a way of developing your skills, before working with specific groups.

It is vital to know your own limitations. If you are leading a group of people out into nature it is important that you feel confident in your abilities. Be honest with yourself about your limitations and seek support if needed. Better to run a successful if limited set of activities rather than find yourself out of your depth or appearing to lack integrity. You will develop experience as you lead more groups. Personal supervision is very useful for considering how you might tackle potentially challenging situations that have not yet occurred (and those that have). You could consider a range of situations you are uncomfortable about and work through your feelings and the options available to you.

Even before your group has got going you can decide on who you want and don't want in your sessions. I mention to referees that my group is open to anyone, except if they think a person might be highly disruptive to the group. In fact I've never had anyone I've had to ask to leave for that reason.

I make it clear that everyone who comes along is a volunteer. Whenever someone has been pressurised to attend they stand out very clearly to me. They either don't turn up the following week or they leave after a discussion with me. I remind everyone who attends the group that the session is voluntary and they don't have to come if they don't want to. They need to be open to trying out different activities and be willing to give things a go.

I want as many people as possible to benefit from ecotherapy. I have accepted some people on a walk as a personal challenge to me – if they are keen to take part. I don't like refusing someone if I can help it and I try to find the benefit in accepting them. A large overweight man with a walking disability meant the group had to walk more slowly and stop while we waited for him to catch up. A blind person with a carer challenged me to think of more non-visual activities we could do as a group.

The physical limitations of those who come along are also worth considering for a moment. I make sure everyone knows what to expect. The leaflet mentions wearing suitable clothing and shoes, to bring water and maybe suntan lotion. At the start of the walk I check if people are suitably dressed and tell them if I don't think they are. Some people who turn up to my walks in London have never walked in meadows and woodland for two hours in their life. With a little advice and encouragement they come back next week fully prepared. There are more details below on what to advise.

*A group pausing to take in the view on an
ecotherapy walk in Dagenham
This is a good place for a walk because the habitats are varied
and include woodland trees, lakes, open grassland and a river.*

Find a suitable venue

I suggest that the following criteria are important although you may not be able to achieve them all for your location.

- **A reasonable size of green space** so that people feel they are away from tall buildings, noisy traffic and lots of people. The bigger the better as then walks can be varied each week and there will be more chance of getting away from other people. However, I have used a corner of the local park, hospital grounds and a big garden to do ecotherapy successfully.

- **Varied habitats**, for instance mature trees, water in the form of a stream or pond, flower meadows. A big plus in winter is a pond where you can feed ducks.

- **Ease of access** with good paths through the area and also places where people can walk into the wilder places and feel surrounded by greenness. Long muddy paths in winter are not much fun, or areas with poorly managed access where brambles and nettles encroach on the pathways.

- **Easy to get to**, as many clients will not be working and have a limited income. A site which is within walking distance of their home or has a bus stop nearby will be attractive as will good free parking.

- If you want people to come back on their own **the place has to feel safe**. Park managers can achieve this by having staff on site or ensuring there are clear sight lines ahead and bushes well back from pathways.

- **Dogs and farm animals** can be very unsettling for some people. Make sure everyone feels comfortable about walking through a field with horses, for example. In that situation I sometimes suggest the more anxious people keep to the centre of the group while the horse lovers walk ahead to greet the animals. Dogs are another problem and best avoided if possible in case someone is nervous. I have found that the typical behaviour of the weekday dog walker is to appear in numbers mid-morning and to disappear to a café by about 11.00 a.m.!

- **Somewhere to meet indoors**, such as a café, means that newcomers can feel safe waiting around and can find you easily. The indoors element also increases the social side of things. People can meet up beforehand and chat and if it is a café then warm drinks are very welcome in winter and soft drinks in summer are also a draw.

- A café or visitor centre is also likely to have **toilets**, another essential.

Check the legal paperwork is in order

You may want to get management on board before doing the paperwork. But if you already meet the other criteria, then it will look more impressive if you come fully prepared when you first broach the idea. The key regulatory paperwork for taking people out is personal and pubic liability insurance, risk assessments and a qualified first aider certificate.

If you work for an organisation such as the NHS it is likely that you will be covered for insurance if you are taking people out as part of your job role, but check first. If you work for yourself as a therapist or counsellor then check your personal and public liability insurance covers you; it should do. A risk assessment needs to be carried out for every site you take people to, but this is a straightforward process. Common sense means that if you take a group out you should warn them to be careful of uneven ground or stinging nettles, for instance. You will, however, need a written risk assessment to be shown to investigators should an incident occur. Within the NHS there is likely to be a health and safely officer who can help you devise a risk assessment form that meets your needs. The Conservation Volunteers (TCV) run short training sessions on how to do a risk assessment for outdoor activities and their website gives advice on how to do a risk assessment. It is impossible to do anything that is completely devoid of risk. Your responsibility as group leader is to take reasonable steps to minimise them. Essentially a risk assessment involves identifying the hazards (e.g. brambles, slippery mud, contaminated water), assessing the level of risk to people (i.e. how likely is it that a hazard will be encountered?) and lastly showing what steps have been taken to reduce or eliminate the risk (e.g. warning people at the start of the walk to avoid brambles and to take care when walking along muddy sections, or maybe leading people through the safest route).

Becoming a 'First Aider at Work' is a requirement for many people as part of their job. The qualification usually requires a three-day workshop and practical exam at the end. It is very useful in all aspects of life to have this knowledge and I would recommend it to anyone who is responsible for working with groups outdoors.

Collate evidence demonstrating the positive effects on people's well-being of being in nature

You can make a summary of the key evidence to persuade a manager whose permission you may need to take people out. You will also need research evidence if you create a presentation to show colleagues and other staff. Later chapters examine some of the most convincing evidence and you can find summaries on my website (ww.andymcgeeney.com).

Following on from the successful campaign to encourage healthier eating with the 'five a day fruit and veg' slogan a mental health equivalent was launched. The 'Five ways to wellbeing' (Government Office for Science 2008; New Economics Foundation 2008) suggests that people:

- **connect** – with the people around them, family, friends and neighbours

- **be active** – go for a walk or a run, do the gardening, play a game

- **take notice** – be curious and aware of the world around them

- **keep learning** – learn a new recipe or a new language, set themselves a challenge

- **give** – do something nice for someone else, volunteer, join a community group.

The ecotherapy advocated in this book meets all five elements.

While you are creating a presentation you could think about how you will *market* the ecotherapy programme. Consider who your target audience is. I suggest you gain the collaboration of community mental health teams, health centre managers, heads of departments, occupational therapists, psychologists, nurses, ward managers, art therapists and, most importantly, service user groups such as Mind and Rethink. A simple leaflet in printed and pdf form can be produced and information can be linked to your organisation's website for further details. The leaflet should have as a minimum: the venue meeting place, where exactly to meet, how to get there by bus, day of the week and times, who you are and contact details, what people can expect including the benefits, and how people should dress. Posters with a colour photograph showing a similar habitat to the venue can be put up in wards, clinics and staff areas. A press release, preferably with a photo, sent to local papers may help. You should consider using social media and links to mental health groups.

It is useful to have participants' contact details in case you can't make a session or you need to call emergency services while outdoors. I ask people to fill in a one-page A4 form which asks for contact details, next of kin and any health conditions I should be aware of like diabetes (in case someone collapses into a coma). I don't ask for their psychiatric diagnosis. I also explain that I like to take photos I can use to show others what we get up to in the sessions. I have a section on the form asking if people mind being photographed and whether they are OK or not with being identified in the image. I usually ask before taking a picture anyway but it highlights the issue at the point of joining the group.

The practicalities of taking the group out

At the start of each session, after I have welcomed everyone, I check that people are suitably dressed for the walk. There is information on the leaflet but some people are not used to spending long periods of time outdoors and don't consider how important it is to be prepared. Beginners most often underestimate how much clothing they need in winter to feel comfortable. They don't get warmed up by walking because we go slowly. The most important advice is for people to wear sensible shoes such as old trainers, a waterproof coat and layers of clothing to regulate how warm they are. Water, a hat and suntan lotion may be needed in summer.

I suggest you consider what arrangements you want to have in place for challenging weather conditions. People differ in what they consider to be prohibitive weather. To avoid any doubt about whether to come or not I tell everyone that I will be at the meeting point (indoors) whatever the weather. On the odd occasion that it has rained or snowed heavily we have responded in different ways. In the worst weather we chat indoors and then do some mindfulness. If conditions change for the worse on the walk we can shelter from a shower or go back to the meeting place, and maybe finish early. In my experience few people join the group in winter. Regulars will have acclimatised themselves from November onwards and will be sufficiently motivated because of what they get from the walks. If they are warmly dressed then after 10 minutes they will have adjusted to the outdoor temperatures. There are some fairly obvious practical points to make regarding cold and wet weather. Everyone needs to be dressed for the occasion – warm layers with a waterproof outer coat, warm hats and gloves, and shoes that cope with mud and wet.

I often get the group to alternate walking fast and then slow. If we stop to do an activity it is wherever possible sheltered from the wind. We also do physical warm-ups every so often such as Do-in Chinese fist massage described in the activity *Physical and relaxation warm-ups*, and stretching exercises. If we do meditation it is in a sheltered place after physical exertion or we do it indoors at the end of the session.

Taking groups out in winter

A common question I get asked is: do you take people out in the winter and when the weather is bad? The answer is: yes, of course.

If ecotherapy is about forming a deeper connection to nature then it has to be for all seasons: not only because the sessions are ongoing each week and it would be disruptive for participants to stop coming, but because so much is to be gained by moving through the natural cycle of the year. The sign of the first snowdrop is all the more exciting after weeks of seeing no new growth. The return of life is a sign of hope and the possibility of change and renewal.

This last point links to the important metaphorical and shared processes in nature. As I have made clear elsewhere we are a part of nature. We participate successfully only on condition that we work with the same ecological and biological laws as the rest of life. By observing nature closely we can learn about ourselves and our own life challenges.

I sometimes ask people to find a tree in the wood which has not been damaged or affected by disease. They come back saying there aren't any. At this point we can have a discussion about our own responses to ill health, damage and imperfection. Who is perfect anyway? Then I may ask the group to go and look at how the trees have responded to life's challenges. We notice that they are nearly all healed and healthy, and they have compensated and adapted to their circumstances. And so we have another observation which is a useful stimulus for reflection on our own lives. Nature abounds in examples of resilience, recovery, and adaptation to circumstances. These processes and ways of thinking are useful in helping us to accept the world as it is. When we are overcome by emotional distress, depressed or anxious an important part of recovery is acceptance. When we understand how things really are we are in a much stronger position to do something about it. All the time we are in a fantasy or wishing things were different we are weakened in our actions.

The last point I want to make on the issue of challenging weather is that I use it positively for ecotherapy. Have a look at the activity *Weather you like it or not* and you will see what I mean. Also at the activities in *What to do in winter* on page 296.

Seasonal changes

At each change of season I will ask the group I am working with to reflect on what is happening in nature. What have they noticed? To give them a start I will give examples of some of my own observations. In winter life is tougher for living things. There is less sunlight, and weather conditions are harsher. Shortages of food for animals make it hard for them to survive. In winter many things are dying and mouldering back into the earth or being passed on as food for other living creatures and plants. Trees store their goodness as sap in their roots; badgers and hedgehogs sleep more in cold weather. These are all adaptations for successfully surviving hard times.

And the question then arises: how do you respond to winter? And how do you deal with tough challenging conditions? Is there anything we can learn from nature? In the ensuing conversations we talk about how we might withdraw and protect ourselves when things get tough, do things more slowly, meditate, occasionally treat ourselves. We might seek support from those that do have more energy to help us sort things out.

We might also consider the ups and downs of life and see the possibility of spring arriving eventually (and another winter of course) and that we need to gather energy in readiness. This is because, just as winter is seen as a season for many things dying, it is also a time of life regeneration, even though it may not be obvious on the surface. Before winter ends there is a lot going on in preparation for spring: bulbs are getting ready to burst forth when the sun returns, butterflies are being assembled inside the chrysalis that once was a caterpillar, and the sap of trees begins to rise in February long before we see the first leaves.

The end-of-year changes are important to us all and that is why we have so many traditional activities to take us through this period. I don't want to get into a detailed discussion about the meaning of Christmas here, only to highlight one aspect: the emotional significance of change and how we deal with it at the turning of the year. Despite many people's self-perception of being fashionable city dwellers who have embraced all that modern technology can deliver, there is still a cultural and personal need to deal with the changes from one year to the next and in the darkest times. We draw on many things from nature to help us get through this transition. We bring in evergreen leaves such as fir, holly and ivy, which can represent continuity of life. We may hang up mistletoe, an ancient symbol of fertility. Fires and lights stave off the feeling that the sun is weak or absent, and to remind us it will return. We eat and drink to remind ourselves we still have sustenance and will survive, even though there is little growing in the fields. The winter festivals of Christmas and New Year, which have their historical roots in pagan festivals, may be a mix of fun and family tensions on the surface, but underneath it is a way of coping with the anxiety of adverse changes in the seasons.

In ecotherapy we can be explicit about what is going on through the seasonal changes and if we acknowledge our intimate participation in nature then the anxiety is lessened. We can also respond to the metaphorical aspects of change in nature and how that is comparable to our own life changes.

I take a small rucksack containing my own stuff and a small first aid kit, and the risk assessment form. I also take a notebook which I use as a diary of who attended and what we do each week. I find the diary useful to refer back to when I'm planning activities. In summer I may take a roll of bin bags for people to sit on if the grass is damp.

Consider what type of ecotherapy leader you are

I strongly recommend all ecotherapy group leaders take a practical course in facilitation. It will give you confidence and you will be able to offer more to participants. There is not space to discuss facilitation in detail here.

I am keen for everyone to develop their own style of ecotherapy. I only want to mention a few aspects of my own style as food for thought. It is up to you to decide whether to follow my approach. Following on from this, it is my belief that when I am leading a group I am enabling others to take personal responsibility. People who have been through the mental health system will have been told by professionals (with good intentions) what to do and how to cope with their 'problems'. My message to participants is that it is they who decide what is good for them, not me. I invite people to connect with nature and see for themselves what happens. I take each individual as they present themselves on the day. I make it clear that anyone can step aside if they do not want to do an activity. I also avoid any pressure to 'get involved'. Some participants do not want to mix with the group. They may even be anxious when too close to others. The freedom to choose how close a person wants to be to others on a walk is possible in a way it may not be indoors in restricted rooms. I also don't often invite the sharing of experiences with the group. I create space between activities, usually by walking somewhere, that allows for internal reflection. If people want to give a response by talking I will listen and respond if necessary. I want the connection between an individual and nature to be central, and not for it to be dependent on my interpretation. From the feedback I have received these ways of working are much appreciated by participants. But as I have said, we all need to develop our own style of working.

Running a session

Ecotherapy is very simple to do, and it has the potential to be developed into something profound.

If you take a group of people out, explain what your aims are and get their agreement to have similar aims, then you are all set up to have an interesting time. You are doing ecotherapy if you are out in a natural environment, and that includes a garden, with the intention of becoming more aware – both in general and subsequently in nature – and to get closer to nature. If being out in nature is good for us the next question is: how can we deepen the experience and feel even closer to nature? Increase the dosage if you like? The answer, at its core, is the use of mindfulness-based activities.

A way of facilitating that is liberating

The style of group facilitation I am advocating throughout this book is one of liberation. The intention should be to enable others to become more aware: aware of their own direct experience of the world and of others. For this to happen the facilitator has to relinquish as much authority and institutional power as possible. The intention is to work with personal power and to empower others to act similarly. The biggest expert on an individual is themselves, not an other. This message needs to be conveyed in the way the group is facilitated.

In the style of facilitation presented here, no one is told to do anything, they are invited. I encourage people to experiment and be curious with what I offer: to road test it for themselves as it were, and not to take my word for what the benefits might be. I tell people that any given activity may work for some people but not for others. If you don't want to do an activity then don't do it. Just step to one side and wait until the others have finished. When I suggest other people do an activity that they might consider a bit strange or weird, I have to be confident about it myself. If I don't fully believe in what I am asking others to do then why am I doing it? What has happened to my authenticity? I also need to read the group very well to ensure that I am taking everyone with me and that people are engaging because they want to. A quietly confident and permissive facilitator will build trust easily and free others to be themselves.

The intention to widen the self

In mainstream Western culture psychological therapies are primarily aimed at working on a person's sense of self. CBT, for example, aims to challenge people's beliefs and assumptions about the world that contribute to their distress: I am not a nice person, I feel ugly, I can't do that. Self-esteem is significant in the West: how much we value ourselves. The intention in this approach is to identify those parts of the self a person is not satisfied with and fix them so the individual can accept themselves and feels accepted by society. Therapy and counselling are much more than this. I'm selecting this key aspect, of treating the self, to make a point. And I am not saying that there is anything wrong with this approach.

A different perspective, which is increasingly being accepted in the West, is to sidestep the issues the self is wrestling with and pay attention to personal experience. Once feelings, thoughts, memories and fantasies are given less attention something interesting starts to happen. They are not ignored but seen as products of the mind, just part of experience.

I have a limited understanding of modern Japanese and Chinese psychology. But I do know that they are intrigued by our obsession with the self, something they pay much less attention to. An example of the Japanese approach is the Kawa model which is much more systemic in its understanding of a person who is distressed. I discuss Kawa in the Activities section.

I do know a lot more about the roots of Eastern psychology and philosophy, particularly Buddhism. Buddhism pays much more attention to what you are experiencing rather than what or who you think you are. The two important intentions in Buddhism are awareness and compassion. Awareness is paying attention to what is being experienced right now in an open non-judgemental way. Compassion comes from the heart and is a feeling of open acceptance of what is experienced. Love is compassion in action. The two conditions – awareness and compassion – are dynamically interrelated. When one experiences increased awareness compassion can come in, and vice versa.

Testing the ideas of awareness and compassion for myself I have found their intentions to be sound. In other words, I have found that when I have the intention to put to one side my concerns over self and I pay more attention to what I am directly experiencing I am more loving. I notice that when I am compassionate to my self then the significance of this same self diminishes. What happens, in my experience, is that I have less identity with my individual self and much more a sense of just living in the world.

In the context of this book, the sense of being part of something more than oneself, of no longer being an isolated ego but a participant in the life processes is what Joanna Macy calls the ecological self. In my work I am aiming to take people from a sense of individual self to an ecological self. From 'ego' to 'eco'. In order to work toward this in a session I typically follow these steps:

body awareness
↓
breath/mindfulness
↓
sensory awareness
↓
attention to the wider world

The steps will become more apparent in the model I am now about to present.

The Mindfulness in Nature model

I use the Mindfulness in Nature model for thinking through the activities (see Figure 3.1). I find it useful as a checklist and as a stimulus to consider what we could be doing. I don't use the model with every group because for a variety of reasons it may not be appropriate. The client group may not be open to some of the activities in each stage. I'm thinking particularly of people who are heavily medicated or agitated who find it difficult to open their senses or settle the mind. The model is a suggested map; an actual session may be more unpredictable.

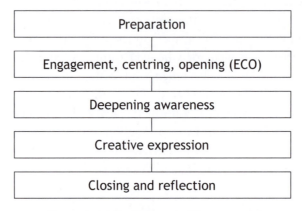

Figure 3.1 Mindfulness in Nature model

Another approach some may find useful is the Flow Learning model created by Joseph Cornell from his work with children and adults (see 'Useful resources' on page 307).

Preparation

In preparation, I gather the group in a place that is not in nature, for example a car park or outside a visitor centre.

I begin by welcoming people and thanking them for coming, maybe acknowledging that by coming along they have made a choice to improve their well-being. I check that everyone is appropriately dressed for the weather and conditions. This is usually not a problem because the printed guidelines advise participants on how to dress and what to bring along. I offer the aims for the session (see below) and set any ground rules. There should be expectations on how to be on the walk and an invitation to join in an adventure.

Sample aims to present to a group

I suggest you find your own words to express these aims.

An ecotherapy session is much more than just a walk in the park. It is finding a way to get a *deeper connection to nature and ourselves*. Consider the following points:

- You have the *choice* to just go for a walk or try out some ecotherapy activities with no compulsion to get involved. Try things out with *an open mind*.

- Ecotherapy works best if you start wanting to *do something for yourself* to improve your well-being (the recovery principle).

- *Respect others* and self-regulate what you share with others about yourself.

- The effects may be *subtle* but can be learnt over time. They are incremental – *listen to yourself*.

- Pay attention to your *body and inner feelings* in relation to nature.

- I am the guide, the facilitator, enabling you to *make a connection to nature*. That's when interesting things happen. This is not therapy despite the name. I am talking to the you that does not need to be fixed or changed.

- This is an invitation to give yourself permission to *trust your feelings, senses and intuition*. You have permission to *enjoy the walk*. Leave behind your work and concerns. Have a day/session for yourself.

Other information I give includes the following. I give timings for the day – when we finish for example. I ask people to turn off mobile phones as they are a distraction to all of us and make it difficult to give yourself fully to the session. I ask all participants to keep sight of me and come to me if they hear the whistle. I ask them to take care and look out for logs and mud underfoot and low branches, nettles and brambles elsewhere. I ask permission to take photos to use for publicity.

Engagement, centring, opening

Having set out the aims and motivated people, walk into a more natural setting; woodland is useful at this stage to contain and surround the group at the beginning, although some space is required for the warm-up activities. The woodland does not need to be big and I have used a group of half a dozen trees and even one big one on its own as a starting place for the activities.

The group at this point is 'in nature' and away from other people, noise and traffic. Your intention now is to begin the process of relaxing, slowing down and opening up. Begin this by focusing attention on the body, followed by the breath, using a mindfulness type of activity. The intention is to sustain an openness of the senses and self to the natural world around us.

My assumptions regarding these steps are as follows. If we can become more aware of our body to begin with then we are more grounded in the here and now, and the physicality of our own nature as flesh. Paying attention to breath (mindfulness breathing) takes us a stage further into being present. It also directs attention away from thoughts in the head to the immediate. Or at least it gives the mind something to do: 'attend to the rise and fall of the breath in our bodies'. One effect of attending to the body and breath is that people slow down and are more able to let go of the recent past and near future concerns. After this state is achieved awareness can expand outwards to the sensory world around us, which is there to explore with new eyes. I explain later in the book how to do a mindfulness activity. (See activities: *Physical and relaxation warm-ups* and *How to meditate*).

Deepening awareness

For many people the ecotherapy session is a sustained break from internal voices and the incessant mental chatter we all indulge in. And it is more than that. This section can take up most of the session and is where you may want to use many of the activities aimed at opening up the senses and reducing awareness of an individual self. Alternatively you may want to walk slowly most of the time and just use one or two activities in a session. The choice of how many activities and which ones to use will depend on how much time you have and also the type and motivation of the participants. With some groups I judge that I can take people to great depths of emotional connection to the natural world. With others, maybe because they are heavily medicated, not feeling resilient, are emotionally fragile or unfocused, I may decide the greatest benefit is just going on a walk.

Appropriate activities for each stage of the model should be evident from the aim of each of the activities.

After each activity I move the group on. I do this to allow time for reflection and integration. It also means that the next activity is arrived at afresh in a different place.

It may be appropriate on the walk to just stop and go through a meditation/mindfulness activity – focus on the breath and let the mind settle again before moving on.

Creative expression

In the Activities section there are some exercises aimed at opening up the senses to nature (classified as sensory) and others to encourage a creative expressive response to experience (creative expressive). You may choose to include a creative activity at any time but it can be particularly effective when people are feeling open to nature. There is no limit to the creative activities that can be encouraged.

The obvious ones are drawing and writing, but music, drama and dance are also worth experimenting with if you have the skills. The environment and intention of the work lends itself to using natural materials in the immediate vicinity: clay, rocks and pebbles on a beach; twigs and branches in woodland; and flowers and grass in meadows. Many people are familiar with the work of the sculptor Andy Goldsworthy, a real inspiration to the possibilities of creative expression by using natural materials (Goldsworthy n.d.). The Bavarian artist Nils Udo works in a similar way (Udo n.d.). I also like the work of Chris Drury (Drury n.d.), but like many land artists, as they are collectively called, his work is often on a grand scale that is not appropriate to the approach in this book.

Closing and reflection

I find it useful to mark the entrance and leaving of sessions. I will do this at the beginning by gathering the group together and indicating that we are about to enter into something special. The first two steps in the model say more about this. At the end of a session it is a good idea to bring everyone together and announce that the session is about to end. Don't let people just drift off; define the ending in some clear way. I may ask people how they feel now or if they have anything to say about their experience of the walk. I encourage people to come back on their own and get in touch with nature.

Bringing ecotherapy into our work elsewhere

How ecotherapy is introduced into the repertoire of client support is going to be different for every practitioner depending on their professional needs and particular circumstances. As well as practical concerns regarding access to convenient green space there are issues to do with the degree of management support available. Elsewhere in this book there are summaries and references to key research demonstrating the effectiveness of ecotherapy. It may be useful to summarise the research findings in order to present an evidence base to your manager. It is to be hoped that the National Institute for Health and Care Excellence (NICE) will approve ecotherapy before not too long. In the meantime here is an approach that succeeded in persuading one psychologist's boss to approve ecotherapy. She told her boss that NICE approves walking and other forms of exercise for depression, and NICE also approves mindfulness.

It is possible to bring ecotherapy into your work in addition to running sessions and workshops. And for those who cannot get permission to take groups out the following suggestions should certainly help.

Your office and counselling room

The room where you invite clients to work with you can be designed to maximise contact with nature. Reminders of the natural world will have a positive effect on yourself and colleagues as well.

The evidence from research shows that just having a picture of a natural scene on the wall can enhance mood and stress levels. Roger Ulrich's work has shown how significant a view of trees from a window is to patient recovery after an operation (see page 105). His work also demonstrates the positive effect on morale when staff have a view of nature from the window. One observation at a psychiatric hospital (see page 101) was that over a 20-year period a record was kept of all the pictures that patients intentionally damaged. None of the images showing a scene connected to nature were touched; the most frequently damaged pictures were abstract works.

Simple changes can be made to your therapy room: a big colour poster of a natural scene in view of the client, for example. A bowl of fresh flowers or a potted plant can make a difference. Conversely the negative metaphor of leaving dead or neglected plants has also to be borne in mind when considering your working environment.

If you are working on a psychiatric ward or in a residential home what is the décor and general environment like where patients have access? Does it remind people of nature? Potted plants can be a bit of a liability in an acute treatment setting but a colleague I know got round this by using plastic pots and cardboard seeding containers. Posters on the wall can brighten up a residential setting and do not necessarily need framed glass but can be laminated.

The person who made my website understood what I was talking about and went back to his office and put a view of trees and blue sky as a screensaver on his laptop. If you want to do the same you can download a natural image for free from my website.

Going for a walk

Indoors the territory of a hospital or therapy room is often perceived by clients as impersonal, medical, owned by the therapist and emphasising the power relationship between client and professional. Outdoors is often perceived as neutral territory, not owned by anyone, for everyone and not just people with problems, full of diversity and life-affirming experiences.

Some people who have been on my workshops have subsequently given me examples of how they have used the outdoors to positive effect on a one-to-one basis. Here are some examples of what they found:

- For some clients in a therapy room the self-focus can be experienced as too intense. Sitting in a therapy session indoors can seem as if the only topic has to be one's personal problems. Walking outdoors invites a range of options in a non-therapeutic context.

- Clients who are reluctant to talk in the therapy room sometimes find their voice outdoors. Nature liberates and reassures.

- In the outdoors it is possible to walk without talking and choose when to interact with another person; silence is accepted.

- When walking outdoors it is easier to choose a comfortable distance between yourself and someone else. By walking in parallel two people can feel they are not being looked at all the time by the other person.

- Some clients who are agitated and struggle to sit still can benefit from the rhythm of walking and movement.

Do you have a local park to go to? If you have your own practice could you use your garden sometimes?

For the client

- As part of creating a case history with the client you could ask about their relationship to nature just as you might enquire about family relationships. What feelings and thoughts does it evoke and do they already use nature for recovery?

- Discuss with a client what the barriers, if any, are that make it difficult to spend time in nature. Explore how these barriers might be reduced or removed.

- Are there ways of connecting a client's existing hobbies and interests with nature? For example, fishing is a good way to spend time outdoors near water. Other possible links are exercise (try conservation work with a local wildlife trust), writing, photography and cycling.

- Get a local map out and discuss with the client places where they could go and be in nature, such as a country park or local park.

- Discuss sensory pleasures with a client and encourage them to participate more in getting enjoyment from their sensory experiences. Explore all the various senses: sight, sound, smell, taste, touch. See in particular the work of George Burns (1998).

- Give activities and tasks to a client which will encourage them to go out into nature.

- Encourage a client to bring back something from a walk in nature, such as a shell, feather or stone, as a reminder of positive times. They could be encouraged to consciously attach meaning to the object when they find it.

- Have clients join a walking group or wildlife club, go on nature workshops run by the RSPB, County Wildlife Trusts, the Woodland Trust, the National Trust and so on.

Resistance to going outdoors

What do we do with clients who, for a variety of reasons, do not want to take advantage of what nature has to offer in the outdoors? They may perceive the outdoors as threatening; too hot, too cold, too wet; boring; and requiring some effort on their part, or they may be agoraphobic. This need not be a problem. There are days, rare ones I admit, when I don't like the prospect of going outdoors. If you sense that a client might benefit from spending time in nature but is resistant to taking up the offer, what are your strategies for overcoming the barriers?

The most obvious response to negativity is to talk through with the person what they think and feel about nature/the garden. How could the activity be made to feel safe for the client and what initial experimental steps could they try out?

An alternative is to just tell everyone in a group 'We are going out now, all of us,' and then see if your command and group pressure works. It could be that once they are outside they do feel OK. I have had people in residential care follow a group out when they see everyone else doing something interesting.

For yourself

You can take time out in nature to recharge your batteries, for example at lunch time or between seeing clients. Exposure to nature has been found to be much more effective as a way of recovering from stress than reading a magazine or sitting indoors (see page 93).

Designing nature into therapeutic environments

The NHS is closely watched by politicians and the public as to how it is meeting targets for improved medical outcomes, reduced financial costs, and increased patient satisfaction. These are the three main measures of how the health service is doing. If anything can be found that helps reach these targets then you would expect it to be adopted immediately. There is now a clear and strong evidence base that bringing nature closer to patients helps meet all those targets (Ulrich 2002). The response to this knowledge is mixed within the health sector. For many the inclusion of gardens into a building project is seen as an additional expense, a luxury, or at best an aesthetic add-on. Fortunately there are some health authorities who do see restorative gardens as a way of saving money and improving patient healthcare and satisfaction with the services. Gardens can improve outcomes for virtually all healthcare buildings: general hospitals, GP clinics, nursing homes, mental health centres and older people's day centres.

It is now well established that there is an interlocking relationship between psychological and physical states in the body. When someone is physically ill they are more likely to be stressed, and when a person is mentally stressed they are more likely to become ill. Just remember the last time you visited a hospital and how you felt. Or recall a period when you were going through a stressful time in your life – did you become ill during or soon after? In reviewing the evidence base for the benefits of restorative gardens the results from research into physical and mental health can be seen as mutually supportive.

The research evidence reviewed in this book points to multiple benefits from exposure to nature, whether by direct experience or from images, in which case it seems particularly important to maximise these effects in healthcare settings.

Research carried out in healthcare settings shows results in line with what we already know in general terms. For example, a study of people experiencing dental fears recorded people's heart rates and self-reported emotional states in the waiting room, and found that people were less stressed when there was a large nature mural compared to days when the wall was blank (Heerwagen 1990).

Restorative gardens

One study carried out 20 years ago, and selected from a long history of positive accounts of restorative gardens, is illustrative of many other studies. The results of observation and interviews from four Californian hospital gardens found that recovery from stress and improved mood was by far the most important benefit for nearly all users of the gardens – patients, family and staff (Cooper-Marcus and Barnes 1995). Patients saw the gardens as a place to escape from the world of treatment and focus on illness. As a consequence it is not surprising that patients and families reported greater satisfaction with the hospital and quality of care because there was a garden, indoor plants and views of nature from the windows. Employees also used the gardens as a way of recovering from the stresses and demands of the hospital.

What make a good restorative garden?

Not enough work has been done specifically comparing different gardens in healthcare settings to be definitive. However, sufficient work has been done on the links between stress reduction and time in nature to draw up the following guidelines (Cooper-Marcus and Barnes 1995; Ulrich 1991, 1999):

A garden is likely to reduce stress and induce a calming effect if it has:

- trees, verdant foliage, flowers and water to look at

- congruent or harmonious sounds such as breeze, water and birdsong

- visible wildlife, for example birds and butterflies

- landscapes with savannah-like qualities, i.e. grassy open spaces with scattered trees.

In contrast, the following qualities receive a negative response from people:

- hardscape is concrete or stark buildings

- hard ground, such as concrete

- cigarette smoke

- intrusive, incongruent urban or machine sounds, such as traffic

- crowding

- perceived feelings of insecurity and risk

- prominent litter

- abstract or ambiguous sculpture.

Gardens which are designed sustainably will be of greater benefit to wildlife and require less maintenance. Big lawns, for example, are high maintenance, requiring regular cutting and weeding. Bushes and small trees on the other hand are low maintenance and can attract a diversity of wildlife if they have blossom, berries and shelter (Carpe Diem Gardens n.d.). If you are designing a therapeutic garden consider stimulating senses in addition to sight. The garden can be made attractive to birds which might sing (bird feeders, nest boxes and cover). Include flowers that give off a beautiful scent (e.g. jasmine, honeysuckle, lavender, rose) and sweet-melling herbs.

Is the garden easily accessible for all? What are the views from the windows? Does it meet the specific needs of the client group? For example, people with Alzheimer's benefit from looped pathways that don't have dead ends and boundaries that contain the space (Shackell and Walter 2012).

Benefits of a restorative garden

The conclusions from research reported in this book are that a restorative garden can bring about:

- faster recovery of physical conditions
- reduced pain
- faster stress recovery
- improved mood, reduced depression
- reduced aggression
- greater patient satisfaction
- increased staff morale, retention and reduced absenteeism.

Consider the following factors when planning a restorative garden:

- sun/shade
- public/private areas
- seating types
- seating to just observe
- looped pathways
- no dead ends
- landmarks for memory
- interest
- colours
- seasonal changes
- easy surfaces to walk on
- edible and non-toxic plants.

Gardens and grounds: improving their ecotherapeutic potential

Take a walk around the grounds where you work and look at the potential you have. Many hospitals and residential care homes have mature grounds with big trees and rich flower beds.

You may have to challenge health and safety decisions made in the past with commonsense evidence for the benefits to patients of having access to the green outdoors. Older people live longer with access to greenery and people experiencing memory loss can improve if they have access to a garden (Takano, Nakamura and Watanabe 2002). Just as with medication that has 'side-effects' a balance has to be struck between potential risks and immediate health and well-being benefits.

Use your own intuition and initial impressions to guide your feel for the place. When you walk around the grounds what feels good? What is boring and unpleasant? What could be improved? Here are some suggestions as to what to look for:

- Are there 'rooms' – distinct areas with a different feel? Perhaps areas screened off by shrubs could create 'rooms'.

- Are there paths that lead you to new experiences, a bit of adventure? You want to avoid creating paths that lead nowhere or to a dead-end wall if some of your clients have memory problems.

- A patio with a flat solid surface area will make walking, sitting and wheelchair access easier.

- Big trees are good for shade, and are also symbols of longevity.

- Flowers, bushes with foliage, fruit and leaf colour should all be included.

- The scent of flowers, herbs and so on is an important element in a garden for increasing sensory awareness.

- Bird boxes, bird tables and feeders could be placed where clients can easily observe living creatures going about their lives.

Ask yourself what you can create/change at minimal cost. Do things in stages, not all at once. Makeovers are not the best idea: change – reflect – change – reflect slowly and in this way nature will have time to give you suggestions.

Carpe Diem Gardens (n.d.) is a company I can recommend if you would like help creating an ecotherapy garden. They have extensive experience of working collaboratively with a variety of community groups, including those who have experienced mental distress. The gardens they create are designed sustainably and to attract wildlife. The garden in the photo below, designed by Carpe Diem for a mental health centre in Dagenham, London, was part of the THERAPI Project I managed while I was at Thames Chase Community Forest. The garden is in a courtyard making it visible to many of the people working there. Note the easy access from the building. The raised beds make gardening for people with limited mobility easier and they ensure that people seated on the benches can get a better view.

Restorative garden attached to the memory clinic in Dagenham

Some suggestions

- Call a meeting of staff, and subsequently patients, and explain the health benefits of ecotherapy and what simple changes can be made to improve everyone's experience of the place. Agree a plan and budget, and keep the manager informed of changes and any positive reports from clients.

- Create a plan of the garden and decide on possible paths, plantings and seating. Take into account the direction of the sun during the day when designating shade and sunbathing areas. Consider ease of access from the building. You could talk with clients about the garden by bringing in garden books from the library.

- Collect seeds from friends' gardens and keep them in old envelopes till spring.

- Ask friends and neighbours for spare plants.

- Trees and bushes are best planted November to April.

- It is worth considering if there is colour in all seasons. Does anyone know if you already have bulbs planted which will come up in spring?

- You could create a sensory area using herbs and other plants with distinctive scents. These are good for sensory awareness and reminiscence.

- Create a sense of enticement just outside the doors to draw people out. Make it easy for people with limited mobility, for example by putting flowers in earthenware pots by the side of the door.

- Think of using tubs and big pots to decorate patio areas.

- Mark out a path with twigs stuck in the grass or dribble sand in lines to see what it could look like. One consideration when thinking of paving stones for paths is that they are heavy, expensive and a potential trip hazard over time, but they are firm and solid to stand on and have clear edges. Alternatives are pea gravel or bark chippings which are probably cheaper and easier to lay, as well as reducing the possibility of tripping over edges.

- Consider bird feeders visible from indoors. Birds like bushes nearby to perch on before feeding. You could also put up bird boxes within view of windows. Make sure they are not in direct sunlight in spring, for the sake of the baby birds who could get hot inside the box.

- Create a pond with water lilies. A pond made like a raised flower bed so the top is waist height is safe and easier to examine close up. The wildlife swimming around under water will be easier to see this way. Water attracts wildlife and is relaxing to look at.

For people who can't go outside
The view from the window

For those who can't or don't want to go outside consider the view from the windows: is it green and busy with birds? What do staff who work inside think of the view? Research shows that staff morale, absenteeism and motivation are better when there is a green view (Lohr, Pearson-Mims and Goodwin 1996; Shin 2007).

*A close-up view of a goldfinch on a bird feeder
just outside the window*

Bringing nature indoors in residential care

For those people in residential care the need for nature to be brought indoors to them is even more important. Ideas can be adapted from this book and you may also want to bring expertise in to help. One organisation you might consider is Rootless Garden. Based in London, they bring plants indoors for people in residential care. 'Rootless Garden is a travelling troupe of garden enthusiasts who use nature as a medium to reconnect generations and promote wellbeing in elderly care' (Rootless Garden n.d.). See also Chalfont (2008).

Part 2

Evidence
A review of the effectiveness of nature on our health and well-being

Chapter 4

The Evidence from Evolution and Ecological Systems

How happy I am to be able to walk among the shrubs, the trees, the woods, the grass and the rocks! For the woods, the trees and the rocks give man the resonance he needs.

Beethoven, letter to Therese Malfatti (summer 1808)

> In this chapter I review the main theoretical explanations for our attraction to nature in the context of our evolution and ecology.

Anyone considering doing or permitting ecotherapy needs to be confident that participants will benefit from the activity. For some time now and with good reason the health service has demanded an evidence base before recommending particular treatments. It is not good enough to offer a treatment just because we have always done so or it sounds as if it should work. However, the process for recommendation, which often relies on NICE guidelines, can be slow moving. Ecotherapy has yet to be recommended by NICE although it does accept mindfulness and physical exercise. Incidentally, 93 per cent of GPs have prescribed anti-depressants against NICE guidelines because of a perceived lack of alternatives (Mind 2007). This is in the context of increasing evidence that these drugs are ineffective.

Is ecotherapy just a good idea that feels right or is there compelling evidence that doing the kind of ecotherapy offered in this book really makes a difference? I want to address this important question by first exploring the ecological, psychological and cultural processes that describe our relationship with the rest of the natural world. If we can establish that being connected to nature is a positive experience for everyone we can then go on to see if a therapy can be formulated that has positive outcomes for those of us experiencing mental distress. For those who want to know more about academic research into the effectiveness of ecotherapy there are now some very good reviews and meta-analyses (Ambrose-Oji 2013; Barton and Pretty 2010; Bragg *et al.* 2013; De Vries *et al.* 2003; Faculty of Public Health and Natural England 2010; Natural England 2009; Pretty, Griffin and Sellen 2003a; Pretty *et al.* 2003b, Tabbush and O'Brien 2003; Bragg and Atkins 2016).

The field of research is growing rapidly and becoming more subtle in its questioning. For a positive review that highlights some of the problematic issues in current research see Hartig *et al.* (2014). I believe, and will demonstrate, that there is a wealth of argument and evidence from our psychological make-up, cultural anthropology, ecology and biological evolution to show that we are intimately a part of nature. This book is directed primarily at mental health practitioners and the research evidence is presented here to underpin the practice of ecotherapy. For those wanting more detailed evidence I strongly recommend delving into the references and further reading at the back of the book. Like all species we have evolved in dynamic response to the natural world around us, and consequently certain natural surroundings have a positive effect on us.

Nature

The word 'nature' has many connotations and shades of meaning. At one level, Nature is everything, the whole universe as an inseparable whole. This is a useful way of seeing things, but for most of the book I'm not going to use this universal meaning. I'm going to use the word 'nature' to mean that which is not human made. It includes all living things, landscape and rocks.[1] I am writing from the perspective of someone who lives in a Western industrialised land with all the limitations that are implied. Some other cultures give nature a different significance to us. In a real sense our views of nature are far from natural but are largely socially constructed. I recommend Castree (2014) for an in-depth discussion of the subject.

Evolution

As Mary Midgley said, 'we are not like animals we *are* animals' (Midgley 2002 [1979]). Evolution is the modern origin myth:[2] it tells of our place in nature and how we came into being like all other creatures. We humans have spent 99 per cent of our time on Earth as hunter-gatherers living intimately within wild places. As an analogy, the time human species have spent on the earth is equivalent to walking through a wild open forest for 2.5 kilometres and taking the last 10 metres

---

1   The word 'nature' has its origins associated with birth. 'Pregnant' comes from the same source. Going futher back, 'nature' has links to the words 'generate', 'kin' and 'kind'.

2   Myth in the original meaning of the word is not a falsehood but a story that profoundly reflects the values and beliefs of a culture.

(since the beginnings of agriculture) out onto cut grass. The Industrial Revolution would equate to the length of your foot as it finished your last step onto concrete.

A similar walking analogy comparing the total time of the whole of life on earth to humanity's time is also interesting. A walk from the beginning of life to the present day would begin in Ankara, Turkey and progress across Europe. It would eventually end up in front of St Paul's Cathedral in the City of London. If you wonder what the last 250 metres might be in the City (the age of modern humans), it would be the walk up from the Millennium Bridge to the door of the cathedral.

If we accept that the physical brain is the primary means by which the mind functions then evolution has a central role in explaining how and why the mind works as it does. Understanding the mind from a neurophysiological perspective has at the same time, of course, to be congruent with psychological and sociological explanations of human behaviour and experience.

A key biological question when examining physical structures and behaviour is: how does this attribute aid the organism's survival, and how did it evolve? The question that attempts to explain why the giraffe has a long neck and the peacock a magnificent tail can also be addressed to the fundamentals of ecotherapy. Why do we feel good in certain natural environments, how does this feeling aid survival, and lastly why did feeling good in certain natural environments evolve? If we accept, and the evidence is overwhelming, that some experiences in the natural world have a positive effect on humans then the understanding of ecotherapy is strengthened if we can also explain how and why these feelings evolved. By saying this I want to make it clear that a full explanation must include sociological and anthropological evidence as well.

Ecological systems

We can begin an understanding of our place in nature by examining human ecology. The word 'ecology' is derived from the root words for 'the understanding of' and 'home'. When we are studying human ecology we are studying our home environment. And as was stated above, our home has been the natural world for 99 per cent of our time here.

Nature is alive, with all that implies, and so are we. Knowing we are alive, and noticing another living being, we can recognise an affinity as we both spend our days surviving in the world. The primary laws we have to obey are the Laws of Nature, the realisation of which can make us feel a participant in Nature and not an observer.

All living creatures and plants are embedded in dynamic ever-shifting ecosystems. In basic physics the second law of thermodynamics says that energy is not lost, it is merely transformed. In ecology scientists use this principle to observe how energy is passed through organisms in a never-ending flow. Nearly all life forms have the basic requirements of needing water, nutrients, oxygen and a suitable temperature to metabolise. They also need to reproduce, and if they are animals they have behavioural requirements to survive and interact with others of their kind. We humans are full participants in these ecological processes even as urban dwellers who buy food and water from shops.

In a way it is strange that even as creative, intelligent, aware human beings it seems we still need continual reminders that we are a part of and are interdependent with these ecosystems that cover the Earth. The air we breathe is transmuted by green plants from carbon dioxide to oxygen. All our food ultimately comes from the soil or the sea and our waste is returned and 'purified' by micro-organisms for re-use. The water we drink every day has been recycling through natural systems since the origin of life on Earth 3.8 billion years ago. Note: the *Four elements: earth, air, water and fire* activity explores these processes further.

If we can grasp that we are intimately interconnected to nature for our very lives, and we add to that idea the driving force of evolution, then it becomes almost self-evident that nature is essential to us psychologically. We can see that all our biological, and by extension psychological, characteristics are with us because of many evolutionary lineages. Many of these traits would have been acquired before human evolution began. We would not have survived if we had not been able to identify and desire to be in the best habitats for our survival.

The connections between our evolutionary heritage and modern life are closer than we might think. Big corporations, when they are after our money, spend billions every year on adverts, logos and brand images. They use marketing to trigger psychological needs in consumers. The signs, symbols and meanings advertisers use are cultural. However, many of these hooks are built on inherited mental pathways from way before our time as humans. Others are more recent and come from the transition by our ancestors into mixed forest and grasslands. Here are some examples of what I am talking about.

McDonald's and other fast-food outlets use the colour red a great deal in their imagery. They do this because red is associated in people's minds with food and comfort. As pre-human primates we evolved to seek out ripe red fruit for food. Plants co-evolved this change in colour by taking on the selective advantage of a signal to birds and animals that the fruit was ready to take away. Red is a good contrast to the green of foliage. And so fruit matures and in the process creates a seductive signal to birds and mammals. It entices them to take away their seeds encased in sugary flesh. Not only is the mind biased towards red but the human eye is physiologically attuned to be more sensitive to red than green. Interestingly red has another association, one of danger. It is likely that the response comes from seeing blood and realising that one is in a dangerous situation. From these examples one can see that our emotional response to colours is built into our nervous system at a very basic level and evolved before humans had arrived as a species.

Green plays its own part in our psychology and along with blue it has a calming effect on the mind. The room in the BBC where people had to wait before appearing on radio was called the green room. It was decorated to induce a relaxing effect on the eye. Imagine trying to remain calm in room painted pillar box red. When people are asked what the most important characteristics of a positive natural place are, greenery and blue sky come very high up the list. Green is used in advertising to equate with freshness as in 'fresh green vegetables'. The pairing of 'fresh' and 'green' seems to occur without thinking. In this and many other ways our response to the natural world is deep in our psychological make-up.

More psychological processes in nature

People become more aware of their senses when outdoors in nature: the colours of plants and sunlight, also the 'lesser' senses of smell, hearing, touch and textures, more readily reach conscious awareness. The senses are actively stimulated when the wind swirls around us, leaves rustle and sunlight flickers through foliage. The multi-sensory quality of being outdoors cannot be *fully* replicated indoors through the media of writing, sound recordings or video, although as we shall see later the evocation of nature through images can in itself influence our feelings.

Memories can be triggered by all kinds of stimuli. The outdoors, possibly because of its multi-sensory nature, can evoke memories of childhood when we were carefree and open to new experiences. Can you remember taking food and making a camp in the undergrowth, away from the rules and control of adults? I have had people at the end of a workshop say with a mixture of surprised new awareness, sadness and hope that the last time they felt that good in nature was when they were a child. There are colleagues working with people who have memory impairments and being out in nature has been found to be a great way to reconnect with the past.

The wild side of us gets permission to come out in wild areas. The poet and activist Gary Snyder has written extensively about the feeling of freedom brought about by being in nature (e.g. Snyder 1990, 1993). Mountaineers talk of the liberation felt when climbing in the mountains high above the seeming trivia and necessary laws of city life below.

The interesting thing is that we find nature beautiful: people will travel a long way to look at and be in spectacular landscapes; a walk in the garden can be enlivened by noticing a particularly stunning blossom; and we can be lost in reverie as we look at clouds or watch the sea swirl around. The particular aesthetics of nature are culturally mediated but it is likely they have their origins in innate psychological processes.

Theoretical explanations for ecotherapy

In psychology there are currently three main explanations as to why we respond positively to natural scenes: Attention Restoraton, biophilia and Stress Reduction. The explanations are compatible with each other and merely emphasise different aspects of our relationship to nature. The first I want to discuss is the Kaplans' hypothesis that when we are outdoors our mind gets a rest from the pressures of modern life, and nature has specific qualities that aid the recovery process (Kaplan and Kaplan 1989). Essentially the Kaplan explanation (ART) is primarily concerned with cognitive factors. The explanation championed by Roger Ulrich is the evolutionary hypothesis which is a development of the biophilia hypothesis proposed by E.O. Wilson. It states that the natural world is the habitat we originally evolved in. We feel emotionally reassured by being in an environment which, in the past at least, would have increased our chances of survival (Ulrich 1993). Ulrich's explanation (SRT – see later in this chapter) pays more attention to emotional factors. The theories are described in more detail with evidence concerning their validity.

Attention Restoration Theory (ART)

Rachel and Stephen Kaplan proposed that nature can immunise against and also help a person recover from the pressures of modern life. They claim their research supports the notion that spending long periods of time on a focused activity such as working on a computer causes stress and that being in nature reduces stress. When we work on a computer we are forcing ourselves to pay close attention for extended periods of time, and in the process we have to continually focus on and filter out irrelevant information. This can cause stress, anxiety, irritability with others and an inability to concentrate.

Attention is the term used when we focus on one thing and screen out other inputs to our mind. Attention is beneficial because it increases our perception, thinking and memory. We do this voluntarily when we actively pay attention to a complex task on a computer by filtering out background noises and so on. However, over a period of time, if we have to sustain complex thinking and filter out anxieties or worries, interpersonal demands, noise and pain, then we become fatigued. A person in this situation shows signs of stress, tiredness, irritability, impulsiveness and a lack of concentration. The Kaplans argue that by spending time in nature we can restore our equilibrium in a way that is more efficient than just resting indoors.

The Kaplans refer to four forms of involuntary attention in nature which restore a person's ability to deal with voluntary attention and overcome fatigue. They noted four *restorative characteristics* of the natural environment on people:

1. *Instinctive fascination* with the natural environment. This is the process of giving effortless involuntary attention to things so that other competing thoughts are easily excluded, for example stopping to notice birdsong or a distant tree.

2. A sense of *being away from* stressful events or thoughts. We give ourselves a break from overused brain activities. The relief experienced when you enter a park in the middle of a city could be one situation.

3. *Awareness of extent or complexity* in the environment, where there is sufficient interest to attract attention and avoid boredom.

4. A *compatibility* between the demands imposed by the environment and the individual's needs and abilities, which lead to a feeling of being *in harmony with a greater whole.*

The natural environment allows for all four circumstances to occur. The Kaplans' research over many decades supports the notion that time in nature restores a person's mental energy (Kaplan and Kaplan 1989).

The Countryside Commission carried out a detailed survey to find out people's attitudes to the countryside in England. They found that nine out of ten people value the countryside. The most important benefits were said to be 'a sense of relaxation and well being' and 'fresh air and peace and quiet' (Countryside Commission 1997). This response is compatible with the study carried out in San Francisco which we will come to in more detail later on (Francis and Cooper-Marcus 1991). What the supporting research shows is that people choose to use nature to recover from stress and to build resilience against possible future stresses in life. For the Kaplans it is stress which causes the reduced cognitive ability they measured.

Many experimental set-ups have been used to investigate whether being in nature aids recovery from stress and reduced cognitive ability more than other comparable situations. For example, in one study young people were given a task which required sustained attention. They were asked to proofread text for mistakes. When they had completed the task they were placed in one of three different environments for 40 minutes, after which their attention skills were measured again. The three environments were a natural environment, an urban environment and passive relaxation (sitting in a room listening to music and reading magazines). Those young people who spent time in a natural environment scored highest on a subsequent proofreading test (Hartig, Mang and Evans 1991). Time in nature demonstrably aids attention recovery.

The main researcher in this study then went on to investigate young people's emotional state in four different environments (Hartig *et al.* 2003). One hundred and twelve randomly assigned young people were compared on their ability to pay attention to a task, their emotional state and their physiological stress indicators (blood pressure). They were either indoors or outdoors, and either in an urban setting or outdoors in nature. The results all show the positive effect of nature in restoring the participants to a healthy physical and psychological state:

- A room with a view of trees was better than a viewless room.

- A walk in a nature reserve was better than an urban walk.

- Attention improved on the nature walk and declined in the urban, with the effect persisting after the walks had ended.

- Positive feelings and reduced anger occurred after the nature walk and increased in the urban.

In another study Stephen Kaplan and colleagues tested participants on a range of cognitive tasks which demanded close directed attention. They then gave them either a walk in the park or a walk through urban streets for about 50 minutes. They then retested the subjects on the same tasks and compared the two groups. A week later the groups were swapped over and given the same procedures. The results showed that after people had had a break in the park they scored significantly better at the demanding mental tasks on their return than when they walked around in town.

A second experiment by the same research team tested ART in a more specific way. The researchers used a similar repeated design and used three tests measuring three different forms of attention: alerting, orienting and executive attention. Work by other people had determined that these three cognitive functions are neurally and behaviourally distinct. They predicted that only executive attention would be positively affected by interactions with nature because it requires much more cognitive control than the other two. After the first task session participants were given a slide show of 50 images to rate, each set being of either nature or cityscapes. Then the tasks were repeated. Both environments in the two conditions were almost identical, the only difference being the type of pictures they viewed during the slide show. The results confirmed their initial predictions. The researchers concluded that interacting with nature did not have a generalised effect on motivation or effort but was effective in restoring directed attention only.

From this and many other similar pieces of good-quality research evidence into ART we can infer important advice on restoring cognitive fatigue. If anyone is tired at work involving focused thinking then we now know one of the best ways to recover. A walk around urban streets near the office or sitting reading a magazine is nowhere near as restorative as a walk in the local park. The importance of designing green space into our towns and cities has never been stronger, not just as an aesthetic add-on but as an essential part of a healthy environment. When it comes to designing hospitals and health centres the arguments are overwhelming.

Two Japanese researchers (Nakamura and Fujii 1990) studied the effects on the brain when a person looks at plants and found that the experiences had a positive effect. In one study they had people look at different things to see what the effect was on brain activity. The different objects were two types of potted plants, *Pelargonium* and *Begonia*, either in flower or not, and a human made cylinder similar to the pots. The people had the alpha rhythms from their brain measured as indicators of a wakeful relaxed state. The results show that the most relaxed alert state was with flowering plants followed by the non-flowering plants and finally the cylindrical pots.

In a further study the researchers took people outdoors and had them look at either a hedge, a concrete fence of about the same dimensions, or a mixed view: part hedge, part concrete fence. The researchers measured their EEG (electro-encephalogram) and the results showed that the green hedge induced the most relaxed states, whereas the concrete fence had a stressful influence.

While the Kaplans' ART hypothesis is supported by the evidence it lacks explanatory power. It fails to fully answer the question: why nature? What is it about being outdoors in a natural environment that has such a positive effect on people's mood and thinking capacity, and why should that be so? The biophilia hypothesis and the closely related evolutionary functional hypothesis tackle this question head on.

Biophilia and an attraction to natural settings

Our ability to think about situations and evaluate them before responding is a characteristic of our species and other higher animals. It is a sign of intelligence. There are other behaviours we have retained in our evolution because they aid our survival by being rapid and unreflective. For example, our fear of heights can be observed in very young babies who will veer away from an edge that has a drop. The template for this behaviour is hard wired into our brains although it can be modified with practice, as any rock climber will tell you.

Fear of loaded guns and electric cables are not hard wired and young children do not show the fear response that they do when confronted with a snake, for example. Over time and pre-dating our species we have evolved rapid unthinking responses that have got us out of dangerous situations. I have mentioned vertigo and snakes; we can add fast-moving small mammals and spiders, closed spaces, open spaces, dogs and running water. The smell of rotting meat can induce a gagging reflex or nausea because putrid meat is highly toxic.[3] We don't show the same response to rotting fruit; in fact someone discovered a long time ago that decomposing fruit produced alcohol and it was fun to drink. But not everyone responds positively to alcohol, suggesting the adaptation is more recent in our evolution than the revulsion to bad meat is.

Interestingly it has been observed among other primates that there is a fascination as well as a fear of snakes. If a member of a troop of monkeys finds a snake a specific call goes out. The monkeys gather to watch and follow the snake until it has disappeared. In human cultures snakes have ambivalent meanings: sometimes power, knowledge and magic, at other times evil and deadly. The most common animal that occurs in dreams across cultures is the snake. Just like monkeys, that which we fear also fascinates us.

We call these rapid negative responses (which can be modified by learning) phobias – more precisely biophobias because they are responses to events or objects in nature.

There is a good body of research from clinical psychology and psychiatry to show that the majority of strong fears we have with respect to objects or situations had survival value in the past for humans: snakes, spiders, heights, closed spaces, open spaces and blood (Costello 1982; McNally 1987). Where the data is available it cuts across industrial societies. When a phobic fear of modern stimuli such as guns is artificially induced it does not persist and is more easily extinguished than negative responses to spiders and snakes.

The evidence so far on depth/spaciousness fears in natural environments (agoraphobia) suggests humans have a defensive/cautious response but not a strong fear of avoidance following aversive experiences of high-depth, spatially open environments. The findings from this research fit well with the assumption that early people in Africa would have done well to be cautious in open savannah grasslands but would still need to proceed in order to find food and shelter.

Edward O. Wilson, a North American biologist, proposed the term 'biophilia'. He defined it as 'the innately emotional affiliation of human beings to other living organisms' (Kellert and Wilson 1993, p.31). He amplified this definition with the statement:

> The human inclination to affiliate with life and life like processes is: innate, biologically based; part of a species evolutionary heritage; associated with human competitive advantage and genetic fitness; likely to increase the possibility of achieving individual meaning and personal fulfilment; the self interested basis for a human ethic of care and conservation of nature, most especially the diversity of life. (Kellert and Wilson 1993, p.21)

---

3   The proteins are broken down into amino acids by microbes, giving off sulphur dioxide, hydrogen sulphide and ammonia, which is what our noses pick up.

Wilson took the view that just as we have biophobias which aid our survival we are also born with attractions to certain aspects of nature which aid our survival. These inborn positive responses can be modified by learning and incorporated into cultural beliefs as we saw above with snakes. An example of a possible modern cultural incorporation of biophilia is the use of rich flower meadows and greenery in the advertising of some shampoos as a way of denoting health and well-being.

The field of biophilia can only be touched on here but it makes fascinating reading. A good starting place for ideas and evidence is *The Biophilia Hypothesis* (Kellert and Wilson 1993). The book sets out the evidence base for the biophilia hypothesis: that nature is attractive to us and this feeling is partly innate. Since 1993 considerably more research has been carried out which validates the notion and gives more detail to the processes. With time the results have become more widely known and are even being appreciated by the medical profession. It is important to recognise that the great majority of the work on biophilia has ignored or played down the sociological processes that could be present in this work. Some phenomena such as a belief in ghosts are universal across cultures but that does not make them necessarily innate. The field will be richer when cultural factors can be included in our understanding of biophilia.

The research into biophilia can be grouped into two overlapping categories: positive attraction/preferences and stress recovery.

Positive attraction/preferences

It seems likely that we have a partly inherited predisposition to be attracted to landscapes that aided our survival in the past: habitats that had fresh water, food and security (Orians 1980, 1986; Ulrich 1993).

One of the basic questions biologists ask of any feature or behaviour they are studying is: how does this aid survival? Although genetic variation is based on chance, natural selection is ruthless in favouring those behaviours that improve an individual's survival. If biophobia and biophilia exist how have they helped our ancestors' chances of survival?

Early hominids evolved in savannah habitat often by lakes (Leakey 1980). Savannah is typified by spatial openness, scattered trees or small groupings of trees, and relatively uniform grassy ground surfaces. Savannah provides higher food sources than rainforest, fewer phobic-inducing creatures such as snakes and spiders, and more open viewing for seeing predators. Lakes are ideal as sources of fresh water, animals to hunt and protein-rich crustacean food.

Literally hundreds of studies across many cultures, both industrial and tribal, have looked at people's emotional response to both urban and natural landscapes. The researchers have more often used slides and film than actual outdoor landscapes to present to people. This is a widely accepted method because it is relative comparisons between different environments that are being made. Measurements of people's responses have been made either verbally, using rating scales, or physiological measures (such as heart and breathing rate, skin conductance and brain activity) that correlate with levels of stress in the body. New technology for monitoring physiological states means that it will not be long before researchers will be able to record changes while someone is outside the laboratory.

The results from all these studies show that modern people prefer elements of green vegetation, flowers and water, compared with concrete and glass (for a review see, e.g., Kaplan and Kaplan 1989). The preferred landscape across many cultures is openness, smooth or uniform grassy vegetation, scattered trees or small groupings of trees, in other words a forest setting with savannah or park-like qualities. Biodiversity seems to play a part. In one study people gave higher ratings of psychological well-being after spending time in parks with a wide variety of plants compared with parks that had low biodiversity (Fuller *et al.* 2007).

English parkland with a savannah-like structure of
open grassland and isolated groups of trees

Natural settings with water are particularly attractive and young children show very positive responses to water. Images of threatening water such as stormy seas or clearly visible pollution are exceptions. Low preferences are also found for restricted depth of view, rough ground textures that obstruct movement and dense impenetrable vegetation. Research in West Africa found that both rural and urban Nigerians give a low preference to the visually impenetrable dense understorey found in tropical rainforests. When the view is of more spatially open rainforest the preferences increased (Chokor and Mene 1992).

It seems that a trip to the seaside really is good for you, and better than a city park stroll (Bell *et al.* 2015). Study results show that stress levels were most reduced by taking a visit to the coast, followed by the countryside, with urban parks reducing people's stress levels the least. Interestingly the only countryside locations that got close to the coastal stress reductions were woodland/forest and moorland/hills/mountains. In fact the closer you live to the coast the better your mental as well as physical health will be regardless of many other factors such as the specific area and personal variations (Wheeler *et al.* 2012; White *et al.* 2013).[4] The explanation for this phenomenon of coastal preference needs more input from sociological studies before we proclaim this as completely biological.

Unimpressive natural scenes are even preferred to attractive urban landscapes lacking nature, although introducing trees and associated vegetation greatly increases preferences for urban scenes. Ulrich recognises that we need more observations to be conducted in tribal cultures and with actual real-life environments, but the overall conclusions from hundreds of studies strongly support the statements presented here. Consistent with the biophilia hypothesis is the statement that our positive responses to savannah-like natural settings are genetically inherited and open to modification by learning and experience.

One last point is relevant to this section. The fact that biophobias and biophilias are thought to be genetically based *and* open to modification by learning could explain an important observation. As I am frequently reminded when I take people on walks in nature, not everyone is attracted to being outdoors in greenery and wildlife. Early positive experiences in nature may well be significant learning modifiers of our innate affiliation to the natural world.

Stress Recovery Theory (SRT): an evolutionary functional explanation of recovery from stress

Roger Ulrich's particular research interest in biophilia is in the restorative qualities of the natural world in response to the experience of stress. His hypothesis is that certain environments in our evolutionary past would have been associated with physical recovery and rapid reduction in stress levels. Being able to easily recognise these environments would have given some individuals greater survival chances. In this way the template for the responses would have become genetically inherited.

The research evidence points to a strong association between experiencing a savannah-type environment and recovery from stress.

From an evolutionary view early people would be concerned about and on the look-out for predators, and also a ready supply of food and water. Feeling safe using these criteria would be important. If an early human was chased by a predator and managed to escape, for example by climbing a tree, the flight response would be experienced as fear, anxiety and physiological changes such as increased heart rate and more rapid breathing. Once the danger had passed it would be important to recover as quickly as possible in order to continue searching for food and water, and find other people to be with. Being able to identify a safe environment would

---

4   See the Blue Mind website (n.d.) for research into the effects of water on our well-being.

be a matter of survival. Knowing that the area you were in was rich in food and water would be reassuring and being able to search the landscape for people and predators, compared to looking at dense vegetation, would help recovery.

There is now a lot of convincing research to show that leisure activities in natural surroundings are important for people recovering from stress as well as meeting other needs. From the evidence of over one hundred studies, people involved in outdoor recreation talk about relaxation and peacefulness in regard to savannah-like settings that show water, open space and scattered and/or large trees as being key factors (Schroeder 1986; Ulrich and Addoms 1981). Similar results come from studies of people's responses to parks among urban settings. People in San Francisco were asked what settings they went to when stressed or depressed. Seventy-five per cent chose outdoor places that were natural environments or urban places dominated by natural elements such as parks, views of natural landscape, lakes and ocean (Francis and Cooper-Marcus 1991).

As well as asking people for their preferred environments for reducing their stress levels in day-to-day life psychologists have gone further. They have generated mild stress in individuals and then observed which environments bring about the best recovery. The results show recovery from stress is faster in a natural environment.

In order to narrow down the range of possible factors influencing a person out in nature some researchers have resorted to using experimental research designs with people indoors. This approach might seem counterintuitive; how can you study the effects of the outdoors on people indoors? However, if the results of lab studies are congruent with observational studies carried out on an outdoors ecotherapy programme then the evidence base is stronger all round. Psychologists have a variety of ways of ethically inducing mild stress in participants, for example by giving people impossible puzzles to solve under time pressure but with a financial reward for success. The psychologists can then give the different groups of people, who are all stressed, different experiences to see which ones reduce stress the best. One of those experiences can be time spent in a green space.

Stress can be measured physiologically in a person's body. We all show increased breathing and heart rate, as well as moist hands, higher blood pressure and tighter muscles when we are psychologically stressed. Roger Ulrich *et al.* (1991) induced mild stress in participants and showed them different videos and then measured their responses. After watching videos of either nature or urban settings with buildings, participants who were stressed showed a significantly faster recovery, as measured by blood pressure, muscle tension and skin conductance, when watching the nature videos compared to those watching videos of buildings. The recovery effect peaked within three to four minutes. Other ratings suggested that the nature settings produced significantly higher levels of positive feelings and lower levels of fear and anger.

Very little has been done on the effect of sounds but there is some experimental evidence, using similar designs to the Ulrich study reported above, that the sounds of nature are also important to stress recovery (Annerstedt *et al.* 2013).

Corroborative work carried out in real-life situations indicate lower physiological stress responses when exposed to images of natural scenes. Two examples from different studies involve waiting to have dental surgery and lying on a stretcher in the pre-op room of a hospital (Coss 1990; Heerwagen 1990).

Bearing in mind the relationship between psychological stress and physical illness it is interesting to consider whether being exposed to views of nature might help people recovering from heart surgery. Roger Ulrich and his colleagues set up a situation for 160 patients who were in intensive care in Sweden to examine this question. Patients were placed in one of six conditions where they could see a picture. Two were nature images (a view of trees and water or an enclosed forest scene), two abstract pictures, and two control conditions (a white panel or no picture). Results show a significant reduction in anxiety post-operatively for the patients who viewed the nature scenes compared to the other groups. These patients also suffered less pain – they changed from strong narcotics to moderate analgesics faster than other groups.

Interestingly the abstract picture groups in this study had even higher anxiety levels than the control groups. This last finding fits with other research that suggests that abstract art, either pictures or sculpture, can increase anxiety among patients who are already stressed (Ulrich 1999). One piece of related research is particularly relevant to mental health workers. An analysis over many years in a Swedish psychiatric hospital recorded strong negative responses by patients to certain paintings and prints. This included complaints to staff and even physical attacks on the pictures. All the pictures which were attacked had some abstract content and in 15 years none of the images of natural scenes were attacked (Ulrich 1986).

Effects on higher-order cognitive functioning

The assumption under review is that higher-order cognitive functioning (i.e. analysis, evaluation and synthesis as opposed to thinking basic facts and concepts) is positively affected by a natural setting. The amount of evidence in this area is limited and so the conclusions are more speculative.

The negative effect of stress on lower-order functioning has been established for many years (Ulrich 1993). Typically people have been tested on simple tasks such as proofreading for mistakes. The Kaplans' theory of ART, attention recovery in a natural environment after fatigue at work, also provides supportive evidence. The positive effects of natural settings on lower-order thinking have also been firmly established.

Higher-order cognitive functioning involves integrating diverse material or associating in a flexible way previously unrelated information or concepts, typically associated with creative thinking. From an evolutionary perspective the ability to think creatively and to deal with complex situations is assumed to have been an adaptive advantage for early humans and to have led to innovation and cultural advance.

A person's emotional state affects their capability to deal with both lower-order and higher-order cognition and to think creatively. Therefore it has been assumed by Ulrich and others that exposure to positive-emotion-inducing environments such as a natural environment is beneficial.

In brief, many studies show that positive feelings significantly boost a person's scores on creativity and higher-order thinking and in contrast negative feelings do the opposite and give lower scores (Isen 1985).

Ulrich argues that exposure to natural environments that were stress free in our early evolution would have had a positive effect on people's ability to be inventive and creative. He admits to being speculative but argues that if we can find the evidence then we will have even stronger support for the benefits of living and working in natural surroundings. Roger Ulrich is asking for research to be carried out to see if modern people are positively affected in their higher-order thinking by exposure to natural environments. There is anecdotal information that many inventive people have had creative thoughts while taking a walk in a natural environment (see the Beethoven quote at the beginning of the chapter, for example). Would research institutes be more productive if they were set in savannah-like parks?

Principles of green exercise

A very useful way of seeing green exercise is to identify the interrelated principles on which many programmes are based. The Mind report of 2007 provides a good summary of this approach (see Table 4.1). The classification could apply to many of the activities described as ecotherapy with different emphases in different programmes.

Table 4.1 Four key principles for describing why people enjoy green exercise activities

Principles	Subcategories	Descriptors
1 Natural and social connections	**A** Social	Being with friends and family, companionship and social interaction, creation of collective identity, making new friends, conviviality
	B Animals and wildlife	Direct bonding with pets (e.g. dogs, horses) and wild animals (e.g. birdwatching)
	C Memories and knowledge	Visiting special places where memories and stories are evoked and recalled (childhood associations), story telling, personal identity, links to myths, stimulation of imagination, ecological literacy
	D Spiritual	Large scale and longevity of nature in contrast to humans, transformative capacity of green nature, oneness with nature
2 Sensory stimulation	**A** Colours and sounds	Diverse colours of nature and landscapes, views of landscape, beauty of scenery, birdsong and sounds of other animals, light (especially sunrise and sunset), visual and aesthetic appreciation of landscape
	B Fresh air	Smell and other senses, being outdoors, exposed to all types of weather, changing seasons, a contrast to indoor and city life, escape from urban pollution
	C Excitement	Adrenaline rush, exhilaration, fun, arising from a physical activity or experience of risk (e.g. rock climbing), sense of adventure
3 Activity	**A** Manual tasks	Learning a skill and completing a manual task (e.g. conservation activity), challenging, fulfilling and rewarding, sense of achievement, leading to a sense of worth and value
	B Physical activity	Enjoyment of the activity itself and the physical and mental health benefits associated with it, makes people feel good, more energetic, less lethargic
4 Escape	Escape from Modern life	Getting away from modern life, relaxing (as a contrast), time alone or with family, a time to think and clear the head, peace and quiet, tranquillity and freedom, privacy, escape from pressure, stress and the 'rat race', recharging batteries

(from Mind 2007)

Conclusions

Even though we are at a developing stage of research evidence and theory I believe we can make strong optimistic statements concerning our psychological connections to the natural world. We are now in a position to say that there is strong evidence from a wide range of qualitative and quantitative research studies, with different designs, that nature has a positive effect on the human mind. People choose to go to green areas to feel better: to recover from stress and lift their mood. People say they feel better in nature and we can measure significant positive changes in their physiology. Time spent in nature has a resilience effect as well as being an effective way to recover from life's pressures.

In Chapters 5–7 I have teased out and separately examined the research evidence concerning key environmental variables and their effects on people. For real people out in nature the effects are dynamically combined. Collectively they underscore the potency of ecotherapy.

If spending time in nature has a positive effect on all of us who choose to be there does it help those of us trying to recover from mental distress and psychosis? I will look at this question after reviewing research into other areas where nature has a positive effect on people.

Chapter 5

The Evidence from Body and Mind Studies

Don't just do something
Stand there.

Anonymous

> In this chapter I review the evidence on the positive influence of nature on physical recovery. I then look in detail at mindfulness and the effects of nature on the mind.

The evidence for the effects of nature on physical health

Our ecological interdependence with the rest of life on Earth is one of the themes running through this book. Trees in particular are symbolic of the natural world. Trees filter air pollution and of course take up carbon dioxide and release oxygen. They also shade us from the harmful effects of UV and keep us cool in summer. Trees may help reduce the possibility of asthma attacks. One in six young people suffer breathing difficulties, and the number of adults admitted to hospital for asthma and related breathing problems has more than doubled in the past 20 years. Asthma drug use has tripled in the past 10 years, and asthma costs eight million working days lost, costing the economy £350 million every year (Baines 2003). More trees in cities could improve everyone's health. We even use tree leaves and flowers as herbs. Lime tea is a good relaxant, while pine oil makes an invigorating bath and fir is sometimes used in saunas.

Room with a view of nature

Roger Ulrich has spent much of his academic career investigating the relationship between our environment and our health, both physical and mental. His most famous and ground-breaking study (Ulrich 1984) was carried out over thirty years ago in a Pennsylvania hospital where he studied patients recovering from gall bladder surgery. Two groups of people were matched on variables such as sex, age, weight, previous hospital experience, tobacco use and so forth. Individuals were randomly allocated to rooms that were identical in all but one respect. A patient's room either had a view of a group of deciduous trees or a brown brick wall. Medical staff were unaware of the study taking place.

The effect of having a view of nature made a significant difference to patient recovery. Those people who had a view of the trees had shorter post-operative stays in hospital, made fewer negative remarks about staff, and had fewer negative minor post-op experiences requiring medication, such as nausea and headaches. Those who had the brick wall to look at required many more painkillers and these were often injections of potent analgesics as opposed to the other group which typically required weaker oral painkillers.

Even a picture works

There have been many other studies supporting this result and Ulrich emphatically makes the link between faster patient recovery and reducing stress levels through exposure to nature. He worked with a colleague at Uppsala University Hospital in Sweden on another very interesting study which showed that just having a picture of nature on the wall aided recovery (Lundén and Ulrich 1990). They studied 166 patients in intensive care who were recovering from open heart surgery and were given a picture on the wall to look at. Each person was randomly allocated to a room with one of these following conditions: a view of nature (either an open view including water or a moderately closed view of a forest); an abstract picture of rectilinear or curvilinear lines; and a white panel or no picture at all as control.

They found that the water scene in nature, compared to all other conditions, significantly reduced anxiety in the post-op patients. Interestingly the forest scene did not significantly reduce anxiety compared to the controls. The rectilinear abstract picture resulted in higher anxiety than the control. The research fits in neatly with the report mentioned earlier of psychiatric patients damaging abstract but not nature pictures.

If the presence of trees supports health recovery then an interesting question to ask is what would happen to people's health if we lost lots of trees? No one knows for sure but there are predictions that *Chalara* ash dieback, *Phytophthora ramorum* on larch, oak, beech, sweet chestnut (Forestry Commission n.d.) and horse chestnut bleeding canker (affecting half our trees – Forestry Commission n.d.) will result in the loss of millions of trees in Britain. We may have some indication of the consequences from a study in the USA. A comparison study was carried out recently (Donovan *et al.* 2013) where some areas has lost tens of millions of trees as a result of being infected with the emerald ash borer. A wide range of demographic variables were controlled for and mortality records over 17 years were compared in 15 USA states at a county level. The results show that there was increased mortality related to cardiovascular and lower-respiratory-tract illness in the counties infested with emerald ash borer. The effect was greater as the infestation progressed and in counties with above-average-median household incomes. The infested states had an additional 6113 deaths from lower respiratory disease and 15,080 cardiovascular-related deaths.

There are numerous other studies showing the positive health benefits of green space in urban areas; see Faculty of Public Health (2010) and Maller *et al.* (2008) for examples.

Nature can help increase physical fitness

We know that taking regular exercise improves well-being. Dog walkers for example are less likely to suffer heart disease. This may be the result of a combination of daily walks and benefiting from stroking an animal companion. Joggers gain psychological benefits from their sport and are said to get a sense of well-being from the release of endorphins into the bloodstream as a result of vigorous exercise.

What is less well known is that doing exercise outdoors in nature can increase motivation. When someone goes to the gym to exercise they go there primarily to get fit. The whole environment is focused on the exercises themselves. The motivation to persist, despite muscular discomfort, depends on the individual's self will. In contrast when a person goes for a walk or runs outdoors they may do so for a variety of reasons only one of which is fitness, for example being outdoors, appreciating nature, getting fresh air. The walk or run in this situation is not just about focusing on pushing oneself to exert more energy. It is a total experience, much of which is a pleasurable distraction from muscular discomfort or measured goals. Even if the primary intention is physical fitness the benefits of the natural environment have a positive role in motivation (Gladwell *et al.* 2013). Two interesting studies demonstrate these effects.

In a commissioned report on a health walk scheme in Reading (Ashley *et al.* 1999) a sample of 476 health walkers were asked to complete the statement 'I will continue health walking because…' Although the walks were designed to 'increase fitness and improve health' this response to the statement was matched by 'a chance to be in the countryside' as one of the two main reasons for continuing on the walks. Even 'watching the seasons go by' was a more important motivating factor than 'socialising', 'energy', 'sleep better' or 'lose weight'.

Walking outdoors may offer other advantages compared with using a gym. A study comparing adults walking indoors to those walking outdoors (Buchanan *et al.* 2000) showed that when asked to walk 'fast but without over-exertion' the percentages of their maximum heart rate and walking speed were significantly higher for outdoor compared to indoor (treadmill) walking, yet their rate of perceived exertion was similar for both. This showed that when the outdoors people walked faster they used up extra energy without feeling any extra effort. It may be partly due to the ground being easier to walk on than a treadmill, but the varied scenery and the natural surroundings (compared to a treadmill and blank wall) may provide a positive distraction from the actual exercise.

A much larger study came to a similar conclusion at about the same time. The four-year study (Bird and Adams 2001) of the first Healthy Walking scheme in Sonning Common near Oxford involved 16,407 participants who went on 1724 walks. The environment was semi-urban. Sixty-seven per cent were female and 49.2 per cent were from the target group 50–75 years of age. The study found that the most popular walks were between one and a half and two miles. What was most interesting was that there was a clear preference for walks that offered a variation in the natural environment, particularly if it had trees. It found that 'Varied scenery was an important aspect of motivation with less attendance on walks with poor contrast and few or no trees' (Bird and Adams 2001). If anyone is thinking of launching their own countryside walking scheme a further observation from the Sonning study may be useful. They found that December was the least popular month for attendance and that April and May were the best, with May being the most successful for gaining new recruits.

At the moment NICE do not have ecotherapy as one of the government-approved forms of therapy for depression (the reasons for this are discussed elsewhere). But they do approve physical exercise (NICE 2008) for mild to moderate depression. NICE also highlighted the need for more research to uncover how the environment influences behaviour and attitudes that have an impact on physical activity and associated health benefits. If walking in nature is one of the best motivators to take up exercise then this is reason enough for someone to get out into somewhere green if they are feeling depressed. While the activities advocated in this book are not physically demanding the experience of going on group walks is a useful transition to joining a Walking for Health scheme. I have had ecotherapy clients go on to join health walking groups and conservation work parties. However, some clients experienced intolerance from others towards their mental state and others found the pace too demanding if they were on strong medication.

Access to green space influences health

Research also shows that if you live in a greener neighbourhood you will live longer. I interpret this to be part of the systemic links demonstrated by Roger Ulrich's work on stress, health and experiencing a green environment (Ulrich 1981). We know that if people are poor then they will have higher mortality rates than those with more income. There are multiple reasons for this: access to more and better quality resources, less local crime and better employment conditions are just a few examples.

However, if you are poor and are living in the greenest area you will have a better mortality rate (Mitchell and Popham 2008). The researchers found that the effect was positive for circulatory diseases. We can link this research outcome to the fact that people are more likely to exercise in green areas (Humpel, Owen and Leslie 2002; Kaczynski and Henderson 2007). We also know that being in a green environment reduces stress levels and has a restorative effect (Hartig *et al.* 2003; van den Berg, Hartig and Staats 2007).

A large long-term study of 3144 elderly people aged over 70 living in built-up areas of Japan (Takano, Nakamura and Watanabe 2002) found that the probability of living longer over a five-year period increased with the amount of accessible green space close to where they lived and the perceived ability to walk in tree-lined parks and streets. One minor weakness of the study is the lack of a clear definition of what individuals defined as green space and what they meant by accessible. The researchers did control for socioeconomic and other demographic factors though. At the same time they found a strong positive correlation between longevity and community involvement. Combining the two main conclusions of the study confirms the health benefits of community-based engagement with nature.

Another study in the Netherlands (de Vries *et al.* 2003) with a sample of 17,000 showed that people who lived within easy reach of green space enjoyed better health, particularly among the elderly, housewives and lower socioeconomic groups.

The evidence for mindfulness in nature

What is this life if full of care,
We have no time to stand and stare.
No time to stand beneath the boughs
And stare as long as sheep or cows.
No time to see, when woods we pass,
Where squirrels hide their nuts in grass.
No time to see, in broad daylight,
Streams full of stars, like skies at night…
A poor life is this if, full of care,
We have no time to stand and stare.

W.H. Davies (Quiller-Couch 1971)

Mindfulness

Mindfulness is a psychological state of increased awareness and attention in the present moment. Historically it is a concept central to Buddhist practice with a two-and-a-half-millennia track record. In modern times it has been popularised as a therapeutic method in Western psychology by Jon Kabat-Zinn among others (Kabat-Zinn 1994). In mental health it is commonly encountered in mindfulness-based stress reduction (MBSR) training programmes. Some practitioners have a more spiritual or religious context than the version promoted within the health service, something I will discuss presently. NICE has approved mindfulness-based therapies for many mental health conditions including depression (NICE 2010). It has been found to be effective for a wide range of other psychological and somatic disorders, including anxiety, ADHD, various addictions, schizophrenia, diabetes, heart disease, psoriasis and cancer (Shonin, Van Gordon and Griffiths 2015).

Mindfulness involves an awareness of one's current experience. This includes both internal (thoughts and emotions) and external (sensory input from the environment) experiences, sometimes referred to as being in the moment. Training in mindfulness is most often done by learning to meditate. It can also be practised in other ways by attending to whatever is happening moment by moment. A person can do this through self-reflection, noticing one's actions by slowing down movement, contemplation of objects or the environment. It is characterised by qualities of:

- delibarate attention to the present moment

- attention and awareness of the senses, body and mind

- openness, curiosity, acceptance, being non-judgemental.

Typically most people live their lives without these qualities of experience and in limited awareness. The mind is often on automatic pilot, responding without reflection to events. I'm sure you will have had the experience of arriving at the end of a journey without being able to remember much of what happened because you were daydreaming. We often say when this happens, 'I was somewhere else.'

Likewise thoughts drawn out of memory can produce emotional memories. Feelings triggered by events can arise which are patterns from the past and bear no relation to what is actually happening. For example, I can be talking to someone on the phone and and all of a sudden they cut the call short. I might feel rejected by the person (depending on the context). I find out later that in fact the person was calling from work and their boss came into the room when they cut off. The feeling of rejection bubbled up from my memory and was not actually related to anything the other person actually said. My mind introduced the negative feeling to an experience. The everyday mind can also flit from one thing to another without really seeing or feeling what is going on. A narrative is then built up in the mind of what happened with only scant reference to external events.

Another quality of being unaware is the evaluative commentary which accompanies and gets in the way of full experience. The judgement about whether an experience is good or bad can take over from being in the experience itself. I might look at a person's clothing and decide, almost unconsciously, to categorise the person into a group I don't like. It's called prejudice, pre-judging. At times I can find myself doing it over the most trivial things, particularly if I am feeling irritable.

Mindfulness training enables people to let go of these mental barriers to direct experience by just noticing them and not getting involved in them. The intention is to be mindful of experience and to put aside judgement as to whether it is a good or a bad experience, as in the thought, 'Oh, I notice I'm disliking the rain,' and then letting go of that thought and returning to awareness of what is happening right now. The mindful process does not involve blocking out thoughts/judgements. That would just put on another layer of judgement. What is required is an acceptance that the 'intrusive' thought is just a part of experience. The important thing is not to get distracted by emotions and thoughts and go off into an extended fantasy or a memory story. If you find yourself going on a mental detour just kindly bring attention back to what is actually happening right now. In meditation this return to attention is often done by witnessing the breath. The breath is an ever-present physical process we all do all the time. No thinking required.

The primary intention in mindfulness is to be aware of this moment, nothing else. In mindfulness training participants are asked to let go of goals *including* the desire to be in a positive mental state.

Stress, anxiety and depression are characterised, among other things, by concerned attention to past and future events, avoidance of current situations, judgemental responses and low mood. All these qualities are challenged by a person being mindful. Interestingly, research shows that MBSR is most effective in dealing with people who have anxiety and mood disorders (Hoffmann *et al.* 2010).

One criticism of mindfulness training as used in mental health is that it is being used solely as another activity or treatment without regard to its broader context. This concern often comes from Buddhists who consider that mindfulness is being made into a technique rather than a way of being. By focusing on measurable outcomes such as stress and anxiety levels the benefits of mindfulness are said to be limited. Buddhists have been using mindfulness for over two and a half thousand years in a particular spiritual and philosophical tradition. The question being asked is: can we extract one element and use it in isolation or do we need the whole Buddhist practice to be effective?

I think Buddhists may have a valid point within the true meaning of the term 'mindfulness'. The traditions of Western psychology grew out of a particular set of cultural beliefs which in many ways are quite different from Eastern psychology. I don't think it is possible to fully appreciate a technique in isolation. Mindfulness is a way of being that goes beyond symptoms and to just focus on being less anxious, for example, does miss its true significance.

I also recognise that MBSR works in Western psychology. I accept that some people may only want to use it as a form of therapy and not go further into the transpersonal aspects. A non-Buddhist version has made mindfulness more accessible to people who hold to different belief systems, particularly in a strongly Christian country such as the USA.

I think it depends on one's intention. Is it to become less anxious or is it to have a better understanding of one's whole being? Also, I wonder how many people have learnt MBSR as a way of coping with stress and gone on to question their whole mode of being in the world. From my own experience mindfulness has a habit of seeping into other parts of our lives in a positive way.

Within the context of this book and my practice as an ecotherapist I am content to see mindfulness as an important way of deepening a person's contact with nature. In turn I believe mindfulness practice in nature will have a positive effect on a person's well-being. In doing so I am not excluding the existential issues it raises personally and which go way beyond symptom cure.

In addition I sometimes need to persuade a sceptical health manager who may have negative assumptions about Eastern religions. With such a person I can refer to the fact that mindfulness has been found to be successful in improving psychological and physiological conditions and functions such as depression, anxiety, low mood, aggression and interpersonal conflict, immune system, heart rate, blood pressure and drug dependency. Research reviews and demanding meta-analyses show a very positive outcome for a range of conditions (see Grossman *et al.* 2004; Hoffmann *et al.* 2010; Khoury *et al.* 2013).

It is also interesting to be aware of the physical effects the practice can have on people. One study exemplifies the positive effect mindfulness can have on the immune system and brain activity associated with positive affects (Davidson *et al.* 2003). A group of volunteers on an eight-week mindfulness training programme were compared with people on a waiting list. Tests were made before and after the eight weeks and then four months later. The results show those who trained in mindfulness had a stronger immune system and increased brain activity associated with positive emotions. The two measured outcomes predicted each other in magnitude.

Rather than go into more details of research evidence on mindfulness here I would encourage readers to follow the references. From my own reading I have found that overviews of mindfulness research point to even greater benefits for psychological states compared to physical and medical changes in condition (Khoury *et al.* 2013).

The clearest evaluation of mindfulness is to learn to do it oneself and experience the results.

Someone leaning against a tree doing a mindfulness activity

Mindfulness practice and forests

There is an excellent if brief review of the research evidence around mindfulness and forests produced by the Forestry Commission (Ambrose-Oji 2013) to which I would direct those wanting further evidence of the benefits. Using strict criteria they review 52 research documents for their report. They are cautious with their final statement given the quantity of positive research they refer to in the body of the report. Their conclusion states that although there are many positive signs for the benefits of being in nature and for mindfulness, more needs to be done to tease out the relationship and benefits of doing both together.

They distinguish between five different mindfulness-based practices using forests:

- shinrin-yoku or forest bathing

- forest walking

- mindfulness and CBT in woodland settings

- forest therapy and ecotherapy

- ecopsychology.

Some of these practices are discussed elsewhere in this book so I will concentrate here on forest bathing and forest walking.

Shinrin-yoku or forest bathing

> Throughout our evolution, we've spent 99.9 percent of our time in natural environments. Our physiological functions are still adapted to it. During everyday life, a feeling of comfort can be achieved if our rhythms are synchronized with those of the environment.
>
> *Miyazaki, a physiological anthropologist and vice director of*
> *Chiba University's Center for Environment, Health, and Field*
> *Sciences, located just outside Tokyo; in Williams (2012)*

Japanese culture takes a more holistic view of the world than most Westerners. The diagnosis and treatment of mental illness in Britain tends to focus on patient symptoms, individual counselling and drug treatment. In Japan the whole environment – family, friends, work and wider environment – is very relevant to understanding a person's condition (see *The Kawa model* in Activities). Hence it is easier for the Japanese to understand that being in a therapeutic natural environment is good for you.

For most Japanese people spending time in the woods is self-evidently a positive experience. The activity even has a name: *shinrin-yoku* or 'forest bathing'. It was coined by the Forest Agency in 1982. It is practised by millions and is prescribed as a therapy for those suffering from stress, depression and other states of mental distress. Shinrin-yoku can be practised in a variety of ways. It can mean just going for a walk in the woods or it may involve more focused activities such as mindfulness, sitting and observing or breathing exercises (Society of Forest Medicine 2014). We will examine the very exciting research that has been carried out in Japan in a moment, after shinrin-yoku has been placed in context.

Shinto

It becomes clear why the Japanese have taken to shinrin-yoku so enthusiastically when one considers the central role of Buddhism and Shinto running though their culture. Shinto is an ancient religion and set of beliefs that go back into prehistory and has strong associations to nature.

In the West the cultural connections with the natural world have been severely damaged because of the Christian Church's antithesis to nature. The traditional Christian perspective so often sees nature as being inspired by the devil and at war with humans. For example, St Martin had a mission from God to attack the devil. He did this by spending a lifetime chopping down sacred trees. The Puritan destruction of pagan sites and the Victorian banning of fertility celebrations such as maypole dancing are other acts of culturally inspired madness. The Japanese have been more fortunate. Their intimate relationship with nature has an unbroken line from the earliest time to today and trees are understandably an important part of the chain. Going out to see the cherry blossom in spring or experiencing autumn colours on the maples is something most Japanese city dwellers would consider important to their lives even today. Although to be more accurate, some Japanese see these outdoor events as an opportunity to party rather than pay attention to the trees or seasonal changes, much as the West 'celebrates' midwinter on New Year's Eve.

Cherry blossom and dew are commonly understood symbols in Japan of the transient beauty of life, in contrast to mountains and pines that embody the eternal. There is a parallel in European literature: the rose and the yew. The rose in Western literature often represents the passing beauty of the present soon to die, and the yew tree signifies everlasting time. T.S. Eliot combines the two images in a very Eastern inspired line: 'The moment of the rose and the moment of the yew tree are of equal duration' (Eliot 1968 [1942]).

To return to the Japanese perspective, they have a term *kami* which means 'the divine in nature' and derives from Shinto and later Buddhist beliefs that just by being out in nature, in a special place, it is possible to gain spiritual insight and even enlightenment. The *kami* can be a mountain, a waterfall or tree, and although it is a focus for attention and respect it is not the equivalent of a Western altarpiece which is there as a representation of God. In the Shinto and Buddhist way of things the *kami* is a manifestation of the divine in itself. In other words, the *kami* is God, and so defines a different relationship between humanity and nature than that of Western theistic religions.

Although the old ways are held more strongly in the countryside people still visit the 80,000 Shinto shrines in Japan, many of which include trees. The rich poetic and artistic tradition of Japan has its roots in the widely accepted inspirational value of the natural world. It is nature which takes the poet deeper into him- or herself. The poet becomes nature's respected intermediary in relationship to the audience; thus it is nature and not the poet that is recognised as the source of a work of art. The trees, animals, rocks and water in nature are the master teacher of the great Japanese poets. The *kami* of trees and rocks do not *represent* anything, they are worthy of attention in themselves and it is assumed that we can learn something from them just as we can from a wise person. In this way nature is viewed as an outpouring of life, a continual process of change without control or disorder. It is a perspective the industrial world has lost sight of and which we as a culture, on the whole, have closed our minds to (Ambrose-Oji 2013).

Japanese research

There is only space here to give an overview and some sample studies to illustrate just how much has been discovered in Japan over the past two decades. The results are congruent with what has been found in Europe and North America and they also add a cross-cultural dimension to the work. It is worth mentioning that Korea has also embraced shinrin-yoku and their own government forestry department is fully supporting it. In 2014 Korea opened a $140 million National Forest Therapy Centre. The Japanese Ministry of Health (unlike the UK government's NICE) actively promotes and recommends walking in natural environments for health. There are 48 official Forest Therapy walks in Japan designated by the government's Forestry Agency with nearly two million people a year using them.

The research work in Japan has been pioneered by Miyazaki and his team working at a university just outside Tokyo and supported by the Forestry Agency of Japan. His team and other researchers in Japan have been able to tease out various elements as to what is going on when a person is doing shinrin-yoku. For example, researchers compared people when they walked in the forest to the same people on another day when they were not working and found, using questionnaires, that stress levels, hostility and depression decreased significantly, and liveliness scores increased while in the forest (Morita *et al.* 2007). Those who were the most stressed achieved the greatest benefits.

In summary the shinrin-yoku research has some very positive messages for all of us (Ambrose-Oji 2013; Suda *et al.* 2001; Tsunetsugu, Park and Miyazaki 2010). There are benefits for people suffering from stress, anxiety, depression, high blood pressure and diabetes. Research has examined psychological states using interviews and internationally validated questionnaires. Today, with the latest technology, it is possible to measure a variety of physiological states in the field. The Japanese researchers have measured brain activity, skin conductance, heart rate, blood pressure and breathing rate. Innumerable cellular and chemical measures of internal states of health have been taken from anti-cancer cells and proteins, NK killer lymphocytes (which defend us from tumours and viruses), and stress indicator hormones such as cortisol, adrenaline and noradrenaline (INFOM n.d.). Today, with the latest technology, it is possible to measure a variety of physiological states in the field.

I offer one example of their research in a little more detail: a comparison was made of urban and forest walks across 14 areas with a total of 168 participants. It indicated significant differences in responses (Park *et al.* 2011). Participants were asked to sit for a quarter of an hour in the selected environment and then allowed to walk for another 15 minutes. Using questionnaires the results show that forests were perceived as being more enjoyable, friendly, natural and sacred. Measures of mood such as depression, hostility, anger, anxiety and fatigue all showed significant positive improvements in forest environments compared to urban settings. They found that the thermal conditions in temperate forests in summer (which they measured in both conditions) are experienced as being more comfortable. They suggest that feeling physically more comfortable in forests is one factor making this environment more emotionally attractive. The authors suggest the results are useful in designing restorative environments in urban areas.

Cultures in the Mediterranean region have known for a long time of the positive effect trees have on people's physical comfort. For example, old roads between villages in Provence are often tree lined and so are squares in the centre of towns. Trees not only provide shade, they act as air conditioners. The temperature in summer will be cooler inside a wood compared to outside a wood because of transpiration. Trees do this by extracting heat from the air in order to evaporate water from their leaves.

Spending time in the forest seems to have a positive effect that lasts some time after the experience. Healthy office workers were taken on a three-day (two nights) stay in the forest and their immune system was assessed by measuring NK activity (cells which attack viruses and cancer cells). The forest experience elevated NK activity by 40 per cent and interestingly the effect lasted at least until they were retested a month later (then it was 15% up). No change in NK levels occurred when people spent a similar time in the city (Li *et al.* 2007). Li also looked at more accessible options and found that NK levels were elevated a week later after spending a day in a suburban park.

The Japanese researchers have looked at the different elements of the environment and the part that different senses play in the effectiveness of shinrin-yoku. They have used both psychological measures and physiological correlates of health, immune system strength and stress levels to build a very convincing body of positive evidence.

Smell

Japanese researchers tested people's response in the lab and in natural settings to certain volatile chemicals found in forests to see if any of them had an effect. Volatile chemicals in plants, including trees, which have an effect on other organisms are called phytonocides. Specific tests were made using volatile compounds found in pine and cedar trees that give them their distinctive aromas. Very mild concentrations had a reported and measured positive effect on people's stress level. Higher concentrations had a negative effect which is what you would expect with any smell that is too intense. We typically experience pine scents in very dilute concentrations in nature. They found that phytonocide exposure significantly aided the immune system by increasing NK activity. They also measured decreased concentrations of adrenaline and noradrenaline in urine which indicate reduced levels of stress. It is generally thought, but by no means confirmed, that the effect of phytonocides is olfactory and not the result of the actual chemicals getting into the blood system and affecting a person physically. Researchers are not saying shinrin-yoku is caused by phytonocides. What they seem to be saying is that the pine aromas have a positive association for many Japanese people. Japan has extensive coniferous forests and wood is commonly used in house building. It is not surprising that resinous wood has many positive associations in Japan. Explanations of how shinrin-yoku affects us are thought to be complex and systemic (Tsunetsugu *et al.* 2010).

Forest walking

We know that walking has a positive effect on mind and body. The Walking for Health schemes which are run by volunteers around Britain are beneficial to those wanting to lose weight, recover from a heart attack, and tackle diabetes and other physical illnesses (Natural England 2009). Walking has also been shown to help recovery from depression and anxiety.

Are there benefits in going for a walk in a wood as opposed anywhere else? The short answer is yes, there are. A comparison was made between walking on a Sunday for a couple of hours in an urban area and a suburban forest park in a big city. Various measurements of blood and urine chemistry were made before, during and after the walk and the following day. Blood pressure was also taken at the same time. The results show a significant drop in blood pressure and chemical indicators of metabolic rates in the group that walked in the forest compared to the urban walkers (Li *et al.* 2011). Previous work by the same research team had found important benefits from forest walking for levels of stress hormones (adrenaline and noradrenaline), anti-cancer proteins and NK cells (Li *et al.* 2011). It is now accepted in the medical world that the neurological, hormonal and immune systems work systemically together. The research by Li and his colleagues suggests multiple benefits to body and mind for anyone, but particularly those of us who are stressed or recovering from heart disease.

What is even more interesting and which confirms the approach advocated in this book is that how you walk through the forest makes a difference. Walking mindfully means that we pay attention to the process of walking itself – noticing how the foot contacts the ground and the body moves forwards in harmony. Attention to relaxed breathing is also encouraged in mindful walking. When mindful walking in the forest is compared to athletic walking, people feel better in themselves afterwards, are more relaxed, their mood is enhanced and also their cognitive ability to work on intellectual problems improves (Shin *et al.* 2013; Wilson *et al.* 2008).

Chapter 6

The Evidence for Specific Environmental Factors

...you hear the lark all day long – not one or half a dozen, nor a score or two, but many scores, and I should say hundreds of larks. Go where you like, to the summit of the highest hill, or down the longest slopes into the deepest coombe or valley at its foot, everywhere you are ringed about with that perpetual unchanging stream of sound. It is not a confused, nor a diffused sound, which is everywhere, filling the whole air like a misty rain, or a perfume, or like the universal hum of a teeming insect life in a wood in summer; but a sound that ever comes from a great distance, out of the sky: and you are always at the centre of it; and the effect is of an innumerable company of invisible beings, forming an unbroken circle as wide as the horizon, chanting an everlasting melody in one shrill, unchanging tone.

William Henry Hudson (1923)

> In this chapter the evidence is reviewed for certain environmental factors which could influence well-being. Specifically we will examine light intensity, the presence of negative ions and natural sounds such as birdsong.

The evidence for the effects of natural light

Blue skies get rid of the Blues

Andy McGeeney

SAD

There are people who become more depressed during autumn and winter. This is called Seasonal Affective Disorder (SAD). For example, a study in Norway found modest increases in levels of depression between November and March among

10,000 men and women (Oyane *et al.* 2008). As an ecotherapist I am interested in understanding what is going on here and whether ecotherapy can play a part in alleviating the symptoms of depression in winter. Does SAD really happen? What are the processes that might influence a seasonal change in mood? And can we counteract the negative effects of seasonal change by using ecotherapy?

In 1984 American psychiatrists began to notice patients who showed a history of recurrent depression which developed in autumn and winter and then abated during spring and summer (Rosenthal *et al.* 1984). It was already known that reduced light exposure leads to increased melatonin in the body and the assumption was that melatonin somehow had a depressive effect on the mind. The researchers carried out preliminary trials to see if exposing seasonally depressed individuals to bright light (with similar wavelengths to natural light) as opposed to dim light would delay the onset of SAD.

Soon after the publication of these results, which were positive in their outcome, it was possible to buy a light therapy box containing special light bulbs that mimicked daylight. People were encouraged to sit in front of the natural light box for set periods every day in order to reduce their SAD. Much research into the effectiveness of light therapy ensued, but the conservatism of mainstream psychiatry to all things non-pharmacological meant that it was not universally adopted. In 2003 the American Psychiatric Association decided to review the efficacy of light therapy in the treatment of mood disorders.

The meta-review laid down strict research criteria such as the use of randomised controlled trials and effective placebo conditions (Golden *et al.* 2005). Most of the studies were flawed according to their criteria and only 13 per cent were accepted for the review. However the twenty studies that made it to the finals indicated some interesting conclusions. The results from the selected research revealed a significant reduction in depression symptom severity with bright light treatment for SAD, dawn simulation (light intensity is gradually increased over one and a half to two hours) and non-seasonal depression. The authors add a word of caution with regard to two issues they did not address. One is safety; no one knows yet the effect of this treatment on the eye, and the combined effects of medication and high light exposure. Second, only adults were tested; different concerns arise when using this therapy with children and older adults.

With further research the picture seems more complex, although the overall link between sunlight and mood change holds up. There could be cultural, genetic and climatic factors at play. For example ,the incidence of SAD in the USA is twice that of Europe, even though Europe is in a higher latitude (Mersch *et al.* 1999). There are positive correlation links between cloudiness and SAD as well as minutes of sunshine, day length and temperature (Potkin *et al.* 1986). A study of Icelandic immigrants in Canada suggests there may be a genetic adaptation which conferred on immigrants lower rates of SAD than among other Canadians (McNair 2012).

If we look at birds and animals we can see countless examples of changes in their behaviour as a result of daily and seasonal changes: what are called circadian rhythms. Reproductive hormones become active in all our native species of birds not long after the midwinter solstice, and by Valentine's Day many of our common woodland birds are already paired up and ready to breed. The trigger for the change in behaviour is daylight. A rise in temperature does have an effect on breeding behaviour but is an unreliable signal for seasonal change. Anyone familiar with the British weather will know what I am talking about! However, daylight consistently gets stronger and the days lengthen from the beginning of the new year, thus providing the body with a reliable indicator of seasonal change. Light fluctuations tell our bodies about diurnal cycles as well as seasonal changes. Melatonin is the hormone involved in circadian and seasonal rhythms. It appeared early in evolution and is found in plants and animals. In humans melatonin is produced by the pineal gland situated deep below the brain but neurally independent of it. As light decreases one effect is that our body produces more melatonin, triggering a desire to sleep. As an aside, in older people melatonin production comes into play earlier and peaks earlier in the night, while for adolescents the reverse is true, which explains a lot about both groups of people's behaviour.

Research shows (McNair 2012) that older people sleep much better if they are exposed to bright light during the day, particularly first thing in the morning (light is also bluer at that time of day). Unlike vitamin D production the light only has to reach the eye to have a positive effect. Even on an overcast day it works because the eye is so much more sensitive to light than skin. Much more light reaches the eye when we are outdoors than if we are even close to a big window.

Blue light is the most reactive wavelength for the suppression of melatonin. The open fires our ancestors sat around and the incandescent bulbs we used to use produce much less blue and more orange light. Modern LED, fluorescent lights and computer screens are cooler and bluer in tone. Harvard Medical School (2012) recommends we should expose ourselves to lots of bright light during the day in order to help us sleep better at night and to boost our mood during the day. They also recommend not using computer screens in the two to three hours before going to sleep.

Researchers in Sweden found that if people working in offices are exposed to blue-enriched white light then their alertness, positive mood, concentration and daytime sleepiness were significantly improved (Viola *et al.* 2008). They also slept better at night. There is some suggestion, though, that their alertness, concentration and performance may have been affected by participants' expectations.

If blue light wavelengths are the most effective in suppressing melatonin and consequently boosting our mood I am also wondering if the pleasure we get from seeing blue sky is in part related to this effect. Studies of people's preferences when looking at photographs of nature show that a blue sky is significant (Pretty *et al.* 2005).

Spring suicide

There is a general pattern of reduced suicide rates in midwinter and a seasonal peak between April and June for Europe and America. Similar patterns occur in the southern hemisphere where the phenomenon has been studied in Australia and New Zealand, in their spring and early summer (Bridges, Yip and Yang 2005).

The strong link between suicide and depression suggests that the increase in suicides in spring and early summer need to be carefully explained in the context of *reductions* in SAD once winter is over. If we accept the research evidence and explanations for SAD that were discussed above then it may help to consider what meaning we give to spring when considering seasonal suicide fluctuations.

It is a common belief that spring signifies change and improvement in nature, a time of hope and renewal. For the suicidal or para-suicidal person who feels strongly that nothing is getting better in their own lives the sight of others feeling even happier could underline their own despair: feelings of being left out and being clearly less fortunate than others.

There is a suggestion that the profiles of those who attempt suicide are different for people who experience SAD. They show much higher levels of anxiety and hostility (Pendse, Westrin and Engström 1999). I'm not clear to what extent this possible difference contributes to the different responses to spring by suicidal people. More work is required to fully explain the seasonal links with suicide. From my own work I can anecdotally report that I have seen the positive effects of being outdoors on in-patients under suicide watch.

Bipolar conditions also have a seasonal fluctuation and seem to be compatible with the SAD research results. Manic symptoms apparently peak in autumn and depressive episodes increase in midwinter (Akhter *et al.* 2013).

Vitamin D

Yet another influence on seasonal mood has been investigated: the link between sunshine, vitamin D and reduced depression. The vitamin D hormone (calcitriol) stimulates an enzyme which synthesises serotonin in the brain (Patrick and Ames 2014). Serotonin is a likely mediator in anxiety and depressed mood levels, being lower in people experiencing these conditions (Sansone and Sansone 2013). Serotonin fluctuates seasonally and is highest at the end of summer and early autumn but lowest in winter and spring (Brewerton 1989). There are additional physical benefits from receiving adequate doses of vitamin D. Falls in older people were reduced by a quarter if they were given above recommended levels of vitamin D (Bischoff-Ferrari *et al.* 2009). Rickets, a bone disease caused by vitamin D deficiency, is making a comeback among children, possibly because many children are confined indoors and if they are outdoors they are protected by factor 50 sun barrier cream.

We know that vitamin D production is increased by exposure to sunlight. It has to be direct sunlight; daylight itself is not effective in producing vitamin D. Could these research results explain the attraction of sunbathing and the desire to be outdoors on a sunny day?

How can you receive a recommended dosage of vitamin D? You can eat 10 tins of sardines or 150 egg yolks, or take supplements every day! Alternatively five to ten minutes of exposure of the arms and legs to direct sunlight (UK estimates) will have the same effect. Less exposure is required at lower latitudes and around midsummer. Exposure of this kind every other summer day should provide enough vitamin D to take a person through the winter. If you are a non-smoker, young or have lighter skin you will need less exposure. However, if you use factor 8 sun barrier cream the exposure time goes up to 140 minutes a day. Maybe applying sun cream after 10 minutes of direct exposure is the answer. There are higher vitamin D deficiency levels among people with darker skin living in northern Europe. The effect can be compounded by cultural dress requirements to keep the body well covered.

In conclusion, the results from research suggest that doing ecotherapy on a sunny day particularly in winter is likely to boost a person's mood and reduce anxiety.

The evidence for the effects of negative ions in nature

Do negative ions, found more in mountains, by the seaside and away from cities, affect our mood?

Ions are charged particles and the molecules in the air can become charged negatively relative to the positively charged earth. For example, negative ions build up at the base of a thunder cloud causing in some instances a thunderbolt to fly between clouds or to the ground. For many years it has been said that negative ions can have a positive effect on a person's health and mood. It has been pointed out that there are more positive ions in cities and around heavy traffic pollution and that mountains and the seaside are places with higher negative ion densities. Could higher negative ions contribute to the positive effects of being out in nature? At the moment we don't know for sure but it seems unlikely.

As with much of the research carried out in psychology the methods used to determine the evidence for the effects of negative ions vary in quality and confidence. One study (Flory, Ametepe and Bowers 2010) over five years and using randomised, placebo controlled trials in the laboratory compared negative ions and bright light for the treatment of SAD. The two placebo treatments were dim red light and low-density negative ions. The results confirm the positive effects of bright light but no significant results were obtained for high negative ion exposure compared to the placebos.

Another study (Goel and Etwaroo 2006) investigated the effects of bright light, high-intensity negative ions and auditory sounds (birdsong with classical music in the background) on both depressed and non-depressed people. They found positive results on depressed mood states for all three conditions. But the results were not significant for anger, vigour, fatigue and sleepiness scores, which are all symptoms of SAD.

The problems with negative ion therapy are that the results of research are generally inconsistent and there is no explanatory mechanism for the effects of ions on the human mind. The dosages of negative ions given out by commercial ionisers are at low levels consistent with negative results from good research. Clearly more research is required before this explanation for the benefits of ecotherapy can be accepted (see Perez, Alexander and Bailey 2013).

The evidence for the effects of natural sounds

How much do natural sounds, particularly birdsong, explain our attraction to nature?

Buying natural sounds

I did an Internet search for 'birdsong and relaxing' to see what research there was on the subject. What came up on the first page were companies selling CDs and DVDs of natural sounds to aid relaxation. The first site was Listeningearth.com (Listening Earth n.d.) and the top line of text was: 'Naturally Relaxing, Time to wind down, surround yourself with the gentle ambience of nature, let go of the day's activities and concerns…'

To one side was a menu of CDs in categories. Under *environments* were these subcategories: waves and oceans, living deserts, the dawn chorus, forests and woodlands, rainforest and the tropics, lakes wetlands and water, frogscapes, insect choirs, beautiful birdsong, nature's symphonies, island life and ambiences. Under the heading *living and listening* were the following listings: rise and shine!, meditations with nature, at work and study, noise masking, naturally relaxing, tinnitus relief, quiet time, travel easy, sleep soundly.

I continued my Internet searching and found that there is an online radio station dedicated to continuous birdsong (birdsong.fm). The station suggests that its listeners can use the natural sounds to help them relax. It is also possible to download all kinds of natural sound effects for free – they are used by amateur filmmakers mostly.

What does this tell us about the interest in and popularity of natural sounds when people pay to listen to nature indoors? The people who purchase the CDs or tune into the radio must be hoping to get something positive from listening to them.

Natural sounds have provided inspiration to poets and musicians from Keats's 'Ode to a Nightingale' to Beethoven's 'Pastoral' Symphony. As we shall see later there is a suggestion that the very origin of music is in nature. All this points to a strong need in people to listen to the sounds of nature and birdsong in particular.

Natural and human sounds

Bernie Krauss, one of the world's leading wildlife sound recordists, has written a fascinating book on sounds in nature and the origins of music in humans (Krauss 2012). At a time when we are losing wild sounds to the noise of modern life he makes a very convincing case for the importance of natural sounds in our evolution. It is a passionate and inspiring book by someone with a musician's ear for the beauty of natural sounds.

He distinguishes between three types of sounds in the environment. The most primal is geophony, the sound of non-living events such as the wind, thunder, rainfall and the sea. Biophony, the sounds of animals and birds, evolved in the context of geophony and changed as different living sounds came onto the scene. In this way what can be heard in many wild places is a natural orchestra made up of an ecosystem spreading its sounds to maximum efficiency for all involved. In a pristine biodiverse habitat he has observed that the natural sounds form a layered orchestral effect made up of different bandwidths. The sound mix varies according to species present, times of day and season. Each habitat type has co-evolved from the sound-making species that have entered or evolved in the habitat. In woodland, for example, some birds sing in a higher tone, others lower, and different rhythms are also employed. Anyone listening to a European dawn chorus will notice a sequence of birdsongs, starting perhaps with a nightingale and ending with cooing wood pigeons some time later. In this way each place in nature evolves a unique orchestral sound specific to the species taking part. If the habitat is interfered with the symphonic balance, complexity and unity are lost.

Finally he identifies anthropophony or human-made sounds, which are now having a negative effect on the natural world's capacity to use sound, and on our own well-being. He has found that 50 per cent of the places where he has made wildlife recordings in the past (and he is very widely travelled) have been lost.

Bernie Krauss shows how human music evolved in a natural acoustic environment over millennia. At some stage in our evolution we started to join the orchestra and sing. Nils Wallin, a Swedish 'bio-musicologist', suggests that song came before speech in our development (Wallin 1991). Krauss gives examples of indigenous people singing in response to the natural sounds around them and of other groups who make music influenced by wild sounds.

The effect of natural sounds on humans

A commonsense view combined with the commercial evidence above would suggest that there are definite positive benefits for people listening to natural sounds, and birdsong in particular. As yet there are very few academic research papers on the acoustic influences, as compared to the visual, in nature on people's state of mind. Much of the research has been done within the context of the Kaplans' ART: the notion that time in nature is cognitively restorative of the stresses of the workplace and modern life (see pages 92–95).

Research in Sweden used the well-established fact that a noisy office environment is bad for people's cognitive ability and stress levels. The researchers then tested to see if playing river sounds was restorative. The results were not conclusive, though a video of a river showed some improvements for people (Jahncke *et al.* 2011). Another piece of work found faster recovery of the sympathetic nervous system (which is active when a person is stressed) when people were played natural sounds compared to a noisy environment (Alvarsson, Wiens and Nilsson 2010). Measurement of parasympathetic activity (activated when a person relaxes) did not indicate any effect. The negative results could be to do with the experimental design or the fact that adults appear to adapt to noise fairly well.

Eleanor Ratcliffe, who is researching the effects of natural sounds on mood and attention, has looked specifically at the relationship between birdsong, stress and attention recovery (Ratcliffe, Gatersleben and Sowden 2013). Her work is at an early stage at the moment but some indications of what is involved have already come to light. Some of her findings from one piece of research are detailed below.

The aim was to gather qualitative data on how people responded to stress and attention fatigue by using natural sounds. The theoretical basis was SRT and ART respectively, that is, that people seek out nature to reduce stress and recover cognitively. People were interviewed and asked to imagine situations where they were either stressed or suffering from attention fatigue and what acoustic experiences would help them recover. Sounds that would not help were also explored. The open questioning steered people towards consideration of natural places such as a park, beach or forest. The results of people's preferences were as follows:

- 35 per cent birdsong

- 24 per cent water

- 18 per cent non-avian animals

- 12 per cent elements

- 11 per cent other sounds such as interaction with nature and silence.

One conclusion is that birdsong is a clear acoustic preference for the participants wanting to recover from stressful or attention-fatiguing situations.

Whether birdsong is restorative or not is the result of many interacting factors. These can be the meanings and associations birdsong has for someone, aesthetic preferences, emotional and cognitive responses and previous experience of nature. As you might expect, when people had positive associations with particular birdsongs this created positive emotions, feelings of attraction and low arousal. On the other hand some bird sounds such as a crow calling, bird squawks and those that sounded aggressive had a negative emotional response and high arousal. The individual meanings people gave to birdsong and the emotional responses that follow are an important factor in whether they experience birdsong as restorative. A crow's call, for example, was seen by some as musically harsh and loud as well as having negative meanings attached to it. The call of an owl can be aesthetically beautiful and yet have associations with horror films. Others might associate particular birdsong with warm summer evenings or positive childhood experiences.

Why is birdsong more attractive than other natural sounds?

The variation in people's response to bird sounds may be another indication that biophilia is partly genetically inherited and also open to modification from experience. It would not make sense to have a blanket positive or negative response to hearing birdsong. Bird and animal sounds are informative about the natural environment and it seems plausible that our ancestors would have found it useful to discriminate sounds. Some examples of cross-species understanding of communication might reinforce this interpretation.

Birds give off different types of alarm calls indicating ground-based or aerial predators. These are similar across bird species and are understood by all. A thin whistle that is hard to locate indicates among woodland birds that an aerial predator such as a hawk has been spotted. Birds respond to the thin whistle by dropping deeper into foliage. A harsh repetitive lower-toned call indicates a ground predator such as a fox or cat. The effect of the latter call is to warn other birds to fly up to safety and to indicate to the predator that it has been spotted and will be mobbed if it stays around. Hunters and modern-day birdwatchers quickly learn these calls.

When the honey guide, an African bird, finds a bees' nest it will make a distinctive call and go in search of a honey badger. The honey badger has evolved to recognise the honey guide's call and will follow the bird. When the badger finds the bees' nest, possibly hidden in a tough tree trunk or underground, it will dig it out and eat the contents. Afterwards the honey guide is rewarded by gaining access to a rich meal of leftovers. In parts of Africa where the honey guide lives local people have learnt to do what the badger does and gain similar rewards.

It seems self-evident that natural selection would have sifted out those of our ancestors that could discriminate by sound a dangerous predator from a harmless or even an edible creature. Being in tune with natural sounds can be a matter of being killed or finding protein-rich food for your family.

Another suggestion is that the presence of birdsong may have indicated to our ancestors that when they went into a particular wooded area they were safe. Birds only sing when they are relaxed and have not been silenced by sensing danger.

There may be other reasons as well. If a large flock of wild birds such as geese or starlings fly overhead most people will express interest and even amazement. The migration of wild animals in East Africa is a major tourist attraction. Why should this be? I think this could be because the sight of large numbers of birds or animals excites interest at a very fundamental level. The large group of creatures gives the message of abundance and in turn indicates a good food supply.

The response to herds and flocks is mainly visual. What about the aesthetics of birdsong? Why would our ancestors have been attracted to a place with many birds singing? It could be that many varieties of song would indicate biodiversity in the same way that a meadow of multicoloured flowers does. Biodiversity in turn indicates a good and varied food supply, and a place where many creatures are surviving well. The converse is often true: a place without birdsong indicates a location with low biodiversity. Hungry birds are not able to spend much time singing, something female birds use in their search for a healthy mate, and early humans may have intuited with regard to habitat value.

The evolution of human language and the ability to discriminate subtle differences in speech sounds may have given us additional advantages when it came to reading the auditory environment around us.

Attention Restoration Theory

The Kaplans consider distraction, effortless attention and novelty to be factors enabling a cognitive recovery from stressful attention. The research by Eleanor Ratcliffe and colleagues (2013) found confirmation of these factors in the reasons people gave for choosing birdsong as a restorative experience. Birdsong was described as a source of fascination, and a welcome distraction from current stresses in life. It was undemanding and a novel source of interest compared to urban sounds. One person found the clucking of chickens reassuring.

I would interpret distraction as a secondary consequence of birdsong. In other words the sound of birds can bring us into the present moment so that we are no longer in a distracted state of mind but in one of full attention. I am reminded of the wild birds in Aldous Huxley's novel *The Island* (Huxley 2009 [1962]) who call out phrases in the forest like 'here and now', and so bring people into the moment.

Previous experience of nature

The Ratcliffe research confirmed something one would expect. There is an association between having frequent positive experiences of nature and birdsong, and helping people feel more connected to nature. When individuals had a limited experience of nature, or a negative connection to it, they tended not to get as much restorative benefit from birdsong.

Noise

Loud noise is inherently stressful for us because we have to use extra energy to sift out the noise from more meaningful sounds. Researchers talk of irrelevant sound effects (ISE), that is, unwanted sounds in our lives. Dealing with ISE results in nervous tension, fatigue, irritation and physiological changes to our body. Many studies have repeatedly shown that even moderate noise in the workplace causes measurable exhaustion, raised blood pressure and negative attitudes after only a few days exposure (e.g. Kight and Swaddle 2010; Kjellberg, Muhr and Skoldstrom 1998). It also seems as if we can appear to adapt to noise but still show changes in our body chemistry which indicate continuing stress levels (Krauss 2012).

Various research papers point in the same direction: noise affects our children's ability to develop cognitive skills such as reading, comprehension, memory, concentration and attention (Klatte, Bergstrom and Lachmann 2013; WHO 2011) and children are more adversely affected by noise than adults. The noise in these studies was from traffic and aircraft. In one study the effect was sufficient to depress IQ points by five to ten points and when the airport was relocated the IQ scores returned to previous levels.

The effect of noise on our mental abilities is thought to be twofold. Primarily it disrupts the ability of short-term memory to process information and secondarily it distracts attention and thus requires more mental effort to keep focused (Klatte *et al.* 2013). Yet another ingredient of ecotherapy is that it takes us away from noise.

Tranquility

Bernie Kauss distinguishes between silence, which is the absence of sound, and tranquillity, an experience of near silence rippled through with quiet sounds. The complete absence of sound is deeply disturbing when people are placed experimentally inside an anechoic chamber which eliminates all external sounds completely.

Chris Watson, BBC wildlife sound recordist, investigated tranquillity. He considers it an important experience for achieving serenity and peace of mind. He asked people what they considered to be tranquil sounds. The answers he received included breathing, footsteps, a heartbeat, birdsong, crickets, lapping waves and flowing streams (in Krauss 2012). There seems to be a connection between these tranquil sounds that creates a base layer of rhythmic patterns. The sounds are not soporific; they gently stimulate the mind into relaxed alertness. Watson refers to research which shows that tranquil sounds affect the limbic system in the brain which in turn releases endorphins, the body's natural tranquillisers.

Unfortunately we have lost our places of tranquillity in Britain. The Council for the Protection of Rural England (CPRE) has been monitoring human-made noise across the country and they have concluded that there are only a couple of places of tranquility left! The USA has vast wilderness areas in its national parks but in the UK with over 60 million people it can feel cramped at times. For anyone wanting to get out to a tranquil place in Britain there are things that they can do. Look on a search engine, find out the aircraft lanes and avoid them. The CPRE have produced detailed maps of noise areas. Be inspired by Robert Macfarlane's wonderfully evocative book *The Wild Places*, an account of his search for wildness in Britain and Ireland (Macfarlane 2007). Be creative in your search. What does tranquility mean to you? I have found that the bottom of small gorges and steep-sided valleys in the north of England can be very quiet because they screen out road sounds.

Many of us have access to quiet places because of where we live and we have money to buy train tickets to get away. But for many in Britain, who are poor and probably the most in need of ecotherapy, the options to experience real tranquility don't exist. Inner cities are noisy, crowded, sometimes threatening and rarely green or buzzing with wildlife. Access to places of tranquility should be a basic right for all regardless of birth and circumstance.

I draw various conclusions from the research to date. Tranquillity is important for our peace of mind and we have lost much of the possibility for achieving it. Not only that but our hearing is polluted with noise at levels which are bad for our health. Natural sounds and in particular birdsong have a positive effect on stress levels and mood. Put together, these results confirm and contribute to a recognition of the benefits of ecotherapy for all.

Chapter 7

The Evidence Relating to Social Differences

In this chapter the focus is on the effects of being in nature for different groups of people. The effects on children, and people experiencing dementia who are mostly at the older end of the age spectrum, are examined first. The next section looks at the benefits to communities of increased natural surroundings. Lastly, and of great importance for the purposes of this book, we will review the effects of nature on people who are experiencing emotional and mental distress.

The evidence for the effects of nature on children

I have included a section on children and nature more as a pointer to other work rather than as a detailed overview. Enough has been written on the research and suggested activities for children to fill another book. I draw your attention to the Resources at the end of this chapter. My own experience of working with children and young people, including Children and Adolescent Mental Health Services (CAMHS) has taught me how important positive nature experiences are to the health of growing minds.

In recent years there have been increasing concerns that children are not spending enough time outdoors in nature and that this is having a detrimental effect on their physical and mental health. In the USA they have medicalised the concept by calling it 'nature-deficit disorder' (Louv 2005). This is a great line for the media but I'm not sure it helps to medicalise a social issue. Regardless of its label there is evidence that children spend considerably less time outdoors in nature and that this has a detrimental effect on their development and well-being.

Children now spend less time outdoors than in previous times. It dropped on average from 86 minutes to 42 minutes a day between the 1980s and 2000 (Pretty *et al.* 2009). Time outdoors for children today is more likely to be organised and managed by adults. The suggestion is that our children should be more 'free range' and allowed to explore in a free, unstructured way our local streets, fields and gardens. It has been said that it would enhance children's social relationships, confidence in risk taking and exploration, as well as connections to nature. The evidence supports this view. Interestingly it also points to childhood experiences in nature continuing into adulthood.

Two major charities in the UK that are keen to encourage people to engage with the natural environment are the RSPB and National Trust. They have both commissioned research and promoted children's activities in nature (Bird 2007; Moss 2013). A review of the evidence concerning the benefits to children of being in nature can be found in these reports. I would also recommend reading the report by the London Sustainable Development Commission (Gill 2011).

What are the key findings? In summary the reports concluded that being in nature was important to childhood, as much as a healthy diet and exercise is. The studies found the strongest evidence for claims about physical and mental health. In terms of the latter, emotional regulation and motor development were significant. They also found a link between childhood experiences in nature and a positive view of nature as an adult. Conversely a lack of positive experiences in nature is associated with 'fear, discomfort and dislike of the environment'. Gardening projects and field trips had an educational impact but the greater personal benefits derived from child-initiated exploratory play experiences in nature. Research found that children who played in wild nature by going for hikes or playing in the woods received more positive long-term effects than just picking flowers, planting seeds or trees.

Of more direct relevance to ecotherapy, it was found there was strong evidence for the positive effects of nature experiences on mental health and emotional regulation. The research was positive for specific groups such as children diagnosed with attention deficit hyperactivity disorder (ADHD) and for children as a whole (Pretty *et al.* 2009).

Forest Schools come out of it well. Forest Schools are defined by the Forest School England network as an inspirational process that offers children, young people and adults regular opportunities to achieve, and develop confidence and self-esteem through hands-on learning experiences in a woodland environment (O'Brien and Murray 2006). The key features are:

- the use of woodland (and therefore a 'wild') setting

- a high ratio of adults to pupils

- learning can be linked to the National Curriculum and Foundation Stage objectives

- the freedom to explore using multiple senses

- regular contact for the children over a significant period of time.

There is good evidence in the O'Brien and Murray review that children improve social skills and self-control. There is also some support for improved self-confidence, language and communication skills for Forest Schools. A core part of Forest School thinking is that children need to spend time away from close supervision so that they can develop their own creative skills in nature.

It is argued that what is needed is for the adults to get out the way more and let children explore nature for themselves. It is increasingly being recognised that vocal individuals who have health and safety anxieties have been in control for too long to the detriment of our children's healthy development. The *Lessons from Berlin* PDF (Lessons from Berlin 2001) is an inspiring example of what can be done using experienced play area designers. The designers made sure in some play schemes that children could not be seen easily in 70 per cent of the areas. The children had bushes and secret pathways to hide in. The adults did not patrol the areas but stayed in one area in case children needed help or insecure children needed someone to be with. Safety has not been compromised and break time behaviour has improved; levels of violence have in fact gone down. The play areas are untidy looking with weeds, brambles and nettles in many places. Children can jump two metres onto a sand pit and ground surfaces are deliberately uneven in places to encourage balance. The insurers have kept an eye on things and are happy with the way things are going.

Research in the UK has found that if a school playground is improved by making it greener then the behaviour of the children changes. A British charity called Learning Through Landscapes commissioned a study to see what effect a green makeover of school grounds had on pupils. They discovered that 64 per of the schools surveyed saw a reduction in bullying when school grounds were improved and 73 per cent reported improved behaviour. Vandalism dropped in 28 per cent of schools, while 65 per cent believed that grounds alterations had improved attitude to learning (Learning Through Landscapes 2003).

I think the harm done to children by restricting their play to the indoors and under close adult supervision has been recognised. My impression is that activities like the Forest Schools are providing more opportunities for children to be in nature. Children are also being taught mindfulness. There are possibilities to adapt some of the activities in this book for children and to take inspiration from people like Joseph Cornell who has created remarkable collection of resources (see Cornell 2015).

The evidence for the effects of nature on people with dementia

The key symptoms of dementia include memory loss, difficulties in thinking and problem solving, leading to confusion and disorientation. The two primary forms of dementia are Alzheimer's disease and vascular dementia, although there are other manifestations. Vascular risk factors such as high blood pressure, high cholesterol and smoking, plus a history of strokes are believed to contribute to vascular dementia. Our knowledge of the causes of Alzheimer's disease is incomplete. This means treatment is focused on slowing down the disease and ensuring a good quality of life. Ecotherapy can make a significant contribution to both responses.

Good-quality evidence for the positive effects of nature experiences for people with dementia exists but is limited at the moment. However, we can place dementia treatment in the wider context. Elsewhere in this book we have reviewed the strong evidence we have for the positive effect of nature on the general population. For example, the implications for dementia patients from Ulrich's SRT on the general population is that our response to a natural environment is deep seated within all of us and is not dependent on higher cognitive capabilities. His work also underlines the fact that nature has great powers to reduce stress (Rappe and Topo 2007). In other words, what is good enough for all of us is good enough for people experiencing dementia. This section considers the specific needs of dementia clients with regard to nature.

The progression of Alzheimer's disease gives us clues as to what the person most needs psychologically and what experiences of nature might help the most. Early on the disease affects memory and the ability to create new ones (older existing memories are less affected). In particular it affects a person's cognitive map or memory for place. A well-designed memory garden can help people who find it hard to orientate themselves by including memorable features and using visual signage as well as words. Later on the disease affects the amygdala which mediates emotions and mood states. A good memory garden would foster positive mood states. This could be done by having benches where the person and their family can sit together and perhaps listen to birdsong or look at a water feature. Deterioration of executive functions controlled by the prefrontal lobes in Alzheimer's disease means that a person finds sequencing events such as cooking a meal or planning a walk difficult. A self-organised garden takes some of the pressure off figuring out where to go. Paths can be in loops, entrances and exits clearly visible and different areas of the garden can feature different colours.

Lastly I want to mention the chiasmatic nuclei which are the cells in the brain enabling us to know what time of day or what season it is. As a consequence they influence our sleep/wake timings. Someone living with Alzheimer's disease can have very disrupted sleep patterns. The change in daylight when we are outdoors tells us what part of the day it is without needing to think about it. Blue light wavelengths, not found at sufficient levels in most in artificial light, but occurring in sunlight, are the main stimuli to our circadian rhythms. The Dementia Services Development Centre in Sterling advises, based on their research, that sunlight could help stabilise sleep patterns particularly for people with dementia (McNair *et al.* 2010). And of course any good garden celebrates the different seasons with spring bulbs and autumn colour (Zeisel 2005). Many of the examples used for gardens equally apply when taking people living with dementia out into parks and wilder natural areas.

One approach taken by those working with people experiencing dementia has been to take what is already known to work therapeutically for this group of people and review how these outcomes can be achieved by being in nature. For example, people with significant memory loss benefit from opportunities to reminisce and to repeat experiences until they become more familiar. Also it needs to be borne in mind that a person may lose some of their cognitive capabilities and still function well in responding to sensory stimulation. Nicky Tann, an occupational therapist working in North East London, has adapted existing activities as well as devised new ones for people living with dementia who are outdoors in nature. An example relevant to memory loss and sensory stimulation illustrates her style of work. People experiencing memory loss are taken to a tree and a discussion takes place about the tree using sensory engagement. Everyone is instructed to take a leaf and explore it. What colour is it? Does it smell? What shape is it? Do you know what type of tree it is? From this sensory encounter a great deal of social engagement takes place as well. Each person then carries their leaf along with them on the walk. Maybe a couple more trees are visited in a similar manner and in the process opportunities to reminisce about the past come up. At the end of the walk the group discusses where they have been using the leaf collection as memory aids (see *Tree leaf designs* activity). In addition the group has some green exercise.

There is some research into the effects of nature specifically on people living with dementia and there are some excellent guidelines on how to create a therapeutic garden for people living with dementia (see 'Some resources for ecotherapy and dementia' at the end of the chapter). I expect that because many people living with dementia have mobility issues and/or are in sheltered accommodation or care homes, more work has been done on the beneficial effects of being in gardens than in wild nature.

Multi-sensory stimulation and dementia

> Multi-sensory stimulation (MSS), previously known as snoezelen (Hulsegge and Verheul 1987), originated as a leisure facility for people with learning disabilities. It is an approach that aims to stimulate the senses through the provision of unpatterned visual, auditory, olfactory and tactile stimuli, therefore providing an alternative to cognitive-based activities. (Baker *et al.* 2003, p.466)

There is some evidence that multi-sensory stimulation is of benefit to people living with dementia although people vary in their response to stimuli. Findings from studies included reductions in agitation, improvement in mood including reduced depression, greater diversity of activity, enhanced well-being and improved interaction with staff (Bossen 2010). In nature we can experience all the sensory modalities mentioned above plus body sense, temperature change and balance.

Even if access to the outdoors is not practical in all situations it is still possible to tap into the positive effects of experiencing nature. The work of Roger Ulrich described elsewhere has demonstrated the positive effects on stress, anxiety and low mood of viewing pictures on a wall and videos of nature. There are online sites selling full-colour posters of natural scenes for very little cost. It is possible to buy DVDs catering for people living with dementia which show nature scenes such as forests and seashores. The DVDs' accompanying advice is to have natural objects such as pine cones and seashells respectively in the room to add more sensory experiences.

Attention is a cognitive function which deteriorates with dementia and the Kaplans' extensive research work on attention restoration clearly demonstrates the restorative function of being in nature. Thus, putting dementia patients in contact with nature has the potential for reducing stress and lifting depression by reducing cognitive demands.

Agitation is another symptom of dementia. The evidence we have points to positive benefits from using outdoor space as a way of reducing agitation (Bossen 2010). The focus of research has been more on activity and being outside buildings rather than contact with nature, however. One study investigated the influence of a wander garden on inappropriate behaviour in a dementia unit (Detweiler *et al.* 2008). The results found that increased exposure to the garden led to reduced agitation but, strangely, increased physical incidents. Verbal inappropriateness did not change. They did record a reduction in falls for those who used the gardens and also decreased use of high-dose anti-psychotic drugs.

One study compared five long-term care homes for people living with Alzheimer's disease, three without gardens and two with. Because of the progressive deterioration of cognitive faculties aggressive assaults can become increasingly more frequent with people experiencing Alzheimer's and this was the case at the homes without gardens. Those with gardens stayed the same or showed a slight decrease in aggressive assaults (Mooney and Nicell 1992).

> In the garden institutions, the rate of violent incidents declined by 19% between 1989 and 1990 while the total rate of incidents fell by 3.5% over the same period. In the non-garden institutions, the rate of violent incidents increased by 681% and the total rate of incidents increased by 319%. (*Gardens for Patients with Alzheimer's Disease* n.d.)

The importance of making sure accessible gardens are part of the design of residential care homes is clear.

Gardening was found to be one of the activities associated with a lower risk of dementia among older people in France (Fabrigoule *et al.* 1995). It is thought to have a protective effect because of the stimulation of cognitive functions. However, more work needs to be done to tease out the complex variables involved in coming to such a conclusion for this and the previous study.

The design of gardens surrounding buildings used by people living with dementia can be used to great advantage if certain factors are considered (Shackell and Walter 2012). Obviously safety is an issue as are ease of access and clear signage (using pictures as well as words). Paths created in loops bring a person back to where they started and avoid dead ends. A view of trees, flowers and wildlife have all been found to make a garden more pleasing. It is also important to consider if the garden features can easily be seen by people sitting down indoors. Raised flower beds are good for people who are outside as well as those inside a building.

Just as we saw in the section on children and nature an overly protective concern with safety at the expense of therapeutic activities can restrict older people's quality of life and mental harmony. There can be greater freedom outdoors than within the confines of the built environment. In an appropriately designed garden a person with memory difficulties can wander unsupervised, pick up and explore things, break twigs, stand and stare, in a way that is not possible indoors. The experience of being in nature can tap into non-declarative memory such as the recall of skills learnt in the past. Implicit knowledge of this kind has the potential for making connections to other memories and for the client to experience expertise.

Specially designed gardens can be used to stimulate the senses. Many residential homes that specialise in dementia care or learning disabilities are creating outdoor spaces that can be explored with all the senses, where plants provide the stimulus through their colour, texture and smell. Sensory gardens may also contain outdoor toys, water features and garden ornaments such as wind chimes. (See also the section on 'Bringing ecotherapy into our work elsewhere' in Chapter 3.)

Smell and autobiographical memory

Smell and memory come from deep within the brain, a primitive area called the rhinencephalon composed of the limbic system and olfactory region. Later in our evolution the amygdala and hippocampus developed to process emotional memories within the limbic system. Very early on in evolution, however, smell was the sense that indicated what to eat, avoid as poisonous, flee from, mate with and nurture. A rat can learn to avoid unpleasant substances from just one negative experience. Maybe you have had a stomach bug followed by a temporary distaste for the smells of the food associated with the illness. Because of its ancient 'pre-intellectual' origins smell is thus a very useful sense when working with people experiencing memory loss. The scent of flowers, cut grass or autumn leaves can be so reassuringly evocative for a person struggling to get used to confusing life changes.

Interestingly, scientists have investigated what is going on when we are aware of the smell of the earth after it has rained. The distinctive scent, which many people find attractive, is called petrochor. It is created by a volatile chemical, geosmin, released by soil bacteria after the ground has been wetted (Royal Society of Chemistry n.d.). The bacteria feed on vegetable matter and are incidentally the source of some of our antibiotics. Humans are particularly sensitive to the smell of wet soil and our noses can detect concentrations as low as 0.5 parts per billion (Polak and Provasi 1992). It has been suggested that our sensitivity evolved as a way of detecting water sources. It could also explain why camels can detect where an oasis is in the desert.

In conclusion the evidence points to two main benefits for people living with dementia of being out in nature. First, nature has a calming effect and a can lift people out of negative mood states. Second, the multi-sensory potential of time in nature means that it can stimulate cognitive capacity and at the same time offer good experiences to those whose intellectual capacity is reduced. These two main factors in turn lead to increased self-esteem in people and even increase the frequency of family visits (Rappe and Topo 2007).

The evidence for the effects of nature on communities

This photo shows a recently created concrete environment in the heart of the City of London. The only concessions to nature – low box hedges – are close cropped, signifying a sense that everything is under control. Although the site and its surrounding buildings use expensive materials no thought has been given to the benefits of providing a green environment.

Concrete environment

Before we look at the direct therapeutic effects of the green environment on people experiencing mental distress I want to complete this part of the evidence review by addressing a broader issue. The issue is whether our urban environment can be designed with nature in mind to improve well-being for all of us. I believe we have the evidence to give a very positive yes to this important question. We can live better lives if we design our neighbourhoods to include green space in community areas. The most compelling evidence comes from a team in the USA who have been working for the past 20 years on this very issue.

In 1993 Frances Kuo set up the Human-Environment Research Laboratory (HERL), with William Sullivan, to study the relationship between people and the physical environment (Prow 1999). Ten years later Kuo set up the Landscape and Human Health Laboratory (LHHL) to focus their work on the relationship between human health and green space.

Kuo and Sullivan's multi-disciplinary team, which is based in Chicago, had the insight and good fortune to be able to observe a natural experiment, comparing people who had green space with those that didn't (Prow 1999; Kuo *et al.* 1998). In the 1990s the city of Chicago built the biggest housing complex in the world. It was a three-mile-long corridor of 28 identical 16-storey high-rise buildings. The new residents who came from tough run-down housing complexes were randomly assigned apartments. Some blocks had trees and other vegetation outside, others did not. Here was a live experiment in the making. The Kuo and Sullivan team trained local residents to interview local people who matched them in gender and ethnic origin. The research team wanted to assess, across a range of factors, if there was any difference between people who lived with greenery near their apartment block and people who didn't.

The results they got were fascinating. They found clear differences between those people who lived with trees nearby and those who had a barren landscape. People with trees knew and socialised more with neighbours, had a stronger sense of community and felt safer than the residents who lived in a treeless outdoors.

Further research delved deeper and they observed that children and adults gathered and interacted more in the places with trees than the barren areas. There were fewer couples disputes in the green areas. And actual violence was also less frequent when people were living near trees. Of 150 residents interviewed 14 per cent living in the barren blocks threatened or used a knife or gun their children; only 3 per cent did so from the areas with trees.

The accumulated evidence you have read so far in this book will make the explanations obvious. People who had trees around them felt less stressed and tense, which meant they were more able to feel safe with neighbours and more willing not only to talk to but help others.

Residents in the barren areas were shown computer-adapted images of their greened-up neighbourhood and then asked to rate how they felt about the images.

The green areas got the thumbs up; people said they would feel safer. The Kuo team also asked the police what they thought about greening up the neighbourhoods. The police response was cautious. They predicted that trees would increase people's fear (potentially a place for muggers to hide?) but the residents disagreed. After emphasising the positive results of their investigations the researchers spelt out an important message for developers and planners: people who live in social housing want trees and yet they are surrounded by concrete, and if neighbourhoods were greened up then everyone would benefit.

Tree lined streets improve well-being
and neighbourhood cohesion

The effect of designing green nature into our cities and towns is not just about making the place look pretty, although that is a good enough reason. It is sensible because it improves people's quality of life, reduces crime and improves community spirit. And if any politicians are reading: it saves money in policing and social work. That is what the city of Chicago believed. As a result of the research programme the Chicago city government invested $10 million in planting 20,000 trees around neighbourhoods.

Another study by the Chicago team found that children played twice as much outdoors if trees were present, they engaged in more creative play and mixed with adults more. The team are now engaged in a more detailed look at the effect on children's learning of greening the school environment (Prow 1999).

These and many other related studies show us that we all need to live in a greener environment for our health and well-being. Town planning is a mental health issue. It means more than just encouraging people who have experienced mental distress to take part in ecotherapy. It strengthens the case for community-based psychological services which actively engage members of communities to green their city. I can predict that the mental health services and social services will make financial savings when local government is given the resources to green our streets.

The challenge is to design cities, where most of us live now, to be fully integrated with nature. The costs to all of us, including politicians, town planners and architects, of ignoring these conclusions can only lead to greater ill health, stress and social alienation. All of these have high economic costs attached to them.

Even before we look specifically at the effects on people experiencing mental distress, I hope one conclusion is clear. The natural environment undoubtedly has a positive effect on well-being, mood, thinking capacity, self-esteem and levels of stress in all of us.

The evidence that nature is good for mental health

Yield to the willow
All the loathing,
All the desire of your heart.

Basho, trans. Blyth (1942)

Let us now examine the effects of nature on mental distress. If we accept that spending time in the natural world is good for all of us it could be argued that we already have enough evidence from people assumed not be distressed. I would agree, and add that the evidence in this section points to even greater benefits for those in greater need. It is a conclusion which strengthens the argument that ecotherapy should be included in the standard treatment for people experiencing mental distress.

Although attitudes and prejudice towards people experiencing severe mental distress are changing in Britain we still have a long way to go (Mind n.d.). The effects of dividing the population into 'normal' and 'mentally ill' is a gross disservice to both groups of labelled people. It is commonly asserted that a quarter of us will experience mental illness at some time in our lives (probably an underestimate). Fifteen per cent of us at any one time are under medication or other treatment for mental illness. Add to that everyone who has at some time felt depressed, anxious or stressed and there aren't many people left in the country (Mental Health Foundation n.d.). Although the greatest need comes from those in greatest distress, we would *all* benefit from knowing how to live more positive lives with increased well-being.

Research challenges

There is now a considerable body of research supporting the benefits of nature on mental health and well-being. NICE has approved both mindfulness and exercise as acceptable forms of treatment for mental illness (NICE 2008). On this basis I believe these are sufficient grounds to justify taking people outdoors on walks in nature to do the kinds of activities offered in this book. However, ecotherapy has yet to be specifically approved by NICE and most health service managers take their lead from the government's advisory body. It is also the case that at a time when the NHS is under all kinds of organisational pressure for change accompanied by cuts to funding all but the most enlightened health managers stick to their statutory duties. This is a very unfortunate state of affairs for people experiencing mental distress, and for taxpayers. The cost of mental health problems to the English economy is £70–100 billion every year (Centre for Mental Health 2011; Chief Medical Officer 2013). Predictions made before the economic crisis were that mental health problems would increase by 14 per cent by 2026. That is 10 million people with mental health problems. The economic case has been made by Mind that millions could be cut from the NHS budget by encouraging ecotherapy (Vardakoulias 2013).

It is assumed that the main reason NICE has not yet approved ecotherapy is that most of the research that has been reported does not meet the criteria of a randomised control trial (RTC), which is called the gold standard of medical research. An RTC is the highest standard required in drug trials, for example, although it is not always adhered to by pharmaceutical companies.

To apply the strictest RTC standards to ecotherapy evaluation is quite a challenge because the components of ecotherapy cannot be isolated from other factors as easily as it is done in a drug trial. To randomly allocate individuals to an ecotherapy programme is difficult because not everyone likes being outdoors. If a researcher only takes on volunteers who like the idea of going outdoors they can be accused of not using random selection. The problem can be got round to some extent by finding a matched group of very similar people on important criteria (e.g. experience of mental distress, gender, socioeconomic position, age, etc.) who do not go outdoors but do something else. A waiting list of people for treatment can also be used to compare similar groups who do and do not experience ecotherapy. Likewise evaluating participants before and after an ecotherapy session is another way.

If we accept the aforementioned methodological challenges there are still some good-quality research results that demonstrate the effectiveness of ecotherapy on mental health and well-being.

Research work on people experiencing mental illness

Mind funded 130 ecotherapy projects across England with £7.5 million of Big Lottery money from 2009 to 2013 under the title Ecominds. They commissioned a five-year independent evaluation by the University of Essex (Bragg *et al.* 2013) as well as an economic cost benefit analysis of ecotherapy by the New Economics Foundation (NEF; Vardakoulias 2013). The University of Essex Green Exercise Research Team is possibly the most important academic centre researching ecotherapy and green care in the UK. The team have produced significant research papers themselves as well as writing evaluated summaries of current research (see all references for Pretty, Hine, Barton including multi-authored entries). The Mind-commissioned research by the University of Essex team is important because it looked at so many ecotherapy projects and participants' experiences. Over 800 people took part in Ecominds. The key findings of the research (Bragg *et al.* 2013) into the effects of ecotherapy in Ecominds can be summarised as follows:

- *Mental well-being:* Using internationally recognised measures of mental well-being they found that the majority of participants had significant increases in well-being and self esteem, by 17 per cent and 11 per cent respectively. The scores brought them up from below average to the average for the population as a whole. Seventy-six per cent of participants experienced an improvement in mood after only one Ecominds session. There were significant decreases in mood disturbance – anger, confusion, depression and tension – after taking part in the programmes of ecotherapy.

- *Social inclusion:* There were significant increases in people's social involvement as a result of taking part in Ecominds. The measured improvement over the whole project was 10 per cent on average with some individuals having improvements up to 89 per cent. Before taking part in the project many people said they did not feel part of the local community; by the end the majority did feel they belonged. There was also a shift in actual behaviour with 81 per cent showing an increase in getting involved in community activities as a result of Ecominds. This is clear evidence that ecotherapy can help improve social inclusion.

- *Connection to nature:* There were significant increases (61%) in people's 'participant connection to nature', that is, the amount people participated in nature over the time of the project. Individual project reviews showed that people thought this was one of the most important parts of the project. Older people were slightly more positive than younger people. Connection to nature showed itself by people spending more time in green places, appreciating it more, and finding a spiritual connection to nature.

- *Healthy lifestyle:* Participants were asked about their own perceived health condition over the duration of the project and 59 per cent saw an average 31 per cent improvement in their health rating.

- *Environmentally friendly behaviour:* Although most people were already environmentally friendly at the start of the project there was still a statistically significant increase in environmentally friendly practices for 60 per cent of participants by the end of the project.

One important conclusion the researchers make from their questionnaires, and which is echoed in my own in-depth interviews with participants, is that all three aspects of ecotherapy – being in nature, being with people and doing an activity or exercise – are equally important and valued. This came out at the end of the project and after taking part in just one session. The research validates the approach taken by this book which encourages active engagement with nature-using groups.

Another significant finding is that ecotherapy had a positive effect on people regardless of the type of ecotherapy project, gender, age and whether the group involved formal therapy or not. The conclusion is that ecotherapy is a powerful intervention to significantly improve people's well-being, healthy lifestyles, social inclusion and positive environmental behaviour regardless of the specific type of ecotherapy used.

In 2008 the UK government commissioned the NEF to develop an evidence-based set of criteria for well-being (NEF 2008, 2013). The result is similar in concept to the five-a-day fruit and vegetables advice for a healthy diet. The Five Ways to Wellbeing are: Be Active, Connect, Take Notice, Keep Learning and Give.

The Ecominds researchers analysed the data and comments they received and demonstrated how the Five Ways to Wellbeing can be encouraged through ecotherapy. By doing ecotherapy participants are being more *Active* outdoors by going on walks and doing exercises, overcoming social exclusion by *Connecting* with others in a group and the local community, *Taking Notice* of nature around them and gaining the mental health benefits from doing so, *Keeping Learning* by gaining new skills and learning about nature and themselves and being able to *Give* by taking part in nature restoration and supporting each other.

Mind has consistently promoted and campaigned for greater official recognition of ecotherapy for many years. Before the Ecominds Big Lottery project, and its 2013 report mentioned above, it had showcased what it saw as an important aid to self-recovery and resilience with a detailed report – *Ecotherapy: The Green Agenda for Mental Health* (Mind 2007). The Ecominds research yet again confirms the efficacy of ecotherapy for all of us and particularly people experiencing mental illness.

Green exercise, self-esteem and depression

Medication is no longer advised for mild depression because of the lack of consistent evidence supporting its benefits (Moncrieff and Kirsch 2005). In addition anti-depressants have side-effects, many people do not like taking them, and they are a significant cost to the health budget. Physical activity on the other hand has no side-effects and is inexpensive. Physical exercise has been found to have a positive effect on depression (see references in Robertson *et al.* 2012) but the long term effects have yet to be recognised (Krogh *et al.* 2011). NICE (2008) recommends physical exercise for mild to moderate depression based on the research evidence.

The case for making significant investments in our parks for all our health and well-being has been made very well in a report by Greenspace (Greenspace 2011). I would highly recommend the report to anyone who is arguing the case that health service savings could be made by greening our towns and cities.

Although NICE now recommends physical exercise for mild to moderate depression it is unfortunately low down on GPs' preferred options for treatment (Mental Health Foundation 2009). As few as 4 per cent of GPs put exercise as their first choice for treating depression and only 21 per cent have it in their top three options. One factor may be that when a GP makes out a prescription for drugs they receive a fee for doing so. They don't typically get a fee for recommending exercise – not an encouragement to offer alternatives to anti-depressants and CBT. If professional support and encouragement are weak, so is the personal motivation to regularly exercise for people experiencing depression. It comes with the condition. Ecotherapy may help overcome the weak motivation by making outdoor activity more enjoyable.

One could argue that although NICE does not yet recommend ecotherapy it would approve of exercise taken outdoors. The term 'green exercise' (coined by the University of Essex team) refers to physical activity in the presence of nature (Barton and Pretty 2010). Does green exercise have increased benefits over and above the positive effects on self-esteem and depression that ordinary physical exercise has? The short answer is yes it does.

When ecotherapy and more specifically green exercise is considered it has many positive aspects which can reduce depression and increase motivation to exercise. Green exercise has the combined effects of exercise, being in nature and social inclusion in a group. A walk outdoors is perceived as being less strenuous than an equivalent time spent in the gym and the main focus is the pleasurable experiences in nature rather than the exercise itself (Bragg, Wood and Barton 2013). Offering green exercise could be a more attractive option to the gym for someone who is depressed. It could at least be a transitional move to more vigorous activity.

Low self-esteem is related to poor performance in school, suicide, alcohol abuse and mental illness in young people. Long-term mood states of anger and fear are linked to physical diseases such as heart disease, strokes, rheumatoid arthritis and asthma, and vulnerabilities of the immune system. There is a clear need to find ways for people with low self-esteem and low mood states to use activities in their lives that create more positive experiences.

Many studies show the positive effects on people's self-esteem and mood from spending time in nature. A meta-study of 10 UK-based green exercise research projects (Barton and Pretty 2010) involving 1252 participants drew the key findings together. The results show big increases in mood and self-esteem over the short term followed by consistent diminishing but still positive returns over the long term.

All the environments improved self-esteem and mood, but being near water had the greatest impact. Both men and women improved their self-esteem equally. Men showed a lower mood level before and after the study, although both sexes improved their mood over time. The young experienced the greatest improvements in self-esteem which diminished with age. Mood was most beneficial to those in the mid age range, not the young and old. Interestingly the greatest benefits were seen in those experiencing mental illness.

Another meta-analysis review, this time analysing randomised control trials for walking and depression (Robertson *et al.* 2012), concluded that there was evidence that walking made a statistically large and significant difference to levels of depression. However,the authors were cautious about making specific recommendations because of the heterogeneous nature of the various interventions.

One suggestion is that the benefits of green exercise might be due to the exercise alone, the outdoors playing little part. We have already seen the evidence for the positive effects of being in nature. The combination of nature and exercise creates greater benefits (Barton, Hine and Pretty 2009). Both are good for you. One study (Barton, Griffin and Pretty 2011) compared three groups of people experiencing mental health problems. One group attended a social club, a second exercised in a swimming group and a third group was set up as a green exercise group (weekly countryside and urban park walks). The social group was used as a baseline comparison at the same time controlling for the positive effects of socialising. The results show that both self-esteem and mood improved after just one session and continued to improve over the six-week observation period. The improvements in self-esteem were significantly greater in the green exercise group. Mood improvements were greatest in the swimming group followed by the green exercise group. One important factor was that the green exercise group was set up for the research project and had a lot of people attending only one session (unlike the other two groups who had been meeting for years). Other studies have compared indoors and outdoors exercise and have found that being outdoors and particularly being in nature reduced negative states and had a more positive effect on mood: feelings of happiness, delight, joy and pleasure (e.g. Ryan *et al.* 2010).

A study in Scotland compared the effects of walking in urban and rural environments on participants' mood and cognitive abilities (Roe and Aspinall 2011). The study also compared people with good mental health with those having poor mental health. The results showed a greater positive restorative effect for both affective and cognitive capacity for both groups who walked in a rural setting compared to an urban walk. As with the meta-study mentioned earlier, those participants who had poor mental health experienced the biggest improvements.

The conclusion from this and many other pieces of research is that if you want to feel better about yourself, uplift your mood and clear your thinking then a walk outdoors in nature is good for you. For those of us feeling particularly stressed or depressed then the benefits of a walk in nature will be even more noticeable.

There is one last point I want to make for those of us who do ecotherapy in all seasons: it seems that even if we don't enjoy a walk, because it is cold and blustery or hot and sweaty, we gain benefits. Work by Marc Berman shows significant improvements in people's creativity, short-term memory and attention even after spending time outdoors in very cold and very hot weather. The work was carried out in Canada which has extremes of summer and winter. Participants said they preferred spring and autumn, but the psychological results were the same regardless of the weather. In other words you don't have to like being in nature to receive the cognitive benefits of being there (Berman, Jonides and Kaplan 2008).

Well-being and more for all

At the conclusion of this chapter I want to put the discussion of mental health into a wider context because talk of mental health often focuses exclusively on mental illness or distress. In other words we sometimes look at well-being as a goal to be attained rather than what should be the norm. In our society, which is so sick at a personal and interpersonal level, many of us strive to attain an absence of stress and do not look beyond this point. We can do better than just be 'average'. Undoubtedly ecotherapy can help us reduce stress, anxiety and depression. It can also build our resilience against future potential stresses. However, it can also take us to even 'better' psychological states.

I am referring to the feelings of awe, wonder, reverence, love and presence that can emerge after time spent in nature, particularly when away from human activity. Some may call these experiences spiritual. As discussed earlier, I would prefer the term transpersonal – going beyond the individual self. In the circumstances under discussion what takes place is not necessarily a religious spiritual process but the dissolution or 'thinning' of the self. I also prefer a term that refers to a psychological state devoid of religious connotations. Others may not agree with me on this last point.

I think it is interesting that religions often use images from nature to convey spiritual meanings. Beautiful flowers, sunsets, trees and seascapes are frequently used for illustration. That is not surprising when the major religions of the world owe their foundations to experiences of awe and wonder in nature. The Middle Eastern Abrahamic faiths of Judaism, Islam and Christianity all found connections to their gods in the desert or mountains. Hindu, Taoist and Shinto religions emphasise humanity's connection to nature, and Buddha attained enlightenment under a tree.

Some resources for engaging children with nature

Berger, R. and Lahad, M. (2013) *The Healing Forest in Post-Crisis Work with Children*. London: Jessica Kingsley Publishers.

Cornell, J. (1998) *Sharing Nature with Children*, 2nd edition. Nevada City, CA: Dawn Publications.

Cornell, J. (2015) *Sharing Nature: Nature Awareness Activities for All Ages*. Nevada City, CA: Crystal Clarity.

Earth Education: Taking kids into nature *www.eartheducation.org.uk*

Love Outdoor Play: *http://loveoutdoorplay.net/category/nature-play*

Mindbodygreen: Teaching children to be mindful *www.mindbodygreen.com*

National Trust: *www.nationaltrust.org.uk*

Project Wild Thing: *http://projectwildthing.com*

RSPB: *www.rspb.org.uk*

Sharing Nature: Joseph Cornell's website *www.sharingnature.com*

Schofield, J. and Danks, F. (2005) *Nature's Playground*. London: Frances Collin.

Schofield, J. and Danks, F. (2012) *The Stick Book*. London: Frances Lincoln.

The Wild Network: Encouraging children to get out into nature *www.thewildnetwork.com*

Thomas, B. (2014) *How to Get Kids Offline, Outdoors, and Connecting with Nature*. London: Jessica Kingsley Publishers.

Wildlife Trusts: *www.wildlifetrusts.org/kids/kids-clubs*

Woodland Trust: *www.woodlandtrust.org.uk/learn/children-and-families*

Woodland Trust Nature Detectives: *www.naturedetectives.org.uk*

Some resources for ecotherapy and dementia

Access to Nature for Older People: *www.accesstonature.org/prod04.html*

Chalfont, G. (2005) *Architecture, Nature and Care: The Importance of Connection to Nature with Reference to Older People and Dementia*. Sheffield: University of Sheffield. This has a good bibliography of evidence-based resources in the field.

Chalfont, G. (2008) *Design for Nature in Dementia Care*. London: Jessica Kingsley Publishers. This is an excellent source for those caring for people with dementia. It discusses all the issues around residential care and increasing connections to nature. Practical and ethical issues, backed by research evidence, are given prominence.

Dementia Adventure: UK activity trips for people with dementia and their carers *www.dementiaadventure.co.uk*

Gardens that Care: Planning outdoor environments for people with dementia (2010) Alzheimers Australia SA Inc. download as: http://dbmas.org.au/uploads/resources/101796_ALZA_Garden32pp_LR.pdf. Clear advice on how to create garden for people with Alzheimer's.

Mapes, N. (2010) 'It's a walk in the park: exploring the benefits of green exercise and open spaces for people living with dementia.' *Working With Older People 14*, 4, 25–31.

Mapes, N. (2011) *Living with Dementia and Connecting with Nature: Looking Back and Stepping Forwards.* Colchester: University of Essex.

Part 3

Activities

Introduction

There is the strength, the marrow, of Nature, in short, all good things are wild and free.

Henry David Thoreau (1991 [1862])

This section contains over 100 ecotherapy activities to enable people to gain a deeper connection to nature. They are based on mindfulness, sensory awareness, imagination and information sharing.

Where do all the activities come from?

The activities come from a broad range of sources. Mostly I just made them up as I was wandering outdoors noticing how I was responding to the natural world. Sometimes I was aware of an interesting experience I had had and thought about how I could make it into an activity. At other times an idea came to me as I was taking a group out and I made the activity up on the spot. If an activity worked I put it in my notebook. Other people I have worked with or read about have also been an inspiration, particularly Joseph Cornell and Joanna Macy. I've made acknowledgements when I've been able to remember where I learnt about the activity. My apologies if I have not recognised someone's contribution to my thinking. Acknowledgements can be made in subsequent editions. There are some activities that have been around a long time and have become absorbed into the folk memory of conservation and wildlife educators; they must have had an inventor at some stage but the name has been lost.

Adapting and updating activities

I cannot emphasise enough the benefit of adapting and changing these activities to suit your needs of the moment. This is particularly important with the descriptive instructions (e.g. *Four elements: earth, air, fire and water*) which need to be personalised so that they become authentic for the speaker. Invent your own – and let me know and I will share it with others. Comments can be left on my website: www.andymcgeeney.com. In the future I will be adding new activities to the site not contained in the book. If anyone else would like to share their own activities on the website they would be most welcome. Full acknowledgement will be given.

Activity format

Each activity is described using the same format of Aim, Need and Instructions. It is important to have the Aim in mind to give intention to the activity. At least ask yourself 'Why am I doing this activity at this place, and at this point in the day with this group?' The Need section states the equipment or materials, if any, that are required to do the activity. It also suggests the best kind of place to carry out the activity. The Instructions should be detailed enough to enable you to carry out the activity. Feedback on how clear the Instructions are would be very useful to me for later editions.

Activity codes

Each activity is coded to make it easier to quickly decide whether an activity is suitable for the group's needs:

 Creative expressive. Encourages creative and artistic thinking.

 Ecological self-awareness. Encourages an expanded sense of self and our place in ecosystems. Enables people to understand something about how the natural world works.

 Interactive/icebreaker. Encourages interaction between people.

 Mindfulness.

 Physical actions, usually as an aid to relaxation.

 Sensory.

 Visualisation, an imaginative narrative to stimulate the imagination and thoughts.

The Activities Listed Alphabetically

Activities listed alphabetically	Coded symbols	page no.
The age of a tree, see Being with trees activities		173
All is experience		163
An apple becomes part of you		164
Attending to the breath		165
Awareness and contemplation		
Blue sky blue mind		165
Eating with eyes closed		166
Just sitting		167
Monologue in a pair		168
Sounds as music		168
Still tree, wandering mind		169
Stretching the mind far and near		169
Today's colour is…		170
Ball name game		170
Barefoot walk		171
Blue sky blue mind, see Awareness and contemplation activities		165
Beach mandala, see Seaside activities		262
Beach scavenger search, see Seaside activities		263

Activities listed alphabetically	Coded symbols	page no.
Being with trees		
The age of a tree	🕸	173
The leaf in your hand	🕸 ✋	177
Tree biological processes	🕸	178
Tree leaf designs	✋ 💡 🕸	179
Tree leaf rubbing	✋ 💡 🕸	181
Tree life history	🕸	181
Trees, their economic importance to us	🕸	182
Birds' feathers, see Seaside activities	💡 ✋	263
Birdsong	🕸 ✋	183
Blind walk	✋ 🧍🧍	184
Blue sky blue mind, see Awareness and contemplation activities	🧘 ✋	165
Bring nature into your home	🕸 ✋ 💡	185
Buried in autumn leaves	✋ 🧍🧍	188
Camera	✋ 🧍🧍 🧘	188
Cat's ears	✋	189
Change is constant, see Change in nature activities	🕸	190
Changes in nature		
Change is constant	🕸	190
Phenology mandala	🕸 ✋	191
Solar arc	🕸 ✋	192
Something to celebrate each month	🕸	193
Changing tides, see Seaside activities	🕸	263
Colour chart match	✋ 💡	194
Colour mosaic with leaves	✋ 💡	196

Activities listed alphabetically	Coded symbols	page no.
Creating a memory of place	🖐️ 👁️	197
Creative activities		
Decorated path	🖐️ 💡	200
Frame a view	🖐️ 💡	200
Leaf blanket	🖐️ 💡	201
Natural cairn	🖐️ 💡	201
Seasonal circle	🖐️ 💡	202
Woodland mobile	🖐️ 💡	203
Dawn chorus walk	🕸️ 🖐️ 🧍🧍	203
Death and life in winter	🕸️	207
Decorated path, see Creative activities	🖐️ 💡	200
Do you know where you live?	🕸️	209
Earth walking	🧘 🖐️	210
Eating with eyes closed, see Awareness and contemplation activities	🧘 🖐️	166
The ecological body	🕸️ 🖐️ 🧘	212
Ecological networks		
Ecosystem milling	🕸️ 🖐️ 🧍🧍	215
Indra's net	🏃 🕸️ 🧍🧍	218
Network of life	🏃 🕸️ 🧍🧍	219
Web of life game	🏃 🕸️ 🧍🧍	220
Ecosystem milling, see Ecological networks activities	🕸️ 🖐️ 🧍🧍	215
Ecotherapy beyond the session		
Using a local map	🖐️ 🧘 🕸️ 💡	221
What can I do on my own in nature?	🖐️ 🧘 🕸️ 💡	222
Experience of nature	🕸️ 🖐️	223

Activities listed alphabetically	Coded symbols	page no.
Find your tree again		223
Folding poem		224
Four elements: earth, air, water and fire, see The four elements activities		225
The four elements		
Four elements: earth, air, water and fire		225
Reflecting on the four elements		227
Walking through the four elements		228
Fox walking		229
Frame a view, see Creative activities		200
Geology of place, see Seaside activities		264
Getting to know another life form		230
Gratitude		232
Hawk and deer		233
Home in nature		234
Honouring our ancestors, see Visualisation		279
How to meditate		235
I appreciate…		237
I notice		238
Indra's net, see Ecological networks activities		218
Inheritance of the wild, see Visualisation		282
Inside/outside me		239
Interview with nature		240
Just sitting, see Awareness and contemplation activities		167
The Kawa model		242

Activities listed alphabetically	Coded symbols	page no.
Leaf blanket, see Creative activities		189
The leaf in your hand, see Being with trees		201
Leaning on a tree, a person		244
Life circle		246
Listening to silence		246
Memory stick		247
Message in a bottle, see Seaside activities		264
A mini-beast's life		248
Mirror exercise		249
Monologue in a pair, see Awareness and contemplation activities		168
Moving water watching, see Watching water activities		290
My connection to nature		249
My special place in nature		250
Natural cairn, see Creative activities		201
Nature makes an appearance		251
Network of life, see Ecological networks activities		219
Nicky's memory cone		252
Off the beaten track		253
Our evolutionary story, see Visualisation activities		284
Phenology mandala, see Changes in naturw activities		191
Physical and relaxation warm-ups		254
Physical relaxation exercises		255
A place, a word, a poem		257

Activities listed alphabetically	Coded symbols	page no.
Poetry for reflection	🕸	258
A question for nature	💡	259
Reflecting on the four elements, see The four elements activities	🕸 🧘 ✋	227
Sea rhythms, see Seaside activities	✋ 🧘	265
Seaside activities		
Beach mandala	💡 ✋	262
Beach scavenger search	💡 ✋	263
Birds' feathers	💡 ✋	263
Changing tides	🕸	263
Geology of place	🕸	264
Message in a bottle	💡 🚶🚶	264
Sea rhythms	✋ 🧘	265
Stone tower	✋ 🚶🚶	265
Seasonal circle, see Creative activities	✋ 💡	202
See with the mind then the heart	✋ 🧘	266
Silent walking	✋ 🧘	267
Smell like a fox	✋	268
Social warm-ups	🚶🚶 ✋	268
Solar arc, see Changes in nature activities	✋ 🕸	192
Something to celebrate each month, see Changes in nature activities	🕸	193
Sound map	✋ 🧘	271
Sounds as music, see Awareness and contemplation activities	🧘 ✋	168
Standing by the river/going with the flow, see Watching water activities	✋ 🧘 🕸	291

Activities listed alphabetically	Coded symbols	page no.
Step out of the river of thought, see Watching water activities		293
Still tree, wandering mind, see Awareness and contemplation activities		169
Still water watching, see Watching water activities		293
Stone in my heart		271
Stone tower, see Seaside activities		265
A story from today in nature		272
Stretching the mind far and near, see Awareness and contemplation activities		169
Survival for a day		275
Texture swatch match		276
The web of life, see Visualisation activities		287
Thisness		276
Today's colour is…, see Awareness and contemplation activities		170
Tree biological processes, see Being with trees activities		178
Tree leaf designs, see Being with trees activities		179
Tree leaf rubbing, see Being with trees activities		181
Tree life history, see Being with trees activities		181
Trees, their economic importance to us, see Being with trees activities		182
Using a local map, see Ecotherapy beyond the session activities		221
Visualisation		
Honouring our ancestors		279
Inheritance of the wild		282
Our evolutionary story		284
The web of life		287

Activities listed alphabetically	Coded symbols	page no.
Walking through the four elements, see The four elements		228
Watching water		
Moving water watching		290
Standing by the river/going with the flow		291
Step out of the river of thought		293
Still water watching		293
What does the river teach us of life?		294
Weather you like it or not		295
The web of life		287
Web of life game, see Ecological networks activities		220
What can I do on my own in nature?, see Ecotherapy beyond the session activities		222
What does the river teach us of life?, see Watching water activities		294
What to do in winter		296
Wild food for ecotherapy		298
Wildlife watching		301
Wind in the willows		303
Witnessing		304
Woodland mobile, see Creative activities		203

The Activities

All is experience

This activity is a challenge to people's experience and beliefs and may be difficult to grasp immediately. It is not easy to understand because it requires heightened sensory awareness and an open way of thinking. I think that even if participants don't get it first time the experience in itself is enjoyable as a sensory awareness activity.

Aim: To weaken the singularity of the individual self and to encourage experience of the ecological self. To encourage the state of being a witness to experiences.

Need: Nothing.

Instructions: Ask the group to stand in a circle, take up a firm stance and close their eyes. The next step is to help people become more aware of their physical body. Talk people through a script something like this, taking your time to give detail:

'I want you to bring your attention to the inside of your body. Can you feel the solidity of your insides, lungs breathing, maybe heartbeat, warm muscles and so forth... Now be aware of your skin as a boundary containing your body - inside is you, outside is your environment.'

Once you think people have had time to settle into this feeling of the bodily self move to the next stage of awareness.

'I want you to shift your attention to your experience of the world outside, still with your eyes closed, take in what is around you now. What can you hear?... Can you feel the breeze on your skin as the air moves around?... Is the sun warming your skin?... Can you feel the solid ground below you?'

Give people time to absorb the different sensations in turn.

Switch attention again back to the inside of the body and repeat the first paragraph of script in your own words. Remind people that their body is what fills their experience right now before moving to the next stage.

'I wonder if it is possible for you to recognise that experiencing your body inside and experiencing the world outside are both in your experience world because of what your body tells you. They are both just different types of experience.

Can you move from experiencing the ground outside you, to feeling the inside of the body, and back again? Your body is part of the world as much as the ground beneath your feet, is it not? Become a witness to your experience.

You know about the inside and outside of your skin only through your bodily senses. It is in your body that you experience the wind and sun on your skin, it is in your body that your ears feels vibrations of air from birdsong, and in your eyes and brain that you make up a view of what is around you.

Both inside and outside are all together in your experience and there is no real difference between them. Move your awareness back and forth between inside and outside and see them both as you having experiences.'

See: *The ecological body, Inside/outside me*

An apple becomes part of you

Aim: To demonstrate the ecological connections between ourselves and the rest of nature by eating an apple.

Need: An apple, a sharp knife and a chopping board.

Instructions: Form the group into a circle and hold up the apple. Tell the group that the apple is presented as a symbol of all the food we eat.

Earth, air, fire and water go into making the apple, as do all those elements in the making of ourselves. Spend some time talking about what the apple is made of: sweet sugars - made, like the rest of the apple, from photosynthesis, mixing water and carbon dioxide with the power of sunlight; a few minerals from the earth mixed in; water from the rain.

'This apple comes from an apple tree and contains within it seeds to grow more apple trees. The apple tree originally came from the Kazakhstan-China border where it was first cultivated and with a lot of help from humans has now spread all round the planet. It has seduced us with its sweetness into propagating its tree very widely.'

Having discussed the ecological link with us, get out the knife and chopping board and cut the apple into pieces, roughly the same number of segments as there are people, including yourself. Pass round the board and ask everyone to help themselves to a piece of apple. Encourage everyone to smell and feel the segment and slowly eat it with awareness focused on its smell, taste and texture. Ask people to imagine eating an apple for the first time. Notice how your mouth automatically responds to the juices by salivating. Suggest they eat the apple piece as slowly and as mindfully as possible.

When everyone has eaten their segment say: *'Where is the apple now? Nothing is lost or gained, only changed. The goodness of the apple is becoming part of us, inseparably integrated. And so it is with all food we eat; it comes from the environment, and then is returned to it once we have eliminated it from our bodies - a continual recycling of matter and energy.'*

See: *Eating with eyes closed*

Attending to the breath

Aim: To create a state of mindfulness and relaxation.

Need: Nothing.

Instructions: After a physical loosening up suggest to people that they stand relaxedly, either with their eyes closed or gently focusing on an object on the ground a couple of metres away. Instruct people to pay attention to the breath as the belly rises and falls. When they find themselves distracted they should return to the breath.

How long you do this activity for depends on the group but you could begin with a few minutes and see how that goes.

The activity can be repeated on a walk at suitable moments in order to bring everyone back to a more mindful state.

I strongly recommend that whoever is facilitating this activity also takes part. By doing so the person is not only modelling the activity but they are becoming more congruent with everyone else's state of mind. After meditating with a group I can more easily speak from that shifted state of mind and encourage us all to stay with it as we move off on the walk.

See: *How to meditate*

Awareness and contemplation

Introduction to *Awareness and contemplation* activities

There are a large number of activities in this book designed to encourage awareness and contemplation. I decided to group these particular activities together because they can be briefly explained and could be used together if the leader wanted to particularly focus on the themes of awareness and contemplation. Do check out other possibilities though.

Blue sky blue mind

Aim: This is an ancient Tibetan exercise I got from reading Ram Dass. It is a metaphor of the clear mind as blue sky with thoughts as clouds floating through experience.

Need: Bin bags, one per person for lying on damp ground (see Instructions).

Instructions: Pick a day when the sun is out, with white clouds drifting across a blue sky.

Ask everyone to lie on the ground and look up. An alternative is to stand on top of a hill looking out.

Ask everyone to get themselves comfortable laying or standing and to look up at the blue sky with clouds. If the sun is behind you, all of you will face in the direction of the bluest sky and ensure no one accidentally looks at the sun.

Explain that the aim is to bring your attention onto a point in the blue sky and allow the clouds to float past your view without paying much attention to them. Eventually the mind becomes blue and you can just allow the clouds to pass by. Let the clouds happen, be aware of them as you attend to the blue but don't be distracted by them.

Afterwards you can discuss the mindfulness metaphor. The mind is like the blue sky and thoughts are like the clouds floating by. In meditation we allow the clouds to appear, notice them and let them float by while we attend to the blueness of an empty mind.

Eating with eyes closed

Aim: To increase sensory awareness, particularly taste and smell.

Need: Either take some fruit like grapes or satsumas or find wild fruit such as blackberries.

Instructions: You can do this activity at the beginning of lunch or, as I prefer, take some fruit such as grapes out with you on a walk. If it is autumn you can invite people to collect a few blackberries before you begin. You can repeat the activity and compare different blackberry flavours.

Take your time over this activity and do it as slowly as possible. Say something like:

'I want you to close your eyes and place the blackberry in your mouth. Don't eat it yet. Notice the shape of the blackberry in your mouth, explore it with your tongue. Now, very slowly eat the blackberry. Notice how your teeth go into action and chew up the fruit. Can you feel the juice bursting out and your mouth responding with saliva to digest it? What do your tongue and mouth tell you about the texture of the fruit? And what of the flavour, is it sweet, sour or what?'

Food for thought: *'You may think that by eating wild fruit you are exploiting the plant and stealing its fruits for free. Quite the opposite. The blackberry has perfected through millennia of evolution ways to seduce birds and mammals, including ourselves, into eating their fruit. They have added sugar which we need for energy and find very tasty. The plants use noticeable colours that contrast with green foliage so we can find them easily. Plants provide attractive fruit so that the consumers are more likely to spread their seeds around. Some fruit, fig comes to mind, even add a laxative so we don't take their seeds too far but do provide a bit of starter compost for the new seedling!'*

See: *An apple becomes part of you*

Just sitting

Aim: To practise allowing things to happen, to be receptive to the world.

Need: Bin bags to sit on, one per person.

Instructions: Go to a wood or somewhere else outdoors in nature as a group. Ask the group to spread out in a loose circle facing outwards so no one can see anyone else.

Ask people to sit on the ground, lean against a tree or sit on a polythene bag. Encourage people to spend a moment settling in, feeling physically comfortable and relaxed.

Talk people through a short meditation of about 10 minutes, with their eyes closed. While everyone still has their eyes closed give the next set of instructions. Say something like:

'In a moment I'm going to ask you to open your eyes. Know that you are in a safe place, I am here looking out for you. When you open your eyes be effortless, allow light, form and colour to come to you. We have spent time, I'm sure, looking and searching, now we can be different. Open your eyes and be a witness to the world happening without the need to do or think anything. The world is just so.'

A variation on *Just sitting* is to do the 10-minute meditation with the group and then suggest people go for a slow but short walk. The instructions are:

'In a moment I'm going to ask you to open your eyes and I want you to go for a short walk. Walk slowly and look around you but without searching for anything. Allow the world to come to you. If something captures your attention sit down and spend some time getting to know the object of your attention. Look at it as if for the first time with fresh eyes, with the wonder of a child. Consider what it is that caught your attention. Then move on.'

You can take the activity further by asking people to draw or write about their experience afterwards.

Just sitting and taking in the view

Monologue in a pair

Adapted from an activity I learnt on a Ronen Berger workshop.

Aim: To express spontaneous thoughts and experiences and be listened to. One person is talking and the other is listening but it is not a conversation.

Need: Nothing.

Instructions: Have everyone choose a partner they feel comfortable with and invite each pair to go off for a walk and be back after a certain time or when you blow a whistle.

The instructions are as follows:

'Begin by walking together in silence and when it seems right one person can begin speaking. The other listens attentively without comment or question. After a few minutes swap over roles. Continue doing this as long as you want or until called by me with the whistle. It is not a conversation. The person talking is to say the first thing that comes into their mind and it need bear no relation to what the other person has said.'

Once people have come back to you hold a discussion on how the experience went. What is it like to talk and be heard but not have a verbal response?

Sounds as music

Aim: To practise just listening without labelling sounds.

Need: Nothing. The activity works particularly well in woodland in spring when there are lots of birds singing.

Instructions: This activity is in two parts. Begin by inviting people to stand or lie with their eyes closed, to relax and pay attention to all the sounds around them. You could begin with a short meditation.

Ask:

'What can you hear, near you and far away? When you hear a new sound give it a name and think of what might have made it, such as a car horn or birdsong. Scan the sound environment until you have labelled everything you can hear.'

After a while ask people to change mode and listen differently. Suggest the following:

'Allow sounds to come to you without making an effort to listen. Drop all the labels now and just listen to sound, don't analyse it or give it a name, just listen to the quality of the sound as if it is music. When you listen to music you might identify a particular instrument but most often I imagine you listen to the beauty or energy of the music for itself. Do this now. Pay attention to the quality of the

sounds and what they evoke in you. After reflecting on a particular sound always return to the "music".'

See: *Cat's ears, Dawn chorus walk, Listening to silence, Sound map, Wind in the willows*

Still tree, wandering mind

Aims: To really pay attention to one thing in nature, and to be aware of how often the mind wanders and needs to be brought back to attending.

Need: A tree.

Instructions: Ask the group to stand or sit some distance from a tree so that they can take it all in; if it's a big tree that might be 50 metres away. Invite people to pay attention to the tree and nothing else. Ask them to begin by taking in all its qualities: its shape, size, colour and movement. Then after a while, they can rest their eyes on one place on the tree, say its trunk, and just be aware of the whole tree. Every time anyone's attention wanders (it will happen frequently) have them raise their hand briefly and then return to attending to the tree.

You could add something to the activity:

'Sit and contemplate the tree and be aware of it stillness, its "isness". It is fully alive and yet it is not thinking, evaluating. Can you be like a tree? Just sit, do nothing else.'

Stretching the mind far and near

Aim: To connect the big with the small.

Need: A raised area of land such as a hill with a view.

Instructions: Take the group to a high point and have everyone spread out so they can see the view clearly. Taking your time at each stage instruct everyone as follows:

'Take your mind far far away to the horizon ahead of you...now slowly turn around on the spot and keep your attention on the farthest distant horizon all the time until you are back facing the same way... Now look up into the sky. Be aware of the big dome of the sky above you...the height of clouds and the blue beyond, how big the heavens are and how small you are in relation to it... See yourself in the centre of this vast dome, contained within it.

Now I want you to shift your attention and switch to something near you, maybe something on the ground or an object you can pick up. Look at the detail of a leaf or feather, how it is constructed and the colour and shapes and forms in it… Take your time with this single object and get to know it… You are looking at one very small part of the universe in all its complexity.

Turn your eyes back to the landscape around you and just think how much detail and complexity there is all around you.'

Today's colour is…

Aim: To heighten awareness of colour.

Need: Nothing.

Instructions: Ask everyone to choose a colour for themselves and then spend the rest of the walk attending to that colour. The idea is that every time a person notices their colour they silently acknowledge it to themselves: 'A different red' or 'Ah, that red there'. You could suggest people begin with a primary colour like red or yellow and on another occasion you can remind people of the activity and get them to choose more subtle colours like browns, orange reds or turquoise. An alternative is for the whole group to observe the same colour.

AWARENESS AND CONTEMPLATION

Ball name game

Aims: This is a great way to start a session. It works at so many levels and is simple to do. It is an icebreaker, it helps people learn each other's names and to loosen up physically. It increases body awareness, being all together in a group, and heightens tactile attention and awareness in a grounding way. It brings people into the present in a fun way.

Need: A ball. I use a ball which is about half the size of a football and soft to the touch. It fits easily into my rucksack.

Instructions: Gather people into a circle with some space between them. Explain what to do:

'This is a game to help us learn each other's names. The instructions are very simple. Throw the ball to someone else and as you do call out your own name.'

When you think you have got everyone's name explain the next stage:

'Throw the ball to someone else and as you do call out their name. If the thrower gets your name wrong say your name clearly before throwing the ball to someone else.'

Stop when you have memorised everyone's name, and others seem to have too.

Barefoot walk

Aims: To increase sensory contact with our feet and the ground and to provide a radically new experience which may push someone out of their familiar way of being.

Need: Preferably a mix of habitats such as meadow and woodland. An old towel or clean cloths in case anyone wants to wipe their bare feet afterwards.

Instructions: I have variations on this activity depending on the habitat, weather, state of the ground and how far I think I can nudge a group into trying something different.

I expect most people at some time or other have enjoyed the experience on the shoreline of taking their socks and shoes off and walking along the sand. Taking our shoes off immediately gives us a strong sensory contact with the ground and a pleasurable feeling in our skin. Sometimes we can be reminded of just how sensitive our feet are, how we can distinguish between different-sized grains of sand and gravel, or how much the temperature subtly changes as we walk along. Cooling the feet in seawater seems to refresh the whole body.

When you are working with a group by the sea or near a river then this activity is fun to do, but it is also not particularly challenging for the group. However, if you try this in other habitats, such as woodland or grasslands, the invitation to take off your shoes and socks is much more exciting. I always offer a choice and some (very few) people decline to remove their shoes and some keep their sock on, but unspoken group conformity usually nudges everyone to give it a go.

If you take the group through different habitats it is an opportunity for people to compare sensations. Woodland can be leafy underfoot or squidgy with soft mud, and in grassland it is amazing how many different types of grass and other plants the feet can distinguish, particularly the thistles!

My initial instructions are some thing like:

'I am going to suggest you all take off your socks and shoes and continue walking. Please take extra care where you walk. I want you to look ahead and see if you can avoid the temptation to stare down at your feet. Trust your sense of touch and take your time. Enjoy the experience.' I take the lead and remove my own shoes and socks and keep my eyes out ahead for potentially dangerous

things like animal faeces, sharp stones and broken glass, but these are rarely encountered if you choose a fairly isolated place.

Encourage people to be mindful and take their time with each step they make.

When I have taken the group fifty metres or so I find a place where we can sit down and discuss the experience. I ask things like:

'How was that, how did you get on?'

'Were you able to not look down and trust your feet?'

'Was it fun? Which places did you enjoy most/not enjoy?'

The ensuing discussion can go in all sorts of directions, from childhood reminiscence to vows to get out more and the importance of finding new experiences which take you outside your comfort zone.

When everyone is back in shoes and socks, ask:

'How does it feel when you put your shoes back on and continue walking?'

It can feel similar to putting rubber gloves on and affectionately hugging someone – you can do it, but something is missing.

This activity is linked in my mind with *Buried in autumn leaves* and *Smell like a fox* because it heightens the sensory experience of nature. It also has similarities to *Off the beaten track* when it challenges us to change the way we are.

Being with trees

Introduction to *Being with trees* activities

There is in my mind undoubtedly something special about the influence of trees on the human psyche. In surveys people say trees are one of the top characteristics of a positive experience in nature. Trees are frequently symbols of the natural environment as a whole in campaigns to conserve nature. In creation myths around the world a tree is often central to the story and a representation of what holds everything together.

I am most interested in how we can enhance our appreciation of trees experientially so I have included a few activities which aim to do that. I am also interested in how, when we are with trees, we can feed the mind with thoughts and ideas to give a more holistic experience. When I introduce information about nature I am not wanting to take people into their heads and away from direct experience. Rather I am planting seeds of ideas that occupy the thinking mind and grow into the relationship with the trees around us at the time. I think this information-giving is best done in small doses, just enough for someone to think: ah, knowing that makes me feel more appreciative of trees or how intimately I depend on them for my existence – and then return to the sensory experience of trees with an enhanced awareness.

I suggest you read through some of the information about trees given in the activities in this section and use it in your own way to supplement the times when you are taking a group out into woods or are by an individual tree. To get you started I describe an activity you can try using a leaf but the information can be used at other times, of course.

The age of a tree

Aim: To measure the age of a tree and reflect on what has happened in its lifetime so far.

Needs: Paper and pens to write notes, a long metric tape measure, or a short tape measure and a long ball of string with knots tied every metre. Copy and take with you Table A.1 and A.2 showing, respectively, tree growth rates and important dates in history. Some big old trees.

Instructions: The instructions below tell you how to measure the height and girth of a tree, and from the latter calculate its approximate age. Both measurements are very simple to carry out in small groups. It is worth looking to see if you can find an old oak in ancient woodland or in an old hedgerow because they could be centuries old. Some housing estates and parks have old trees, relics of ancient hedgerows that once surrounded farmland before the houses were built.

Tree height

Give the following instructions or demonstrate first.

'Stand some way from the tree so you can see all of it, top to roots, without tilting your neck. Find a straight twig or pencil and hold it up in front of you at arm's length (keeping it at that distance), twig pointing vertically up. Walk backwards until the twig looks the same visual height as the tree.

Then rotate the stick to horizontal (still at arm's length) with one end level with the middle of the foot of the tree.

Get another person to walk from the base of the tree and to stand level with the end of the stick. You can take your arm down now. Measure the distance from the standing person to the middle of the tree - this equates to the tree's height.'

Tree age from girth

'Get a couple of people to run the tape measure or string round the tree at breast height or 1.5 metres to be exact, avoiding branches and big bumps. Note the measurement on a piece of paper. Divide this figure by the annual growth rate for a given tree - see Table A.1. If you can only say whether it is

evergreen or deciduous then use 3 or 2.5 respectively as an annual growth rate. To be more precise use the Tree growth rates table.'

Table A.1 Tree growth rates

Species	Annual growth rate of girth in cm
Sycamore	2.5
English Oak	1.5
Cedar of Lebanon, London Plane, Douglas Fir	7
Scots Pine, Horse Chestnut, Lime	1
Yew	0.7

Now comes the interesting bit. Maybe you have asked the group to guess the age of the tree before measurements began. What do they think of the result, was it less or more than they expected? Who was closest?

Your simple calculation will give you the estimated year the tree was seeded. What was happening in the world of humans in that year? What has taken place in history during the life of this tree – internationally, nationally and locally? I have created a timeline or chronicle of events for the past 400 years (see Table A.2). You can add to it by referring to local events or famous people and events that may be of interest to the group. The Internet is an obvious source for this kind of information.

Table A.2 Important dates in history

Years ago	Date Event
400	1570 Francis Drake sets sail and discovers West Indies for Europeans 1588 Defeat of Spanish Armada 1600 Great Britain population four million 1605 Guy Fawkes Gunpowder Plot fails to blow up Parliament 1607 First English colony in Virginia 1616 Shakespeare dies 1651 English civil war ends 1666 Great Fire of London 1697 St Paul's Cathedral London completed by Wren

Years ago	Date Event
300 250	1701 First daily papers in England 1704 Isaac Newton's *Optics* published 1705 Halley describes a comet 1707 United Kingdom formed by union between English and Scottish parliaments 1719 *Robinson Crusoe* (Daniel Defoe) first English novel published 1721 J.S. Bach Brandenberg Concertos composed 1746 Battle of Culloden, Bonnie Prince Charlie defeated 1764 Watt's steam engine invented, beginnings of the Industrial Revolution 1770 Cook discovers Botany Bay, Australia for Europeans 1777 US constitution written, previous year the US declared independence 1786 Mozart composes *The Marriage of Figaro* opera 1792 French Revolution
200	1805 Battle of Trafalgar, J.M.W. Turner's *Shipwreck* painted 1807 Slavery abolished in Britain 1808 First census of Great Britain: population eight million (= London today) 1813 Jane Austin writes *Pride & Prejudice* 1815 Battle of Waterloo, Napoleon imprisoned 1825 Beethoven's 9th symphony performed; first public railway 1840 Maoris surrender to British forces 1841 Great Britain population 18 million 1838 Queen Victoria begins reign 1840 First postage stamp
150	1845 Texas founded 1859 First oil well; Charles Darwin wrote *The Origin of Species* 1860 First public flush toilet 1861 Charles Dickens *Great Expectations*, L. Pasteur theory of germs, William Morris wallpapers 1863 Football Association founded 1876 Telephone invented by Alexander Bell 1878 Microphone invented, electric lights on in London 1882 Women get the right to own their own property 1885 Daimler and Benz build first motorbike and car respectively 1887 First gramophone player 1889 Eastman makes celluloid roll film; Eiffel Tower erected 1890 First tube in London 1899 Magnetic recording invented; aspirin first made

Years ago	Date Event
100	1900 Freud *Interpretation of Dreams* published; Brownie camera; Labour Party founded
	1901 Queen Victoria dies; instant coffee invented
	1902 Boer war ends in South Africa
	1906 Great Britain population 40 million
	1908 Ford Model T: first car assembly line; electric iron and paper cup invented; first commercial oil field in Middle East
	1914 First World War
	1917 Russian Revolution
	1919 First Atlantic flight; first helicopter
	1922 First BBC Radio broadcast
	1930 Ancient woodland double what it was in 2010
	1939-46 Second World War
50	1960 Beatles; anyone aged 50 in 2010 born now; Great Britain population 52 million
	1961 First person in space: Yuri Gagarin
	1965 First home video recorder
	1971 Email and PC available
	2010 Great Britain population 62 million

(Taken mostly from Mellersh 1995. The 'years ago' in the table was calculated for the year 2010, chosen as a round number benchmark; over time this will need revising.)

A slice through a Scots Pine Pinus silvestris showing yearly growth rings
This photograph can be used to illustrate the growth process in trees.

The leaf in your hand

Aims: To give information about trees so that people appreciate how significant they are in their own lives. To enable people to appreciate the sensory qualities of a leaf and its structure.

Needs: A selection of trees in woodland or park; maybe an identification book on trees; a whistle; one leaf per person.

Instructions: Ask everyone to go off into the woods or parkland and pick a leaf from a tree that they like the look of. Ask them to take their time getting to know the tree they have selected. Maybe notice its size, height, girth, colour, age and distinguishing features. Why did they choose this tree? Do they know what type it is? It doesn't matter if they don't know its name though. When they think they have got to know the tree, or when you call them back with a whistle, have everyone show the group their tree leaf and maybe talk about its characteristics – shape, colour and so on. They can also say why they chose that particular tree. If there is time and it is a small group you could go round and visit each person's chosen tree.

It is useful for the next part if you have your own chosen leaf with you as a prop. When I am running a group I say different things at different times and most of it is in my head, but if you are unfamiliar with the information I suggest you make up a narrative beforehand and talk it through with groups until it is in your memory.

Have everyone hold their leaf and look at it as you talk them through this section. Say something like:

'Look at the leaf in your hand. It is a thin green sheet with a tough stalk which attached it to the tree. What shade of green is it? How does it compare with other tree leaves?

Look at the shape and structure of the leaf. Does the shape help you know what type of tree it has come from? How would you describe the shape? If a raindrop fell on your leaf it would make the leaf heavy and collectively a lot of wet leaves could be quite a weight for the tree to support. Trees have evolved to enable water to roll off easily, and get to the ground and its roots before the sun comes out. How do you think your leaf would do that? (Hint at waxy coating or pointed tips.)

Notice how the two sides are different. Feel the texture of your leaf. The top side may feel tougher and waxier which makes sense if the leaf has to protect itself from rain and things falling on it. The top side is designed to absorb red sunlight - the green is reflected back and gives it its colour.

Turn your leaf over and look at the underside. Notice any difference in colour and texture? The leaf has a network of veins which both support the structure like umbrella spokes, and are a means of transporting water and other substances to and fro. Interestingly, the overall structure of the veins on a leaf look like the branches on a tree. That is because they have a similar function of supportive structure and transportation. Something else to consider: the negative image of an X-ray of our lungs looks like a tree in winter. Both leaf and lung are designed to transport gases across their surfaces.

If you were to look at the underside under a microscope you would see tiny holes that look like green pairs of lips. These are called stomata and they control the in- and outflow of gases. Stomata allow carbon dioxide to flow in and oxygen to be given off at night.

Does your leaf have a smell? Would you want to eat it if you were an animal or is there something in its smell that puts you off? Crush part of it in your fingers and smell again. Some plants have bitter toxins which we recognise as making them inedible.'

After talking about the leaf itself I might continue with the life history of the tree up to the point of maturity (if you have an acorn in your pocket and you talk about an oak tree that adds interest). At other times I might begin with the structure of the leaf and talk about its ecology (see the following activities).

Tree biological processes

Aim: To increase awareness of how a tree lives.

Need: A tree, maybe a particularly old or impressive tree.

Instructions: Share the following information with the group:

- Trees need water, light, warmth and soil with nutrients.

- *Transpiration* of water – the drawing up and evaporation of water through a plant. A mature oak can draw up 70 litres per hour in summer or 151,000 litres in a year (about a third of that for a mature birch).

- The water in a live tree weighs more than the timber (80-90% by weight).

- *AirCon* – a mature oak can absorb ten times the heat of a 1kw bar fire. Forests moderate extreme temperatures. They use the absorbed heat to power water movement. Woodland is cooler in summer because of this and the shade trees give.

- *Photosynthesis* – the magic of mixing of water and CO_2, using sunlight to create sugar. $6 H_2O + 6 CO_2$ = sugar $C_6 H_{12} O_6$ and surplus $6 O_2$. A mature oak can produce 230kg of wood every year out of mostly sunlight, water and fresh air!

- *Minerals* are taken from the soil to build more complex substances, often with the help of fungi.

- Trees lay down *wood* for strength and protection. Wood is essentially made of chains of sugars to make up *cellulose and lignin*, the tough parts of wood.

- Trees absorb the CO_2 we and other animals breathe out. In turn trees liberate oxygen from the process of photosynthesis every night. One oak provides enough oxygen for two people. There is a *symmetry of gas exchange between our breathing and trees*. Both use a metal as part of the key substance that captures the vital gas. We use iron, colouring our blood red; trees employ manganese in chlorophyll which gives leaves their green colour.

- *Cleans air* – a beech wood of one hectare (100mx100m) attracts five tonnes of dust per annum.

- *Stops floods with roots* – 85 per cent of rainwater is held by the soil in a forest. One hundred per cent of rainwater is lost down the drains in cities. Trees are often planted for flood alleviation. One oak can have five miles of roots in total.

- Trees are part of a wider ecosystem of energy flow. Our two species of oak, when mature, *can support 423 species of insect*. When you consider this information you can see the necessity of having all the life forms present before it is possible for us to hear a dawn chorus in May. In an oak-dominant forest the rich supply of moth caterpillars provides abundant food for the songbirds to live and breed. Birdsong is the sound of the forest singing.

- *The biggest and oldest life forms are trees.* Bigger than a blue whale is 'General Sherman', a giant sequoia (*Sequoiadendron giganteum*) living healthily in California. It holds the record for the oldest tree with the biggest volume at 83.8 metres high and 1487 cubic metres. It is estimated to be 2200 to 2700 years old – but other trees are even older and wider. In human history 2500 years ago we were building the pyramids of Giza, the ancient Greeks were developing their civilisation, and in Britain we were living in the early Bronze Age.

Tree leaf designs

Tree leaves are ready-made material for learning about trees and creative activities.

Aims: To explore the sensory qualities of leaves and get to know our common species.

Needs: A wood or park with a variety of native trees. A set of paper bags to collect leaves in, one for each person (saved from the vegetable section of the supermarket). A tree guide (Usborne Spotters Guides are pocket sized and don't have every tree in Europe to confuse beginners). The Woodland Trust do a good leaf handout which can be downloaded or saved on a smartphone. You will find lots of other activities to do with trees on their website.[1]

---

1   See www.naturedetectives.org.uk/download/hunt_leaves

Instructions: This activity can be carried out any time of year but is maybe most suitable when the leaves are dropping in late autumn and people are aware of the fall.

At the beginning of the walk you can give out paper bags and suggest that everyone might like to see how many different tree leaf shapes and types they can find on the walk. You can begin the activity by picking up a leaf you know the name of or can look up in the book with the group. Pass it round and point out the different qualities of the leaf in terms of visual features: shape, size, edging, colour, texture, smell. Is the possible parent tree nearby?

At the end of the walk the group can gather round and discuss their finds. What do they like about the leaves they have, the texture, colour and shape? On the last point it might be interesting to ask why different leaves have different shapes. What are the advantages of certain forms? For example, pine needles have a small surface area and are tough which means they will survive better in very cold and very hot climates. The pointy bits on a leaf speed the water dripping off the leaf surface.

Table A.4 Leaf shape

Shape	Leaf
Classic leaf shape/oval	beech, hornbeam, blackthorn, sallow, alder, elm
Round	hazel
Ace of spades	lime, birch
Lobed	oak, hawthorn
Long and thin	willow
Palmate	field maple, sycamore, horse chestnut,* ivy
Pinnate	ash,* rowan,* elder*
Needle	Scots pine, larch, yew
Scale like	cypress
Spiky	holly

*Compound leaves – made of groups, not single leaves on a stalk.

Laminated leaves

I went on a walk with an occupational therapist colleague, Nicky Tann, and a small group of people experiencing memory loss. We decided beforehand that we could manage focusing on three species of trees each week. As we walked along we came across an oak in the park and asked if anyone recognised the tree and some did. After passing round a leaf from the tree and pointing out the sensory features mentioned earlier we moved on and whenever we came across another oak we made reference to the original leaf find and made comparisons. At the end of the walk we reviewed the session and in particular the leaves we had collected.

The following week we all met up again and decided to begin by revising the previous week's finds. What I wasn't prepared for was the brilliant idea that Nicky had of laminating the leaves. She encapsulated each leaf with a name tag written on paper between two sheets of heat-welded plastic (she had a machine for laminating worksheets in her office). The laminated leaves meant that we could preserve the leaves' original shapes and colours without damaging them and pass them round the group. Each week we added one more leaf to the collection.

See: *Tree leaf rubbing, Colour mosaic with leaves*

Tree leaf rubbing

Aim: To work creatively with tree leaf shapes.

Needs: A box of wax crayons, sheets of plain A4 paper and clipboards. A selection of tree leaves found in a wood or park.

Instructions: Have everyone make a collection of different tree leaf shapes and towards the end of the walk find somewhere to sit down. After talking about different leaf shapes and other characteristics you can demonstrate how to do a leaf rubbing. Take a leaf and turn it over so the veins are facing upwards and place it on the clipboard. Cover it with a sheet of plain paper. Position the leaf under the paper where you want it to show. Press down firmly with fingers either side of the leaf and rub lightly with a crayon over the leaf area, being careful not to move the leaf underneath. If it works well you will have the shape of the leaf and its veins appear as a wax image. The process can be repeated many times with different leaves and colours.

See: *Colour mosaic with leaves, Tree leaf designs*

Tree life history

Aim: To remind people of the life story of a tree.

Need: Woodland or a place where there are trees of different ages.

Instructions: Share the following information with the group:

- A tree starts as a *seed*, which is packed with nutrients and all the genetic material needed to grow a tree. The seed needs the right conditions to get started and continue to grow. Principally these are fertile soil, water and sunlight.

- *The seedling grows* into a tree, putting down one ring each year. It could take many human lifetimes to mature, centuries even. A tree cannot move and must adapt to where it grows. Some oaks can reach 800 years, yews more than 1000 years.

- *A bud* is developed in winter which then opens up in spring in response to sunlight. A mature *oak has 700,000 leaves*, equivalent to the area of two tennis courts. These act like solar panels to energise photosynthesis and to act as cooling fins to facilitate evaporation.

- A leaf could be *eaten by a caterpillar* and then if this is found by a parent bird and fed to one of its babies the goodness of the leaf could become part of a baby bird, which in turn could be caught by a sparrowhawk. When the hawk dies its body returns to the earth where it decomposes back into soil. The soil in turn may give up its nutrients to a growing tree.

- *In the autumn*, if it is a broadleaved tree, the tree takes much of the goodness out of the leaf and then cuts off the life supplies to the leaf at its base in order to survive the winter. Cold nights and sunny days give the brightest colours.

Trees, their economic importance to us

Aim: To enable people to be aware of how our lives are so dependent on trees.

Need: A place with trees although it doesn't necessarily have to be a wood.

Instructions: If you are reading this indoors my guess is you are not more than an arm's length from something grown by a tree. Consider this possibility:

The book you are holding is made of trees.

The ink is made from fossil trees.

The chair you sit in, the bed you sleep in and the floor you stand on may be made from trees.

The cradle and the coffin are made from trees.

Money doesn't grow on trees, it's made from them.

Trees give us a significant supply of oxygen.

Trees take in carbon dioxide and help reduce climate change.

Trees provide shade in hot countries.

Trees give us wood, which is used to make beams and floors in houses, fuel, paper in books and magazines, spoons and furniture, for example.

Trees give us coffee, tea, wine, olive oil, margarine, chocolate, fruit, nuts, vanilla, cinnamon, quinine, turpentine, maple syrup, latex rubber, coal, amber and aspirin.

Share some of the above ideas with the group. Then say something along the lines of the following:

'Trees guided our evolution all the way. They influenced the way our bodies and minds function. Without trees we would not be human. We evolved in woodland edges with our limbs adapted in earlier times for climbing trees. Our grasping hands and forward-looking eyes with stereo vision both made sure we didn't fall out of the tree canopy. The trees created conditions for the later evolution of hand–eye coordination. A major reason why we are so intelligent and can make sophisticated tools is because of this combination of hands and eyes. To these qualities derived from an adaptation to trees we can add our colour sight. We are biased towards being attracted to reds and yellows which developed in our early primate search for ripe fruit.'

At the end of the *Being with trees* activities everyone has a leaf they have got to know quite well. Do they want to take it home or leave it here in the wood?

If people want to take the leaf home with them they could leave it somewhere on a windowsill and notice what happens to it each day, how it changes once it is detached from the tree. Or they could place it between two sheets of tissue paper and press it under a pile of heavy books for a few months, or dip it in melted candle wax which will preserve the shape and colours for a longer time.

However, some people may want to leave their leaf in the wood to be recycled by an important hidden group of life forms in the ecosystem, the decomposers – bacteria, fungi, worms and bugs. They perform the essential task of breaking down the leaf into simpler substances that can be taken up and re-used in building complex things again like trees and animals.

See: *Buried in autumn leaves; Leaning on a tree, a person; Interview with nature; Wind in the willows; Colour mosaic with leaves; Tree leaf designs; The age of a tree*

BEING WITH TREES

Birdsong

Background

Birdsong is one of the most powerful connections we have with nature, something which even non-naturalists say they get a lot of pleasure from listening to. Poets have been inspired by songsters including the nightingale, blackbird and skylark. Maybe less inspiring are the calls of birds like the crow and sparrow; they are considered less musical which raises the question: did music originate from listening and imitating the more tuneful songsters? Some think music developed out of using the earliest whistles as an attempt to imitate the tunes of birds and that rhythm was derived from dancing and the heartbeat. Whatever the origins of music the human ear finds much birdsong beautiful and inspiring to listen to.

Many Western classical composers have drawn on the notes and rhythms of songbirds. If we just look at some of Beethoven's music we can see the connections. I am not only referring to the obviously imitative 'Pastoral' Symphony 'Scene by a brook' (nightingale flute, cuckoo oboes, quail clarinet). You can hear the rhythms of a blackbird in the opening Rondo of his violin concerto - ta ta tatadi. There is a Cetti's warbler in his second symphony, among with many other examples. Some of it could be coincidence - the white-breasted wren in the USA sounds like the fifth symphony's themed rhythm - but some inspirations from birdsong were most definitely intentional. In the nineteenth century most composers would never be too far from the countryside and we know that Beethoven went for daily walks in the Vienna woods.

Why do birds sing? In summary, the sun increases in strength in spring leading to more warmth and light, which leads to green leaves budding out and to caterpillars hatching and eating the new leaves. In turn the abundant insect food makes it the best time for songsters to attract a mate and have babies.

Male birds use song to advertise themselves to females, who are attracted to males that can sing well and for long periods. Woodland birds tend to be territorial, and in dense foliage it is easier and safer to let others know you are around by singing rather than by having bright colours. As well as attracting a mate, a songster can let his male neighbours know his territory is occupied, and that they should keep a distance.

Aim: To increase awareness and enjoyment of birdsong.

Need: An area of scrub, parkland or woodland between late winter and summer where birds are most likely to be singing.

Instructions: New research suggests that birdsong may have a therapeutic effect on people; see pages 124-30. Encourage your group to stand in silence and listen to birdsongs, maybe after a mindfulness session. The group could discuss their responses to the birdsong and whether they think it has a therapeutic effect, which could just mean they get enjoyment out of it.

See: *Cat's ears, Dawn chorus walk, Sound map, Sounds as music*

Blind walk

Aim: To heighten the senses other than sight - particularly touch - and to encourage trust.

Needs: An open area with varied habitat of mixed trees, bushes and so on. The ground should not be too rough or uneven. Blindfolds, one for each pair. You can make them out of old material or use coloured scarves. Some people don't like wearing a blindfold, they can just keep their eyes closed.

Instructions: Suggest to the group:

'Choose someone you feel comfortable with and pair up. One person wears a blindfold, the other is their guide. You will swap over half way.

Take your partner on a guided walk around this area, taking them to interesting experiences of touch and texture. It is an opportunity to give pleasure and be playful. Take it very slowly and with care.

The sighted person needs to be the eyes of their partner and to make sure the ground is safe, and to warn them when a change is coming up such as a dip in the ground. Check out for overhanging branches and prickly plants.'

Debrief in the group once everyone is back. What was it like to be led by someone else? What did you discover about nature, about yourself? What was it like to lead someone else who was blindfolded?

See: *Camera*

Bring nature into your home

Aims: Many people are not able to leave their home easily and be in nature. This section is for them and their carers. Consider the options by asking two questions: how can I bring nature closer to where I live so that I can see it from indoors, and how can I bring nature into my home?

Needs: The resources you need are described in the text below.

Instructions: Read the advice given for each section below.

How can I bring nature closer to where I live?

What does the view from the window in the living room look like, or from the kitchen when you are doing the washing up, or anywhere indoors where you can sit comfortably? Imagine you are a bird visiting the outside of your home. Does it look enticing? Is there food, somewhere to hide?

I live in a flat and have a *bird feeder* filled with sunflower seeds just outside my office window. It is suspended from a piece of string from the soffit underneath the gutter above. You could use a bracket above the window if you live on the ground floor. As long as I don't make any swift movements the birds come and go. Wilkinson's sell cheap feeders and their sunflower seed is a good price as well. You can get transparent plastic feeders that stick by suction onto the outside of a glass window but I've never found they stay up for long.

A *bird table* can be made out of an old wooden drawer screwed to a pole. The sides of the drawer give the birds something to perch on and stop food getting blown off onto the ground where rats can feed on it. Make sure there is a hole drilled into the bottom of the bird table to allow water to drain out. Birds love a shallow bowl of fresh water they can drink from and have a bath in.

A *bird box* sited out of reach of cats and too much direct sunlight will give you hours of pleasure. A pair of birds will go through the stages of reproduction from courtship displays to nest building, feeding the young, and fledging. Put the box up in early winter as pairing takes place early in the year and the birds may use the box as a roost in cold weather.

Usborne Books publish a very reasonably priced bird guide to help you identify the different species.

Planting bushes that have berries in winter will attract a lot of birds such as blackbird, mistle thrush and song thrush as well as winter migrants such as fieldfare and redwing.

A good gardening book will give you ideas on how to plant a garden so that the trees and herbaceous plants look attractive all year round. Think about how your garden can become attractive to a range of animals such as butterflies and moths, bees and hoverflies, which will in turn be fed upon by insect-eating birds. (See Resources below for more information.)

How can I bring nature into my home?

Maybe it's not possible for you to get out easily, or you would just like to bring the natural world closer while at home. Here are some ideas for bringing nature indoors and to increase the sense of well-being. Experiment and see what works best for you.

One idea might be to put up *pictures* that are inspiring. Research has shown that people in hospital get better more quickly if they can see a tree outside their window or if they have a picture of nature on the wall.

You could go to a store like Ikea and buy one of their framed prints. If you cannot afford to do that find pictures in a magazine such as *BBC Wildlife*. Cut the pictures out and stick them up where you can see them regularly.

It is possible to download rights-free images from search engines and photography websites which are not covered by copyright. These pictures can be printed off and placed somewhere where they will be regularly seen.

You could use coloured pens/pencils/paint to create a picture of your own.

Window box

A window box securely tied outside a window and planted with flowers or salad makes an attractive sight. It provides a transitional point between the home and the garden.

Another option is to bring *stuff in from a walk* – interesting pine cones, pebbles, bits of wood, colourful leaves – to create a nature table. Set aside a small area on a windowsil, for example, and regularly change things you find on your walks that remind you of the positive experiences you had out in nature.

Press leaves or flowers between two sheets of tissue paper, and press these between two pieces of wood or under a heavy book/old catalogue/telephone directory. Leave for a month or so to dry out.

Pick a bunch of wild flowers and put them in a jam jar by the window. In late summer bring in dry grasses.

The Woodland Trust website has a sheet for identifying common tree leaf shapes; see below.

Ask someone for a plant cutting and plant it in a flowerpot filled with earth. Make sure it is well watered until it produces new shoots. Or buy a potted plant and watch it change over time.

How to make a bird feeder

You will need a small plastic drinks bottle and cap, a twig about 20cm/8″ long, ball of string, pointed scissors.

Make two small holes with the scissors opposite each other near the top of the bottle below the cap. Thread a length of string (50–60cm) through the holes and make a loop by tying the two ends. This is the string to hang the bottle up from a branch or hook.

Make another pair of small holes opposite each other near the bottom of the bottle and push the twig through it to make a perch on each side.

Make a square hole above each perch, about 4cm up, for the birds to access the seeds. The hole should be small (less than 1cm) and when you cut the bottle leave the bottom section of the square still attached and push it into the bottle; this flap will help stop seeds running out.

Fill the feeder with sunflower seed kernels and hang up. Top up regularly and keep it clean.

Resources

Royal Horticultural Society: Ideas for attracting wildlife into your garden *www.rhs.ork.uk*

BBC Earth: A rich source of information and ideas of things to do in nature. Regularly updated to reflect the seasons in Britain *www.bbc.com/earth/uk*

RSPB: Advice for a wildlife-friendly garden *www.rspb.org.uk*

Woodland Trust: The UK's leading woodland conservation charity. They protect woods, plant trees and inspire people to go out and enjoy local nature *www.woodlandtrust.org.uk*

Buried in autumn leaves

Aim: To have some fun, to experience being cared for by another and to relax.

Need: A woodland with lots of dry leaves in autumn. Beech wood is good.

Instructions: You can run these as separate exercises or have the first one as a warm up for the second. I can't remember where I learnt this activity. It's good fun for all ages.

Sensing leaves

The group gathers up a big pile of leaves to form a rectangular shape on the woodland floor. Everyone is invited to take off their shoes and socks and feel the leaves with their bare feet. After a while ask the group to disperse the leaves with their feet.

Bury a person in the woods

Ask everyone to choose a partner they feel comfortable with. Each pair goes off into the woodland and takes it in turns to bury the other person in leaves! You can offer a polythene bin liner to lie on if someone is not sure. The person being buried is asked if they want their face and eyes covered or left open. After the person is buried the burier sits nearby while the buried enjoys the experience. Don't rush this bit. There is no talking throughout and the pair swap over when the leader blows a whistle.

Camera

This is inspired by a workshop I went on run by Joseph Cornell and described in Cornell (2015). It is one of his best inventions. Joseph Cornell is an inspiration to anyone working with people in nature, particularly children. I am in sympathy with his passionate approach to connecting to the natural world and have borrowed, adapted and invented lots of activities as a result of his pioneering work.

Aim: In this activity there are elements of trust, giving positive experiences to another, and having senses other than sight heightened. This is a very popular activity and one which is a pleasure to do whether you are the giver or receiver of the experience.

Needs: An area which is easy to explore underfoot, that is to say not bumpy and uneven. A location that is varied to look at.

Instructions: I demonstrate the activity first by using one of the participants as the 'camera'. You can say something like this to the group:

'I will explain what is involved and then you can choose someone you feel comfortable to work with on this activity.

One person is a "photographer" and the other is a "camera". You both get to do each role when you swap over. The camera shuts their eyes and links arms with the photographer who takes the lead in slowly exploring the surroundings and finding interesting things to "photograph".

When the photographer finds something interesting, and it could be a landscape or close-up shot, they position their partner correctly, even tilting their head if it helps. They then lay their free hand on the "camera's" shoulder. This is the signal to the camera to open their eyes and look. The camera must immediately shut their eyes when the photographer takes their hand of their shoulder.

The photographer can vary the exposure from a long gaze to a very brief two-second shot. The first time the photographer gives only a short exposure it usually makes the camera look seriously at the next shot in case they lose it!

An important warning to the photographer: you are the eyes of your blind partner so walk slowly, looking out for overhead obstacles as well as uneven ground or fallen branches. Tell your partner about any obstacles coming up.

Swap over when you are ready.'

You can discuss people's experiences afterwards. Issues of trust and seeing things differently often come up.

Statements for the camera

In his book *Sharing Nature with Children* (1998) Cornell suggests a variation on the *Camera* activity. While the camera has their eyes open the photographer reads them a quote relating to nature. You can make a selection of about ten quotes from poems to inspiring text that mean something to you. The quotes from chapter headings in this book could be a start. Print enough copies for everyone.

See: *Blind walk*

Cat's ears

This is an activity I remember inventing after reading a book by Bernie Krauss, *The Great Animal Orchestra* (2012). Krauss is a wildlife sound recordist and was watching a clouded leopard in Sumatra. The leopard was using its mobile ears to scan the environment. Krauss was intrigued to experience something of the hearing of the leopard. He went back to camp and made a pair of big cat's ears out of paper, put a small microphone in each paper pinna (the outer part of the ear) and clipped these to his glasses. He then listened through his headphones and was amazed at how much more he could hear with big paper ears.

Aims: To increase hearing ability and to imagine what it is like to be an animal with more acute hearing.

Need: Nothing, unless you want to use paper (see below).

Instructions: There is a low-tech version of the cat's ears Krauss made, which I use when I'm listening acutely to a quiet sound, for example a woodland bird some way off or an animal rustling dried leaves. It is my hands! If you cup each hand behind an ear you can change the shape of your hand and direct your ears towards faint sounds. Bending the pinna seems to be the crucial thing to do. It really does make a difference. If you are out with a group you can share this technique with everyone. It is particularly useful if the bird is hard to locate or is some way off.

This skill, and a few others in this book, are related to the skills our hunter-gatherer ancestors would have been familiar with.

Changes in nature

Introduction to *Changes in nature* activities

Changes are happening all the time in nature. The weather, diurnal changes or the passing of seasons are examples. Much of the delight from being in nature comes from observing these changes. Here are three activities which encourage an increased awareness of change.

Change is constant

Aim: To become more aware of changes in nature.

Need: Nothing.

Instructions: For people who feel stuck in their lives it can be a personal challenge to realise they live in a world of constant change. I use any opportunity I can to remind people that in nature changes are occurring all the time. For a group that meets the same time every week I might point out the change in quality of light from the previous week or mention the height of the sun above trees at the start and end of the walk. Other things I do to bring natural changes to people's attention is to get them to remember what it was like in the same place a few months ago: 'Remember the bare trees three weeks ago? Now we can't see through the branches for leaves.' Or I point out green shoots in February and say, 'Look, see how the green is ready to come up again. We will come by here in a month and I'm going to remind you to look again to see what has changed.'

Fresh leaves begin in late March where I live and keep coming at least until the end of May. April is the time the world goes green in Britain. So watch buds of different species change and become leaves. Where have all the buds gone? They have not gone anywhere, they have changed just like everything else. Cow parsley can froth up along lanes and hedgerows in spring and then fade even more quickly. Did you notice? The Japanese, whose rich culture acknowledges change in nature more than we do, celebrate the ephemeral nature of cherry blossom every year.

The possibilities of being aware of changes in Nature are endless.

Stand for five minutes in woodland with eyes closed and listen to the sounds of the world moving on.

- Place your gaze on a shadow and be aware of its passage across the ground as you sit still.

- Notice the equinoxes and midwinter/summer turning points.

- Notice the moon phases shifting from dark to D shape to O to C shape (DOC).

- Notice temperature changes moment by moment as the sun slips in and out behind clouds, or through the seasons.

All our lives are created and moulded by the changes in nature, cause enough for celebration.

See: *Bring nature into your home, Colour chart match, Dawn chorus walk, Death and life in winter, Wild food for ecotherapy*

Phenology mandala

Aim: To increase awareness of seasonal changes in nature by observing when events first occur.

Needs: A3 size piece of paper, pencils, pens.

Instructions: Phenology is Nature's calendar, the times when recurring events in nature take place, often in relation to climate. Examples are the earliest snowdrops or sound of the cuckoo in spring. The first phenologist in this country was Robert Marsham who wrote down his 'Indications of Spring' from 1736 until his death in 1798. In recent years scientists have analysed records to demonstrate the effects of climate change. Flowers open and birds nest 11 days earlier than they did 30 years ago.

If you have a regular group you can make your own phenology chart as a reminder of natural changes throughout the year. You can do this by drawing a big circle on an A3 piece of paper and then draw radiating lines to make 12 monthly divisions. At the end of each session the group can fill in things they noticed that were different from the previous month, and special observations such as the 'day we saw two peregrine falcons'. You can also do this as a recording activity on a smartphone.

The timing of the arrival of spring depends on a lot of factors: how far north you are, altitude, soil types, weather patterns and orientation, but on average the opening dates of flowers like violets and primroses move at about 3km a day northwards.

Check out Nature's Calendar[2] for more information and how local records can be used by scientists.

Solar arc

Aim: Working with change. To become aware of the movement of the sun and changing light.

Need: A place with a good view of the horizon both east and west where the sun rises and sets. Study a map beforehand to find a hill that might be suitable. You can use a compass and protractor if you want to be more precise in where the sun will travel. There are apps which show you the direction of sunrise and sunset from any given place. The more basic ones, which will suit your needs in this activity, are free.

Instructions: Find a place in winter where it is possible to see the sunrise and sunset on the same day, maybe looking over the sea or distant land from a hill top. On 21 December, the shortest day of the year, the sun rises at 08.03 and sets at 15.51 where I live east of London. During the day's activities, whenever it occurs to you, look around and observe the quality of light through the day until sunset.

If you have a protractor, compass and the website Build It Solar[3] you can work out where the sun will travel during any day. For example, for a town near me the results are:

On 21 December, the sun will rise 58 degrees east of due south and set 58 degrees west of due south.

On 21 March/21 September, the sun will rise 91 degrees east of due south and set 91 degrees west of due south.

On 21 June, the sun will rise 126 degrees east of due south and set 126 degrees west of due south.

The trick is to check the weather forecast and find a day when the horizon is clear at sunrise and sunset on the same day.

2   See www.naturescalendar.org.uk
3   See www.builditsolar.com

Something to celebrate each month

Aim: To acknowledge and celebrate the monthly changes in nature.

Need: A table showing the 12 months of the year and spaces next to them to fill in events.

Instructions: As the seasons change there are natural events that remind us of the changes taking place in nature. The examples given here were created from observations made in East London where I work. The events and timings will not be the same if you live in a different latitude or climate zone. I encourage you to discuss with your group what natural events are worthy of celebration in your area. Maybe you can find ways to creatively express these monthly changes.

Table A.3 Something to celebrate each month

Month	Look for
January	Snow, ice and frost. Footprints in snow. Put up bird boxes. View the stars. See dawn and dusk. Build fires. Look for signs of death and new life. Snowdrops, hazel catkins.
February	Signs of spring coming – pussy willow, bluebell shoots, birdsong and courtship, big starling roosts, frogs and toads gathering, yew smoke (from blown pollen). Plant a tree (Nov–March). Feed the ducks.
March	Woodland blossoms begin – blackthorn, wood anemone, celandine. Hibernating butterflies wake up – brimstone and peacock, tortoiseshell. Birds on the move – leaving for Scandinavia or arriving from Africa. Snakes basking after hibernation, shedding their skin. Buds swelling, some new leaves.
April	Warblers arrive, cuckoo calls, nesting birds, bluebell woods, violets, orange tip butterflies. We can nibble fresh shoots.
May	Flowers abundant, white may blossom and cow parsley everywhere. Trees fresh and filling the view in woods. Dawn chorus, and birdsong at dusk. First dragonflies.
June	More flowers – dog rose, honeysuckle. Blue and brown butterflies, skylarks. See the tide go out and in on one day.
July	More flowers, e.g. knapweed. Glow worms, burnet moths, dragonflies, swifts leave at end of the month.
August	Willowherb in flower, blackberries. Grasshoppers and bush crickets.
September	Berries abound – hawthorn, conkers. Swallows leave.
October	Fungi, deer rut, spider webs. Redwing and fieldfare arrive. Woodland colours.

Month	Look for
November	Sloes, hips and haws. Geese, swans and ducks arrive from the Arctic and the north of Europe. Leaf fall.
December	Owls at dusk. Look for winter visitors: fieldfares and redwings, geese and ducks on lakes, wader flocks on marshes and coast. See sunrise and sunset on the same day.

CHANGES IN NATURE

Colour chart match

This idea originally came from me mulling over the autumn colours and wondering if we could make a colour chart like the ones you get in a paint shop but using real leaves. My idea was that we could cut squares of coloured leaves and stick them on paper and then give each colour swatch an imaginary name. I then changed the activity slightly to make it easier to do and came up with this one.

Aim: Sensory awareness. To increase awareness of different colours and tones in nature. A small group activity.

Needs: You will need roughly one set of all the items below for each small group or team of three or four individuals:

- Two sheets of A4 stiff grey card. The stiff back of stationery pads are useful for this and other activities requiring a firm surface to write on outdoors. A bulldog clip will secure paper to the card.

- A set of paint chart/swatches collected from a DIY store such as B&Q, Wickes or Homebase. Make sure you have the same number of sets of the same colours as you will have teams. These will be used to make your own colour swatch cards.

- A pair of A4 plain transparent wallets with one side open. These are to keep the A4 cards protected.

- An A4 record sheet (see below).

- A glue stick.

- A pen or pencil.

Instructions for preparations beforehand: You need to make one A4 colour swatch card per team. Cut up the sets of paint chart swatches you have collected from the DIY shop into individual rectangles. Stick a selection in rows onto an A4 card. Make sure you have the same selection of colours for each A4 card.

I suggest you begin with a selection of the basic colours of the rainbow. Then add a couple of unnatural colours such as day-glow pink or high-visibility green. They may be impossible to find but it will provoke discussion. Then have a couple of rows consisting of two colours in subtly different tones, for example greens from dark emerald to light pastel green, or pink to scarlet, crimson and maroon.

Give a number to each colour. Cover each colour swatch card with an A4 transparent plastic wallet to keep it dry and unmarked.

For the A4 collecting card place the second sheet of A4 card into a plastic cover to protect and flatten any collected items. Again make sure the number of plastic-covered cards matches the number of teams.

The A4 record sheets should have a list of numbers down the left-hand side, matching the number of swatch colours on the colour swatch card. Leave plenty of space between the numbers to allow for writing and to stick things on it. The record sheets can be printed out or written with a pencil on plain sheets on the day. They can be clipped to one of the plastic-covered cards.

Instructions on the day: Ask people to get into teams. There needs to be the same number of teams as you have colour swatch sets.

Give out one set of colour swatch cards, glue, pens and so on to each team.

Explain that the aim of the activity is to go in search of colours in nature which match *as closely as possible* the colour swatches.

When someone finds a match everyone in the group has to agree to the match. They can either glue the object to the record sheet or write its name.

Challenge the groups before they leave to be as precise as possible by pointing out at the start how some colours look very similar. Matching any old green leaf with a green swatch is not good enough. Can they find the precise shade of green in nature that is on the card? That is why you will have made some colour tones very different and some very similar as part of the challenge.

Ask everyone to come back to you when they have completed the activity. They can take their time and enjoy the process; you will call them after a while if everyone is not back.

Meet up as a big group and compare results. What did people discover? Did people have disagreements? How easy or difficult was it to be precise? Do people have a favourite colour? Do certain colours remind you of anything?

One response is to note how difficult it is to exactly match colours in nature – there are more colours than there are colour swatches. Fashion designers, photographers and film makers use Pantone charts to match colours.[4] Someone who is used to looking closely at colours, a photographer, artist or dressmaker for example, will most likely have a greater sensitivity to tones.

Colour blindness is not uncommon and that can provide an interesting discussion on how we see the world differently.

See: *Colour mosaic with leaves, Texture swatch match*

---

4   See www.e-paint.co.uk/pantone_colour_chart.asp

Colour mosaic with leaves

A walk through woodland in late autumn to admire the yellows, oranges and reds of the trees around us is an opportunity to use an activity that encourages us to really look: to look at the subtleties of tone and take in the changes happening around us.

Andy Goldsworthy has produced some beautiful works of art made from aligning shades of coloured leaves on the ground. I find his books a continual source of inspiration for activities in nature.

Aim: To increases awareness of the autumn colours.

Need: An area with broadleaved trees in mid-October to early November (also May to August – see below).

Instructions: Explain to the group that we are going to create something using the natural colours of the leaves we find around us in the wood or park.

People can do this individually, in pairs or a group, stopping to admire the trees and discussing the different tones or shades of one colour as you all walk along. How many reds are there? Can you find a pure black or white? Check, have you got every colour in the rainbow?

When everyone has a good collection of leaves find a flat open area the group can work on. The first time I did this we used a solid wooden bench top but you could use an area of river sand or bare earth. Mud on a path also makes a good base. This is your canvas on which you can work creatively with the colours you have collected. The possibilities are endless but to start with you could make a colour chart: a disc of colours with the lightest tones in the centre getting darker nearer the rim, the colours changing subtly around the circumference. You could also make patterns, snake designs, mandalas. Have a look at what Goldsworthy has done. After taking a photo you can leave the 'artwork' for others to admire.

A line of coloured leaves, graded from black through
yellows to reds and purples, on a bench

Summer mosaic

In the Peak District, Derbyshire between May and August, most often around Whitsun, over sixty communities decorate their local wells using natural materials. A big framed wooden board is constructed around the wellhead onto which is smeared a thick layer of clay. Coloured materials (petals, berries, leaves, etc.) are pressed onto the clay to create a mosaic, which at a distance looks like a painting.[5]

You could try making a summer mosaic using flowers, leaves and berries around a puddle of mud. Obviously it makes sense only to use plants which are very common in your area; a mosaic of orchids, however beautiful, could not compete with the intact wild flowers themselves, and it would be illegal! White may blossom from the hawthorn bush is a good contrasting medium to use on the mud around a pond.

See: *Colour chart match, Tree leaf designs*

Creating a memory of place

Adapted with thanks from the work of Sophie Jeffery.

The use of visualisation is commonplace on relaxation recordings. The intention is to place the listener in a relaxed state by evoking an environment which is likely to be associated with calmness. Many of the recordings take people via their imagination into nature. There is a good deal of research evidence supporting this process as an effective means of relaxation.

In this exercise we ask people to choose their own special place in nature which feels relaxing and to create a memory of it for future access. The instructions encourage people to really pay attention to their chosen environment and use all their senses to create a positive memory.

Aim: As an aid to relaxation and to create a positive memory from nature which can be accessed elsewhere at times of stress.

Needs: An area of mixed habitats, preferably with some woodland, open grassland, and water such as a stream or pond, a set of instruction sheets, one per person, a whistle.

Instructions: The process begins by taking the group to an attractive peaceful place in nature with a choice of habitats such as woodland, meadow, stream or open water. The group is then taken through physical and mental relaxation activities before explaining the instructions and giving out the sheets of paper.
You can say something like:

'In a minute I am going to ask you to head off and find a place you feel drawn to being in, a place where you feel comfortable and maybe relaxed. In this immediate area we've got a range of habitats to choose from: the river, the

---

5   See www.peakdistrictinformation.com/features/welldress.php

grassland, the wood and so on. In your chosen place I want you to create a good memory of it so that at other times you can recall the memory and the positive feelings that come with it. It is a bit like the way positive feelings can come back when you look at a photograph of yourself on an enjoyable holiday. You could use this experience when you're trying to relax. You will be able to close your eyes and think of that place and how much you enjoyed yourself or felt safe there.

The process is very easy to do. I am going to give out instruction sheets to help you. First of all I want you to go for a walk around here and find a place you feel comfortable and maybe relaxed in. Then spend about 20 minutes creating your memory. I will blow a whistle to call you back here.

One good way to create a memory for yourself is to focus on all the different senses. This is so you can later recall what you saw, heard, smelled, tasted and touched, as well as the feelings that accompany the experience.

I've got a sheet here which will prompt you to focus on all those things. You can write or draw on the sheet if you like to help remind you later. Or you can just create a memory in your head.

Take your time and be creative, maybe begin by standing or sitting and doing some of the relaxation breathing we have just done. If you don't fancy doing this, perhaps just find a nice place to sit and relax. When you've finished, head back to this area. I will blow the whistle when time's up.'

Creating a memory of a place

Take your time doing this activity and go with how you feel about a place. Explore until you find somewhere you feel drawn to being in, at ease and safe.

You're going to create a memory for yourself. You can use this memory in the future if you are trying to relax. It needs to be a rich memory so that you could close your eyes and imagine yourself back here.

One of the best ways to create a memory for yourself is to focus on all the different senses. This is so you can recall what you could see, hear, smell, taste and touch, as well as your feelings.

Later you can use this sheet to prompt yourself to recall all the sensory experiences. You can write or draw on the sheet to remind yourself of all these things later. Or you can just create a memory in your head.

Start by spending a few minutes relaxing in this place. Focus on your breathing and let any thoughts drift away.

What can you see?
Take in the whole picture – what view do you have? What things make up the view? What can you see close up? What shapes and colours can you see? What are the plants and animals that live here? What can you see that you like?

What can you hear?
Close your eyes and explore the sounds around you. Which direction does a sound come from and how far or near is it, do you think? Do you know what makes each sound? Which sounds do you like?

What can you touch?
What can your hands touch? Spend time exploring the different textures and shapes - rough or smooth, soft or firm, wet or dry.

What does your body feel like?
Feel your feet or bottom on the ground. Can you become aware of your whole body? Can you feel the air on your body?

What can you smell?
Reach around yourself and explore the different smells in your place. Try smelling the air, plants and trees, the ground, yourself.

What can you taste?
This is a tricky one! Be adventurous within limits!

How does it feel to be here?
What emotions do you have? What thoughts come up while you're here? Is there anything you want to try to remember? Any words of wisdom for yourself?

Join the group after about 20 minutes or when I call you with the whistle.

Later - when you want to evoke the memory

Let's imagine you are somewhere else, at home maybe, and you want to go back into your mind to your special place in nature. Make sure you are on your own and won't be interrupted. Sit down and take yourself through a physical relaxation exercise such as the tighten/relax muscles routine. Then see how well you can evoke your memory of the special place in nature. Go through all the senses: what does it look like, how does it sound, feel, smell, taste, how does your body feel, and what emotions are associated with the place?

CREATING A MEMORY OF A PLACE

Creative activities

Introduction to *Creative activities*

I find that creative activities such as drawing, poetry and sculpture are particularly appropriate towards the end of a session. It allows for an opportunity to reflect on the day's experiences and to integrate any thoughts and feelings.

The activities described here are only a small sample of the possibilities available to you when taking a group out in nature. Many of the activities below use natural materials such as leaves and stones. For some people this is a novel revelation in creative expression but for others it can seem strange and they may need time to adjust to it.

In the Mindfulness in Nature model, Chapter 3 (page 70), there is further discussion on creative expression in ecotherapy.

Decorated path

Aim: To create decorations from natural materials.

Needs: Natural materials, string and scissors.

Instructions: This is a variation on the *Seasonal circle* activity. Using natural found objects such as flowers, leaves, berries or twigs a group can decorate a path with individual or small group creations. Mud on the path is good for pressing leaves and berries onto the ground. Branches at the sides of the path enable things to be tied above ground with string, grass or rush stems.

Frame a view

Inspired by someone on a workshop. The idea is to find an interesting view and share it with others. This activity is most easily accomplished in woodland where the frame can be suspended from a tree branch.

Aim: A fun way of viewing landscape.

Needs: String and scissors, fairly straight twigs and branches. A woodland area.

Instructions: Tell the group:

'I want you to find something of interest or a view in the landscape and then frame it. The frame can be made of twigs and branches tied with string at the corners and then suspended from a tree, tied to the top of a stake in the ground

or held up in the right position by the person who made it. Come back here when you have finished making your frame or when you hear my whistle blasts.'

Everyone goes off into the woods to look for an interesting view to frame. Call people back after 20 minutes. The group then walks around the wood looking through each person's frame and listening to any comments they may want to make.

See also: *Colour mosaic with leaves, Life circle*

Leaf blanket

Inspired by Andy Goldsworthy ('Sycamore Leaves' in *Parkland* 1988).

Aim: Creative use of natural materials.

Needs: Plenty of big flat colourful leaves, thorns broken off from a hawthorn bush and a horizontal branch on a big tree.

Instructions: The activity works best in autumn when there is a ready supply of colourful leaves. Large tough leaves work best, such as maple, plane or sycamore. The leaf blanket is made more easily laid out on the ground first, with leaf stalks pointing up from the top row of leaves. The leaves are joined together in rows using the thorns, as you would use a large pin to join two edges of material together. Leaf stalks can be used to join leaves up in a similar way. Once the blanket is complete it can be suspended from a horizontal branch of a tree. The autumn leaves look particularly colourful in sunlight, creating a stained glass window effect.

Natural cairn

Aim: A creative exploration of natural materials.

Needs: You will need a good supply of materials for making the cairns. What you use will depend on the environment you are in and what you can find. By the sea and rivers there is often a good supply of boulders, pebbles and driftwood. In woodlands you can find fallen branches and twigs.

Instructions: Artists like Andy Goldsworthy and Chris Drury use natural materials as the medium for their work. If you can borrow books from the library or check their images out online you will find many ideas for inspiration. I am going to focus here on one theme they work with, towers. Chris Drury has created towers made of boulders, slate, bones and wood, some with a fire inside. They remind me of the stone cairns you see on mountain peaks or way markers on the route up. Some are made with a wide base on which a narrowing tower is built; others are carefully constructed by balancing boulders vertically one on top of the other. We have had everyone make mini towers out of pebbles on the beach. We had a competition to see who can use the greatest number of stones and who has the highest or the most artistic cairn.

You can also use wood to make towers out of logs or short branches with either a square or triangular base.

Environmental artists for inspiration

See website and book references for:

Chris Drury

Andy Goldsworth

Nils Udo

Richard Shilling

Seasonal circle

Aim: To celebrate the changing seasons.

Need: A variety of habitats.

Instructions: At any time of the year there are certain natural indicators of the season and the changes that are taking place. There are different flowers in May as opposed to August, different leaf colours in late October and the darkness of February. A way of recognising and acknowledging these changes is to make a display of things that signify the appropriate season. We do it in midwinter for Christmas with a fir tree, and holly, ivy and mistletoe decorations. At the end of winter some people bring hyacinth or crocus bulbs indoors in expectation of spring.

The suggestion for this activity is that everyone is asked to go and search for things that remind them of the season we are in at the moment, and to bring them back together. A flat open area where the group can gather round is most useful but you may see other opportunities such as a tree stump on which to place decorations. I have often used a circular pattern, beginning in the centre and inviting people to add their own objects until a wide disc is filled. Some people may need encouragement to participate – the idea of using natural materials in an artistic way is strange to some.

Any materials can be used: twigs are good for defining space, flowers and berries are obviously colourful, fungi are also distinctive. Circles of leaves of the same colour and size look good.

After the seasonal circle has been created time can be spent discussing the display, how people feel about the changing seasons and anything else that arises.

Woodland mobile

Adapted from Danks and Shofield (2005).

Aim: A creative activity.

Needs: Cotton thread and scissors. Straight twigs and other natural materials.

Instructions: The activity can be done by individuals or pairs working together. Quite a bit of trial and error is required to get the cross bars/twigs to stay horizontal once things are tied onto them.

Either an existing horizontal twig of about 40cm can be used or a twig of a similar size can be suspended from a bigger branch above. From the first twig other twigs or items can be suspended using cotton threads. If the items are tied loosely to the upper twig they can be slid along it until a balance point is found. Almost anything can be suspended from the mobile's twigs as decoration, depending on where you are. In a woodland, feathers, bones and flowers look good; on the beach, seaweeds, driftwood and found rubbish can be used.

CREATIVE ACTIVITIES

Dawn chorus walk

Why a dawn chorus? In the early morning it is too dark to feed and thus birds have time to sing. It is also important to remind neighbours you are still around first thing because unoccupied territories get taken over quickly. The singing also stimulates the female to lay an egg in the morning.

One of the special things about living in the temperate zone of the Earth is the seasonal changes and in particular the sexual buzz of activity among birds in the spring. The ultimate experience is the collective outpourings of our woodland birds in a dawn chorus. Before the sun rises, male birds, in a roughly predictable sequence, declare their presence to their neighbours and seek to attract passing females - that is the practical reason for it happening but the experience is something else.

I really don't like getting up early in the morning but I make sure that at least once a year I set the alarm for 3.00 a.m. and stagger out in the dark to bathe in the sounds of a wood coming alive as the sun comes up and a new day begins.

An alternative to getting up very early is to do a dusk chorus. Birds sing before going to roost for similar reasons they do first thing in the morning, but the experience for us is different. The chorus is less intense and it fades out to darkness. The psychological effect of being in the dark before dawn and then hearing the chorus swell as the sun comes up is just incomparable. Nevertheless, for practical reasons it may be easier to organise a group event in the evening. The same practical tips apply - see below.

Aim: to get the most out of experiencing a dawn chorus.

Needs: A wooded area with birds. Things to bring:

- Food and drink - can be left in a car, but some should be taken in a rucksack on the walk.

- Warm clothes - thick coat and layers, gloves, hat and so on. Dress as if for a winter's day (seriously, in May before dawn it can be near zero degrees and people will be standing around a lot).

- Torch, for emergencies only. Human eyes are adapted for night vision after 20 minutes of darkness.

- Folding chairs or bedroll to sit on. A carrier bag is the minimum.

- Insect repellent.

- Mobile with number given to everyone who is coming.

- MP3 player with birdsong, if you want to identify songs later.

Place: The best places for a dawn chorus can be checked out by doing a dusk chorus a week before. Ideally you want a mature woodland with open spaces, clear safe paths, easy public access and minimal light pollution. A country park or nature reserve is a good starting place to check out. Your local county wildlife trust may be able to suggest the best place to go to and listen to nightingales or wood larks.

Time: Not a rainy day: bad for you and the birdsong. You need to arrive in the wood when very few birds have started singing and where you plan to stay at least one and a half hours before the official sunrise. You wouldn't arrive half way through a music concert would you? For calculating sunrise times see websites such as Earth System Research Laboratory.[6] This site easily and automatically gives you sunrise and sunset for any location in the world. Early May is good. National Dawn Chorus day is usually around the first Sunday in May. On 4 May in southern Britain sunrise is at 4.27 a.m. If you leave it much later in the month you will have to get up earlier and earlier and eventually some birds sing less

---

6   See www.esrl.noaa.gov/gmd/grad/solcalc

once they have a mate. Going a couple of weeks earlier means you may miss some late-arriving migrants.

Instructions: The whole experience of being outdoors for an extended period of time in the dark will most likely be a novel experience for a lot of your group and this means the session can be made a special event.

Having done your research on the best place to hear a dawn chorus you need to agree a place to meet that is easy to find. It may be better to meet in a safe public place and walk to the woods rather than meet in woodland edge in the dark. A short flyer with a map of how to get there and some advice on what to wear and bring is a good idea. Remind people that they need to be on time because once the group has left the rendezvous site you will be very difficult to find. People need to bring their own snacks and warm drinks; you could be outdoors for three to four hours. Agreeing to go for breakfast afterwards can be part of the experience.

Once people have arrived and you have checked everyone is suitably equipped you can give advice on how to get the best from the experience, which may include the following points:

- Stay together.

- Keep torches off, use only in emergency; after 10–20 minutes your eyes will adjust.

- Keep warm.

- Slow down considerably, move quietly and be unhurried.

- Avoid the temptation to chat. If you have to mention something whisper or point.

- Become more aware and use your non-visual senses, particularly hearing of course.

When I take a group out for a dawn chorus walk I encourage people to slow down, open up and enjoy the sensory experience as they would a music concert. I don't spend time naming each bird while the chorus is in full flow. But I might point out certain birds on the walk back, if there are questions. Do you need to know which instrument is playing in an orchestra to enjoy the music? No, but it adds interest if you do. I think the learning and the immersion in sensory experience should happen at two different times. If you have a regular group you can talk about different birdsongs during the daytime sessions. I copied birdsongs from a CD onto an iPod to help me learn, and you can also listen to birdsong on various websites such as the RSPB's. Birdsong is generally too high and fast for humans to imitate easily and so birdwatchers have come up with memorable phrases and hints to make it easier to distinguish different species in song. I have created some notes to help you learn birdsong in the outdoors when combined with sound recordings.

How do you know what bird is singing?

Here are some notes on the most common resident birds you are likely to hear singing in spring, followed by a few summer migrant visitors.

Thrushes

Blackbird: leisurely, cool and black suited. Varied phrases with a pause between. Flutey, deeper, mellow and relaxed. Phrases often begin with a pure whistle and end with a harsher rattle. High perch.

Song thrush: repeats 'words' three to five times in a loud, clear insistent way from a high perch. Some sounds are musical, others harsh; not as smooth as a blackbird.

Mistle thrush: repeats whole songs, not words. Musical like a blackbird but not as smooth, more hurried, has a wistful, clear, loud song with pauses. Song post is high up on a tree top, often late in the evening. One of its names is storm cock.

Robin: thin rippling short phrases, each one different as a jazz player, sweet. In autumn there is a different song that is plaintive and particularly melancholy to our ears.

Wren: a single song sung with tremendous energy and hurried speed with trills. No variation usually. A rattle in the middle and a more musical trill at the end. Usually sung low down in bushes; 103 notes in 8.25 seconds.

Dunnock: flat-sounding scratchy warble, short and fast but not as high pitched as a wren. Lacks the wild enthusiasm of a wren.

Collared dove: three notes with the rhythm of 'will *ow* tree'.

Wood pigeon: cooing, 'buffing the silver' rhythm.

Starling: whistles and clacking metallic sounds, can mimic human sounds like phone dialling tones.

Tits

Great tit: two notes, 'tee-cha', forceful, strident, less stressed, cheerful. Lots of variations even with one bird. Foot pump imitation.

Coal tit: two notes, 'weechoo', 'peechi', sweeter, softer, faster, higher pitch. Bike pump imitation, squeaky. Contact call – 'wee-tit'.

Blue tit: complex long notes in trills. A high-pitched song sometimes described as 'tsee-tsee-tsee- chuu-chuu-chuu'.

Goldcrest: song is thin, high-pitched, 'sisey, sisely, sisely', spluttered flourish. Associated with conifers. Call is high pitched, intense, short series see-see-ssee-see.

Finches

Chaffinch: a single song repeated between breaks and made up of an accelerating rattle of 'chip-chips' ending with a fast, more musical flourish. In a poem by William Allingham called 'The Lover and the Birds' he gives the song as: 'Sweet, sweet, sweet. Pretty lovely, come and meet me here', a reasonable imitation of the rhythms rather than actual sounds. Sung up in a tree.

Greenfinch: wheezy, trilling song, twittering with harsher 'zzzz' in the middle.

Goldfinch: can sound like distant tinkling bells. Trills and rippling notes, beautifully upbeat. Sung from a tree.

Migrant summer visitors

Cuckoo: nothing needs to be said! Can you see the bird though?

Willow warbler: a flowing, slippery descending warble, more insistent louder middle section, then fades towards the end. Repeated with pauses as it moves through the branches.

Chiffchaff: sounds a bit like its name, more like 'silp-salp'. Sung inside tree branches as it feeds.

Blackcap: a beautiful flowing warble that seems to take time to get going but becomes more flutey towards the end. Sung hidden in a bush.

On a dawn chorus walk you may also encounter bats and other mammals and moths, and get a chance to observe the stars and moon.

Further resources

You and your clients might like to experiment with using birdsong recordings indoors to see if they have a positive effect on mood and relaxation levels. They can be used as a quiet background to another activity. The best recordings to use are those which are general habitat sounds such as woodland or coast. These type of recordings also tend to be longer. One example is *Brecklands Dawn Chorus* by Andrew Flintham (2008) Overthrill Records.

See: *Birdsong*

Death and life in winter

Aim: To be aware of life and death as coexisting processes, and of life in winter.

Need: Nothing. Open woodland is good for this activity.

Instructions: Begin by asking the group to explore the wood and look for things which are dead. Tell them that if there are small objects they can bring them back with them. Big things can just be noted. Tell them also that you will remain where you are now and that when they have finished, after about 10 minutes of exploring, they are to return to you.

Discuss as a group what you have found. On one occasion we found leaves, feathers and wood, and we talked about non-organic things like Coke cans and bottles as well. From these observations it is possible to discuss how life and death are inseparably intertwined in nature. The following points might help your discussion:

- Fallen leaves are dead but the trees are not: an obvious point but it is significant if you are in a wood in winter thinking there is no life. The word 'dormant' is a better description of trees in winter. Trees shed leaves after removing useful nutrients, just as we shed skin and hair, as an adaptation to living. Deciduous trees no longer need broad leaves in winter when there is less light and their structure makes them vulnerable to frost.

- The fallen leaves are very soon alive again with bacteria and fungi and may have more cells in them than when they were on a tree.

- When a creature dies the bacteria which begin the process of decomposition are already on and in the body of the animal. The microbes have been breaking down and disposing of dead cells on the live animal, now they are continuing the process on a bigger scale. We have millions of bacteria doing the same on our own bodies.

- The soil is alive. There are more living cells in a spadeful of soil than there are human cells in your body. When we stand in a wood and look around we not only see the living trees but the soil we are standing on is also alive. In many ways the soil has more life than the trees above ground.

- Our bodies are kept alive by continually renewing cells. As some die others take their place. The process is known as *apoptosis*. It is a very sophisticated process of continual organised dying, as part of keeping the bigger body alive. It is quite unlike traumatic cell death as a result of injury. In brief, apoptosis (or programmed cell death), once triggered either internally or externally, results in the cell signalling its intention to die. Once the cell has started to break up specific cells come along and eat up the remains very quickly. Over 50 billion cells in your body died yesterday and the same will happen today. In this way virtually all your body cells are replaced after a number of years. There are some exceptions but even in these cells the molecules are exchanged over time.

- There is absolutely zero waste in nature. Everything that dies is food for another living thing. The elements that make up all living things, including yourself, have been circulating through ecosystems for millions of years.

- We can talk of Britain as a country made up of so many millions of people who are being born, living and dying so that after 120 years none of the original people are alive and yet the culture still exists. Something similar is going on in your own body as cells are born and die, and yet you continue to exist.

After this contemplation of life in death the group can go on another walk together. The task is to look for evidence of life in the wood. Explain that the wood may not seem as alive as it is in summer, but based on what we have just discussed and what we may find, the wood is very alive right now. Take your time and have everyone point out life around them. Examples can be the soil we have just spoken about, the trees, bramble and elder (often green in winter) birds and small creatures.

What happens to all living things eventually?
They die.

What happens to all dead things eventually?
They come alive again, taken up as part of the life process, food for new life.

Do you know where you live?

Adapted from Devall and Sessions (1985).

How well do you know the area where you live? Jennifer Owen didn't get beyond the garden gate in Leicester when she began in 1980 to study all the wildlife she could find in her garden (2673 species). She wrote a book about it, *Wildlife of a Garden: A Thirty-Year Study* (Owen 2010).

Aim: To reflect on how much we know of the locality we live in, particularly the natural world.

Need: A set of printed handouts of the questions below. Or you can read out the questions to the group and discuss.

Instructions: Discuss the questions in the following list. You may need to do some preparation to make sure you can answer all the questions.

How many people live next door to you? Do you know all their names?

Were the stars out last night?

What phase is the moon in today/last night?

On what day of the year are the shadows shortest where you live?

From where you are reading this, point north.

From what direction does most of the rainy weather come from in your area?

Where does your drinking water come from? Where does your water supplier source the water?

What is the name of the river nearest your home and where is its source and ending? Does it flow into the sea, another river or a lake?

What are the main geological events or processes that created the land forms where you live?

What type of soil is near your home?

What are the main plant communities in your area?

What was the land used for in your area 100 years ago?

What did people live on in your area before agriculture?

Where does your domestic rubbish go (general waste and garden waste)?

What is the largest wild or semi-wild area near your home?

Name five edible plants in your area.

Name five trees in your area. Are they all native? If you cannot name them describe them.

Name five resident birds in your area.

Name five migratory birds in your area.

What species of animals, birds and plants have become extinct in your area?

What spring wildflower is consistently one of the first to bloom in early spring in your area?

Common Ground is an organisation that promotes a sense of place, combining nature, community celebrations and the creative arts.[7] If you want to get together with others to celebrate the distinctiveness of your local area Common Ground has lots of ideas of how to go about it.

Earth walking

Adapted from *The Box* (Terma 1992).

Aim: To increase awareness of our bodies and the process of walking.

Need: Nothing.

Instructions: This activity can be done barefoot.

Walking is something we just do without thinking and we may only become aware of the process when something goes wrong like a foot injury. In this

---

7   See www.commonground.org.uk

activity we bring walking into our awareness in order to become aware of the moment-by-moment changes in our experience. Because our bodies are constantly available they make good sensations to bring to the attention of the mind.

Here is a script you can adapt for your group. Maybe use it after you have done a standing meditation:

'We are going to walk with awareness of walking. The focus is not on getting to anywhere but on what our bodies are doing. You will need to walk very slowly in order to give your full attention to the process of walking. I will talk you through. We will be going in this direction (indicate a general direction that doesn't have major obstacles like logs, brambles, steep ground, etc.).

Your body has to hold you up against gravity trying to pull you down, and when we walk we have to shift our weight from one leg to the other. Begin walking and looking ahead, not downwards; trust that your feet will tell you about the ground.

Can you feel your feet inside your shoes? Be aware of your shoes on the ground and how the feet roll to fit the land. Don't change anything consciously, only be aware... Notice how your shoes touch the ground; do you end on the soles of your feet or are shoes an extension of you feeling the ground beneath? Where do you begin and end? (Give people time to tune in to feeling each stage beginning with the ground through their shoes/feet.)

Now feel the ankles as your extremity, as if the end of your shanks were the end of you, touching the earth. Feel them adapt to the earth as you continue walking.

Now be aware of your knee joint and how that is an ending to you and how you can adapt to the earth through your thigh bones and muscles. Be aware of your hip bones gently rolling. Feel your pelvis like a basket gently rolling across the earth with legs below. What are you carrying in this basket? This is where you generate seeds or eggs for birthing the next generation, absorb goodness from your food, eliminate unwanted matter.

Now change awareness to your spine, from base tail tucked under, right up to the shoulders and neck. Feel it bend and give like a sapling tree as you walk.

Add arms to your awareness as they swing in rhythm to the spine and the chest moving onwards. Be aware of your heart and lungs, protected in the rib cage. They adapt to your pace as you walk, fast or slow.

Lastly feel your skull and head atop your spine moving with the rest of your body... Feel your jaw hang from your skull. Feel the head as a lollipop, gently sitting on top... Now feel it as a balloon holding the rest of the body lightly up from the ground.

Can you feel your body all together now from feet up to crown, moving as one across the earth?

Experiment with walking slowly with awareness over different terrain (rough, smooth, twiggy, grass, hard soil, etc.). How much can you know of the ground from your feet?

If you feel like it take your shoes and socks off and continue walking barefoot on the grass. Now do you feel connected?!

If it helps you can add words to your walking. Up until the early twentieth century almost everyone walked everywhere. If people walked long distances they would sing songs to keep their spirits up. Today many of us need to drop our energy levels down a bit; we have plenty to keep us energised. As you do your Earth walking you can experiment with repeating a word or phrase that you think might encourage your awareness, such as slowly saying "relax" or "slowly" with every step. Maybe a word will come to you as you walk with awareness.'

See: *Barefoot walk, Silent walking, Fox walking*

The ecological body

Aim: To raise awareness of how our bodies function for our well-being and the connections our insides have with the outside world.

Need: Nothing except the script below.

Instructions: You can use the following words as a starter and then adapt them to suit your own needs. My intention is to draw attention to our bodies and how they function, draw connections between us and nature, and to remind people to appreciate their bodies and what they do for us.

I often use these activities after we have done a mindfulness session and people still have their eyes closed. You could contemplate one part of the body in a session, or if it is a longer workshop refer to all the parts described here at different times throughout the day.

Lungs

'Take a big breath. Begin by pushing the air out of your lungs from the base of your chest, and then relax and let the air return of its own accord. Do that again in your own time twice more. How does that feel?

Return to normal breathing and become a silent witness to your breathing. Feel the air moving in through your nose, throat and lungs. There is nothing you have to do to exchange air, you can trust your body to breathe in and out, over and over for the rest of your life.

We share lungs with many other creatures on the evolutionary family tree from lungfish to all four-legged creatures and birds, not forgetting that nearly all life needs oxygen to exist.

We could not stay alive without air for longer than four minutes. But consider how easy it is to be alive.

As you witness your normal breathing consider this information. We have two lungs hugging each side of the heart and protecting it from shocks. The lungs are directly connected to the heart. Oxygen is absorbed by the inner surfaces of both lungs whose total surface area is the same as half a tennis court. Fresh, bright red, oxygen-rich blood is pumped around the body from the heart. Then the darker blood returns to the lungs to release its carbon dioxide before once again going back to the heart.

The air we take in is warmed by our nose and two bronchiole tubes leading to each lung. The lungs in X-ray look like a white twin-trunked tree, upside down.

It is red iron in the haemoglobin which holds the oxygen in our red blood cells. Haemoglobin transports oxygen to every single cell in our body with every breath. A mirror substance to our blood-red iron is found in plants. The metal manganese gives plants their green colour and is the key substance that releases oxygen from the leaves of trees. The used air expelled from the lungs passes over our vocal cords; by subtle contractions we are enabled to speak, shout and sing.

Still keeping aware of your breathing, open your eyes and look around.'

Heart

'I want you to pay attention to your heart now. Relax and take your attention to the middle of your chest deep inside. Feel or imagine your heart beating gently…as it has done for your whole life. The first rhythms you were aware of was your mother's heartbeat above you. You can now tune in to your own heartbeat. This is one of the primal rhythms of nature. A heartbeat is a measure of seconds, just as the path of the sun is a measure of a day, and the seasons mark out the year.

You can imagine the arteries in your body going to the lungs to get fresh air and returning to the heart, which then sends blood to the whole body. Bright red blood carries oxygen for energy, and also food, to every cell in your body. The heart makes sure all of you gets the warmth from the centre of your body.

Your blood passes through your liver and is cleansed of any toxins before making its way back to the heart again.

The blood cleanses you in other ways. It takes CO_2 back to the lungs. Any waste products are carried to the gut for elimination. Your blood takes other unwanted substances and water to the kidneys for removal from the body. Take time now to appreciate your heart and how it does so much to keep everything flowing and alive in your body… The heart is seen as the source of love. Now I want you to sink deeper into your heart and imagine love accumulating in your heart with each beat… I wonder how you visualise or feel the love in your heart. Is it a warm feeling or a rich colour? Or what? Feel with each breath your love growing, expanding beyond your heart to fill your chest and beyond. Maybe it reaches your toes and fingertips so your whole body is filled with love…a letting go and a true acceptance of what you are…just as a mother accepts her young child. Stay with the feelings, they are a recognition of your aliveness as a human being.

Now you can imagine this love flowing from your heart to the world beyond you. Imagine love streaming out to people you know…friends and family you feel close to… A strand of it could go to someone who you think could do with a bit of extra loving right now… Anyone else who needs to be sent some love? Let it flow out to them right now…

With those feelings of love still flowing, open your eyes.'

Skin

'Become aware of your skin. Maybe start with your face and hands, which are exposed to the air. What is your skin informing you about the world around you now?

Is the air moving around you? How strong is the wind and from which direction is it mostly coming? What temperature is it today? Warm or cool?

Can you become aware of your skin under your clothes and what difference it makes to be covered up? In our culture we reveal or conceal our skin according to various customs. For most of our early evolution in Africa we were naked and lived in the open. How would that be, do you imagine?

We are most aware of our skin (part of us) when it makes us aware of the world around us (not us): a change in temperature; a sharp thorn; a caressing touch. Our skin informs us of the outside world and brings it closer to us. And it is a boundary to our body, holding us in. Just as a shoreline is the meeting place between sea and land so our skin is the connection between us and everything else outside.

Through our sense of touch we feel the world. In our awareness skin is simultaneously both us and our environment. In this way the illusion of separation is created in our minds.

One last thought to contemplate. The cells that make up our skin only live for a week. Our body is continually, and in an organised way, growing new skin and also shedding itself. It does this by cells "choosing" to die. They are not diseased but they have had their time after only seven days. In fact billions of our body cells are silently and unknown to us dying every day, in order that the whole system that is us continues: a perfect example of how life and death are one and the same process.'

See: Inheritance of the wild

Ecological networks

Introduction to *Ecological networks* activities

Inspired and adapted from the work of Joanna Macy and others unknown.

All three of these activities aim to enable participants to consider ecological networks and how we are part of them.

They can be used in sequence or individually. They are adapted and inspired by other people's work I have experienced at different times.

Ecosystem milling

Inspired by attending a workshop and adapted from Macy (1983).

Aim: A good icebreaker because it has many elements to it that set the feel for a day workshop. It gets people moving around and interacting without words; it has elements of childlike fun, and real depth of feeling if people are willing.

Need: An open space free of debris where people can move freely, such as a woodland clearing or a circle laid out with dead branches in a field. People need to be close up while they are milling. If the circle space needs to be reduced you can do this by moving the boundary branches, coats and bags further in.

Instructions: Talk the group through the various sections of the activity using this script to get you going before you learn to create your own version. Speak the script slowly, particularly the Hand section where people need time to tune in to their sense of touch. They also need to process their emotional response to what is an intimate encounter with a relative stranger. If you think you are speaking slowly go even more slowly. The overall structure of this activity is alternating periods of milling followed by an interaction with another person.

Milling

Encourage the group to start walking in the designated area by milling around in different directions, criss-crossing the circle – discourage everyone from going round the same way by role modelling walking across the circle. Use your intuition as to how long each stage lasts but keep the energy going and allow time for people to process the experience. No talking allowed.

The script:

'Begin milling around in the space we have, taking care not to touch anyone else. Keep moving and don't talk. How does your body feel today? Relax and let go of all concerns. Feel the ground beneath your feet. Are you breathing? Feel your diaphragm rise and fall as you walk. Keep moving round.' I join in to act as a role model.

Crowd

'No talking, keep moving, circulate and pass each other like extras on a film set – imagine a very crowded street in London. Weave (leader demonstrates)... Feel annoyance as if everyone was in your way. Imagine you are hurrying to get your Christmas shopping done and everyone else is a nuisance. Be silent and avoid eye contact.'

Notice each other

'Slow down a bit, relax. Look up. As you pass by notice each other and briefly make eye contact with everyone. Be aware when you look at another person that they are alive like you in the year 20XX. Keep moving, milling round.'

The world

'Now I want you to pause in front of someone else, someone you don't know. Face them and go palm to palm like a high five and hold it there. Make and keep eye contact... Imagine what this person might feel about what is happening to our world - the destruction of the natural world, the human population explosion, wars and drought. Just take note without speaking, say goodbye without speaking and pass on...mill... Take another person's hand. (Repeat previous instructions two or three times if you wish; take it slowly). *Begin walking again, milling.'* (This allows some processing to take place.)

The hand

'Pair up with someone you feel comfortable with and face each other... You will both get a turn at doing this activity. One person closes their eyes and offers their right hand to the other person to hold. Just relax, let go and enjoy someone holding your hand. That's all you need to do. If the other person were to let go of your hand it would fall down. Relax as much as you can.

The Holder can listen to my instructions as follows... You may want to close your eyes too. Gently lift and hold the other person's hand. Cradle it and feel its weight... Slowly flex the wrist joint and notice how easily it moves. Imagine you have never seen or felt a human hand before in your life... Be open to the discovery of something new in Nature... Move on to the palm and fingers, becoming aware of bone, muscle and skin all held together in such complex ways. This hand is unique in all the world.

Feel the energy, warmth and intelligence in this hand and consider what it is capable of... The opposable thumb and fingers for picking things up... Notice the sensitive fingertips for contacting the world, other people... Remind yourself of what it can do, it can grasp a tool...a pen...a gun... Open your imagination to its history, revisiting its evolution over millennia from a fish's fin, to a reptile's front foot, to a monkey's hand... How it developed in the womb like a fin to become a human hand... After birth how it reached out to meet the world to explore and do things... This hand learned to grasp a finger...hold a spoon...tie shoe laces...write its name...and throw a ball... This hand learned how to comfort another and give pleasure... With thanks, let go of the hand. You can both open your eyes.

Without speaking swap over and continue to listen to my instructions.

Gently take hold of your partner's hand in your own hands... This hand you hold is unique in the universe. Feel its warmth and vitality, how flexible the joints of the fingers are and how soft the skin is... The fingertips are ultra-sensitive, patterned in a unique way for each person... Are you aware of its vulnerability as well as its sensitivity? It can reach out and touch as a way of knowing the world... It has no protective armouring and is so fragile, it can so easily be crushed or burnt... Be aware of your desire for it to be healthy and whole so that it may do its best... It has many tasks to do in the future that your partner has no idea of... It may be the hand that creates new things...or mends what is broken... It may help and support other people, offer a helping hand in a time of crisis, confusion and distress... It may be the hand that holds you in your last moments of dying, communicating reassurance, wiping a brow.

With gratitude let go of the hand and open your eyes.

Find a way of saying thank you to your partner and move on. Return to milling.' (At this point people will definitely need time to process – you will see it in their eyes and slow pace to allow time in the milling.)

Tag

'Mill around as before. Now put your left had behind your back, and as you pass a person try to touch their right hand with yours, without being touched back. (You demonstrate by tapping someone's hand to get the energy up and going.) Quick now!'

Same people

'OK, now stop tagging, slow down, begin to just circulate among each other, mill around... As you pass a person now take a moment to face them straight on. Put your raised hands together palm to palm, shoulder height, and look into each others eyes...

As you do, be aware how alive this person is...how their heart beats like yours...how they breathe the same air and are alive today. And they feel the same sun's warmth, drink from the same well, eat from the same earth. Lower your hands and move back to milling. Move on and mill around... Mill around and then find another partner.' (Repeat instructions again.)

Let go to death

'Find a partner and face each other, maintain eye contact. Place your hands palm to palm as before. You may let the possibility arise in your mind that the person in front of you will one day die... like all living things... and be reabsorbed into the earth... And can you know in yourself they will have the courage to let go... Just look, be open, don't speak... Without words say goodbye, lower your hands and move on. Go back to milling.'

Better place

'Face another, place your palms together at shoulder height...and let the possibility arise in your mind that this person may play an important part in making the world a better place...that they will find their passion, which is within them now...and move with their passion to express it in the world... Lower your hands and say goodbye.

Now move on... Continue milling slowly. As you walk notice how a human body feels on the inside... Feel the ground beneath you through your feet... Up through your legs and torso, adding your arms and head...and now feel your whole body moving easily. How alive and beautiful you are. Stay with the feelings. It's part of what makes you human.'

Discuss the experience

'Come to a stop now...form into groups of three or four and take it in turns to talk over what you have experienced.'

I sometimes let the group move off in silence, walking to the next place. This can allow people to digest their experience on their own.

See: *Indra's net, The Web of life game, Network of life*

Indra's net

Aims: To create a reflective moment after the Web of life activity using a mythic story.

Need: The text of the story below.

Instructions: Stand in a circle and read the story below.

'Indra's net was created by the chief of all gods at the beginning of time and space when he released water and light to create the universe.

Imagine the most wonderful infinite network of strong silken threads, like a dew-covered spider's web of gossamer, stretching on for ever and ever in all directions. At each node or meeting point on the threads Indra left a shining pearl. When you take a moment to select one of these supremely beautiful pearls and look attentively you see something truly remarkable: you can see all the other pearls in the net reflected perfectly on its shimmering surface. And in every pearl is reflected the one you are looking at now.'

The story of Indra's net has its origins in early Vedic and Buddhist literature at least one and a half millennia ago. It is offered as a way of understanding our interdependence on each other and the rest of the universe.

Another variation on the story has Indra tie a silver bell to each node on the infinite network of strong and sensitive threads. He did this so that when any living being moved it could not happen without ringing all the other bells on the net.

Network of life

Aims: To physically represent the interconnections within simple ecosystems. Also a useful warm-up activity for the group.

Needs: A ball of wool or string (green garden string is good). Enough space for the group to mill around comfortably.

Instructions: Tell the group standing in a circle that we are going to create our own net. Have everyone stand in a close circle, shoulders touching. Take the end of the thread from a ball of wool or string and pass it to someone to hold tightly as if their life depended on it. Ask an ecological web question (see below) and pass the ball to the person who answers the question. They have to hold tight to the thread which has crossed the circle and pass on the ball of wool or string to the next person who answers a question. Continue with the process of asking and answering questions as a group until everyone is holding the thread at least once. Eventually you will end up with a network of thread criss-crossing the group circle with everyone connected by a thread and an ecological link to everyone else.

Ecological web questions: Link one person/part of life to another. One way to begin is for the first person holding the thread to answer the simple question: What do plants grow in? Answer – soil. The next question could be: Can you name a plant that grows in soil? Then: What eats that plant? Then: What eats them? And what eats them? Or what else do they need to live? Or what is a related animal? I hope you get the idea. After a few turns people get the idea and may offer their own connections.

When the network has been created with everyone holding the thread you can try a few experiments. Holding the thread tight what happens if someone gently pulls their threads: how do others respond?

What if the people who feel one of their threads pulled also pull the other thread – passing on the disturbance as it were?

Then ask what happens if one of the living things dies out, is extinct. Have that person 'die' and fall slowly to the ground while still holding onto the thread. People will be tugged, everyone is affected.

Web of life game

Aims: As a warm-up to get people physically moving about. To encourage people to understand the dynamic nature of ecological networks.

Need: An open area of flat ground with sufficient space for people to move around freely.

Instructions: Give the following instructions to everyone:

'When I say start I want all of you to move around in this space we have. While you are moving around I also want you to secretly choose two other people in the group, and without them knowing, position yourself equidistant from both of them. As they move, so you have to adjust your position to make sure you are the same distance from both of them. Does everyone understand? OK, begin.'

If it is a big group then people have to keep continually adjusting themselves to the two other people each of whom are also adjusting to their pair. Some groups keep moving for some time, others reach an equilibrium and slow down to a standstill fairly soon. The bigger the group the better it works.

After a while stop the group and ask them how they fared. They were part of a simple system where the parts had very simple rules of equidistance which kept the whole group alive and moving. You can draw comparisons with living systems such as cultures and ecosystems and the interconnections and interdependency between all the elements.

You can ask the group to begin again, choosing a new pair to track. Before they begin walking have everyone close their eyes and you touch the shoulders of one person. Explain that this person is a rogue participant who does not have to obey the rules. What happens now when they open their eyes and play the game?

Stop the game and discuss what happened. Repeat the game for the third round. When people have moved around for a minute or two explain that you will touch a certain individual's shoulders and they are to count to 10 and fall to the ground as if dead – the person has become extinct. How many you eliminate depends on the group size and what effect you want to create in the group. What happens?

Ecotherapy beyond the session

Introduction to *Ecotherapy beyond the session* activities

This section is designed to help you think about how you might incorporate ecotherapy outside of the session.

Using a local map

Aim: To encourage people to continue with the activities outside the session.

Needs: For this discussion bring a local map which includes where participants live. An OS map in the Explorer series is very detailed and does give some street names. They show rights of way and green space.[8] A local street map is easier for people to interpret but it may not highlight green space. A combination of maps is probably best. A local bus and train map is also handy. Internet maps on a laptop or tablet can be used but they are often harder to view outdoors.

Instructions: After running a group for a few weeks and when people have learnt various activities I make time to discuss how people can take ecotherapy away with them. We begin by looking at suitable places to visit to do ecotherapy. It is surprising to me to find out how many people don't know their neighbourhood. Some routes may be very familiar but many of us drive or walk through areas without exploring what else is going on. Where is your nearest woodland, river, pond, hill top?

I find that some people will have explored local parks and open spaces but many haven't so we begin by looking at a map to see what the options are. On an outside table or in a café I spread out a map of the local area and get everyone to tell me where they live and I then mark their location with a pencil. We then have a conversation about the various green spaces we can see on the map and try to evaluate their suitability. Some places may be near home, others may be more attractive because people feel safer there, others have more wild areas but they require a bus ride.

A lot of confidence building may be required. What are their concerns about going there? Is it finding the place or who else is there or what? Encourage them in overcoming their challenges. When I have discussed why people don't go out more often on their own to the local park I get a variety of responses. The most common are: How do you know you are allowed there? Who else might be there, is it safe? What do you do there?

---

8   See www.shop.ordnancesurveyleisure.co.uk

Encourage people to just go for a short visit at first, check out the place and see who else is there. Do they feel safe? What can they do? Maybe they can go with a friend just to explore the park at first. The purpose of the walk is always to get a deeper connection to nature, not to arrive at a goal, and so there is no need to hurry. In fact the intention should be more often to wander aimlessly, noticing whatever catches your eyes and ears.

It is surprising how small an area is required for someone to feel they are in nature. Often a quiet garden with screening trees is all it takes to feel absorbed in nature.

Annihilating all that's made
To a green thought in a green shade.

Marvell, The Garden (1621–1678)

What can I do on my own in nature?

Aim: To extend activities beyond the session.

Need: Suggest your clients wrap up more than they would when going out for an ordinary walk, and maybe take a carrier bag for sitting on the ground or to collect any spontaneous foraging finds. Take binoculars, a notebook or just nothing.

Instructions: Offer the following advice:

'Just walk. Don't think about anything else, be open and aware of all that is around you in a receptive way. Go for a wander.

Just sit on a park bench, a log or the ground. Everyone else will be wrapped up in their own world and even if they do notice you it will not be something of interest for them. Do some of the activities described in this book.

Attend to your breathing and do a mindfulness session or contemplate a single thing such as a leaf or stone.

Watch wildlife carrying on. If you sit motionless leaning up against a tree for long enough wildlife will get used to you and carry on their business unafraid. I have had a herd of deer move through woodland in front of me after I had sat against a tree for 20 minutes. The wind was coming towards me and away from the deer. One of the older does kept an eye out for me in case I moved. It is best to do this alone as there is always a temptation to talk or point out things when someone else is there.

Take a sketch book and draw the patterns you see in nature. Take a notebook and write words that evoke how you feel and what you sense, make them into a poem.'

Experience of nature

Aim: This activity encourages people to connect with the memory of a strong experience in nature. It can be used at the start of a session to ease people in or as the beginning of a creative session.

Need: Space to sit in pairs. Maybe something for people to sit on such as bin bags.

Instructions: Ask people to pair up with someone they feel comfortable with and sit down together. You can say something like:

'I want you to take it in turns for a few minutes each and tell your partner of a special time in nature, of a strong experience of being in nature, something that stands out for you, that remains with you today.'

The discussion can be extended if desired. For example, you can say:

'As a result of reflections on a special time in nature can you identify what it was that made it special? Is it possible to find those conditions or state of mind elsewhere? If so where do you know already?'

This activity could be a precursor to a creative activity in which participants write, paint, draw or photograph what a special place in nature means for them.

The activity can be done indoors if the session has to be changed because of bad weather.

Find your tree again

Inspired by and adapted from an activity called 'Meet a tree' devised by Joseph Cornell.

Aims: To encourage the use of the non-visual senses in a fun way. Trusting in another.

Needs: Blindfolds (scarves will do), enough for all the group in pairs. The location needs trees or woodland with a mix of trees, and a forest floor that is easy to walk around in without getting tangled up in brambles or fallen branches.

Instructions: Explain that the activity involves working in pairs with one person blindfolded. Ask participants to choose a partner. They will each take it in turns to have a go at the activity. Give a blindfold or scarf to each pair and say something like this:

'One person is to put on the blindfold when I have finished explaining the instructions: they are the Searcher. Their sighted partner is the Lead.

The Lead carefully takes their partner blindfold through the woods to a specific tree. Do it in as roundabout a way as possible. In the process make sure your blindfolded partner is safe, particularly underfoot and overhead. Go slowly.

When you have reached the chosen tree the Searcher is left to get to know their tree through all their senses except sight: touch, sound, smell and taste. Take your time. When the Searcher feels confident they know their tree and is ready, the Lead takes the person back to me here and removes the blindfold. The Searcher has the task of finding their tree again with eyes open. The Lead goes with them and if the Searcher gets completely lost or has no idea the Lead can offer some hints to help them.'

Remind people to swap over when they return to you and to leave discussion until later. When every pair has completed the activity you can discuss how it went. How did they find their tree? Which senses did they use? What helped? What about the trust issue, did that work? How did it feel to rely on someone else?

Folding poem

I have adapted this activity from a workshop by Joseph Cornell, who in turn got it from the North Carolina Outward Bound School (also found in Cornell 2015). If you have ever played Consequences you will understand how the activity goes.

Aim: To create a poem after spending some time in nature.

Need: Clipboards, lined paper and pens for everyone.

Instructions: Ask everyone to get into groups of three and issue a clipboard, paper and a pen to each group. Tell them they are going to write a group poem on a theme they have to agree on before they start writing. They will have 10 to 15 minutes to write a poem of six lines. If they finish before time is up they can continue with a longer poem. Show them a sheet of paper you have prepared earlier with the line instructions (see below).

The first person in each team writes the first line of the poem, then passes it to the second person to read. This person writes one line that responds to the first writer's line, then writes another and then folds the poem so the third person can only see the last line they have written. The third person writes a line responding to the second person's last line, then writes another; and then folds the poem so that the next writer sees only the last line. The first person writes the last line of the poem, making six lines in all.

1	Person A	writes one line on the agreed theme.
2	Person B	reads and responds by writing one line and folding the paper to cover up the first two lines.
3	Person B	writes a new line and passes on the paper.
4	Person C	reads line 3 and responds by writing a line and folding the paper to cover it up.
5	Person C	writes a new line and passes on the paper.
6	Person A	reads line 5 and responds by writing the last line.

Each group is asked to read the composite poem to the group.

The four elements

Introduction to *The four elements* activities

The four elements activity began as a spontaneous statement I made after a mindfulness session. I began talking about the interconnectedness between ourselves and the trees around us, the exchange of gases that allows us to breathe. Later on I was looking for a way of filling people's minds with information that would be congruent with what we were doing at a sensory and emotional level, something to keep the 'mind' happy rather than going off somewhere else – not that this is primarily a thinking exercise; the intention is holistic. I also wanted an activity that linked our selves with the wider world ecosystems. I found my copy of *Thinking like A Mountain* (Seed *et al.* 1988) with the Gaia Meditation by John Seed and Joanna Macy in it and things fell into place. Like many of the activities in this book the four elements continues to evolve as new ideas arrive and new information comes to my attention. Maybe you can take them a stage further.

Four elements: earth, air, water and fire

Aim: To allow people to slow down and fill their minds with ideas that make clear the interrelationship between themselves and nature around them. If this is followed by a silent walk it can be a very profound experience.

Need: An open space with level ground. Small bowl and bottle of water; a candle, joss sticks and lighter; a heavy stone; big feathers.

Instructions: This activity has elements of a ceremony to it. There is a defined structure and a repeated process shared within a group. It is a celebration of what makes up nature and of our place in it. It encourages a shared way of seeing the world.

I begin by explaining, in the manner of a prologue, the thinking behind the activity:

'In all cultures around the world and throughout history people have put forward explanations of what the world is made up of. A very common understanding is that the world is made up of four elements: earth, air, fire and water. In modern scientific thinking we talk of solids, gases, liquids and energy. We are going to pay attention to these four elements and how we are made up of them.'

The next stage is about paying attention to the qualities of each of the fundamental elements and making explicit the interconnected processes between the world and ourselves. Lastly I draw on four metaphorical and symbolic links between the elements and body, mind, emotions and spirit.

I have been brief with the information here. I encourage everyone to add their own knowledge to this activity. Start the process by going through each element in turn. Do this by offering an object to represent it, for example a single heavy stone to represent the earth. Talk about the element's qualities and slowly pass the object around the group. When the object has returned to you, place it in the centre of the circle as a point of focus.

Earth, of which our physical body is a part, symbolic of our physicality

Pass a heavy stone or handful of soil around the group.

If you know what type of rock it is and where it has come from talk about its age and what has happened to it. Create a sense of amazement at how long the rock has lasted and how it has changed though time. I use a 300-million-year-old volcanic rock that originated in Norway, was pushed by ice to Scotland and smoothed by the sea until I found it.

Remind people that we are made of earth. Think of how food passes through us and how we are literally what we eat. When does this morning's breakfast become you? For how long is it you? Over seven years we change virtually all the molecules in our body. The physical you standing here is not the you of a decade ago.

Once the stone has gone round and been placed in the middle I ask people to become aware of their bodies. I talk them through the *Physical relaxation exercises* activity to shake their limbs and stretch themselves, or maybe use the instruction to tense and then relax sets of muscles and to progressively let go of tensions in the body.

Air, linked to our breath, symbolic of the mind's thinking

Pass round a feather to represent air, or a lighted smoking joss stick. Be aware of air and breathing; the same air is recycled in the world among all beings and green plants. With each breath we take in air that has been through innumerable plants and animals and other people over millennia.

Raise people's awareness of their breathing. Ask them to take a deep breath, let the air out with a sigh, then repeat. Ask them to notice how we usually breathe without awareness or conscious effort and become aware of air passing through the nose, chest and abdomen. Say something like:

'Air goes to every cell in the body. Breathe deeply, then relax. Focus on the belly rising and falling. Be a witness to thoughts and sensations, let them pass by and then return to breathe. Open the mind to new ways of thinking that describe and explain our deep interconnectedness.'

If we have trees nearby I talk about the interchange of oxygen and carbon dioxide between us and trees, our interdependence. I then move to do a mindfulness session with the group standing in a circle attending to their breath.

Water, linked to our body fluids, symbolic of emotions

Pass round a small bowl of water.

You can refer to its qualities of lively movement and purity. We are 70 per cent water and so is the surface of the planet. It is the source of all life: we cannot last more than a few days without it. The water on the planet is the same as the water from the time of the origin of the earth. It is possible to drink a glass of clean water knowing that it has been through many organisms and waterways and each time it is purified by micro-organisms.

I encourage everyone to bring their emotions into awareness.

Fire, linked to our body heat and symbolic of the human spirit, passion

Pass around a lighted candle. People will have to be protective of the flame to prevent it from being blown out.

All our energy ultimately comes from the sun. The sun gives light to plants which feed animals. The sun drives weather systems and sea currents with its warmth. We burn our own internal heat. Be aware of your own warmth. A life burns. Underline the intimate connection we all have with natural world just by being alive.

I remind people to bring their spirit of aliveness to the present moment. As a freethinker I make no reference to metaphysical spirits. I speak rather of the fire within us, the passion that drives our expression of life.

After the objects have passed round the circle and been placed in the centre I remind everyone that this is it. There is nothing in nature except the four elements. There is nothing in you except the four elements and all are flowing seamlessly through us. Rest for a moment's contemplation and then move the group out into nature for an exploratory exercise.

If you have a weekly group you may just want to use one of the elements in a session. You could talk about air before or after doing a mindfulness set, or the water element could be talked about while standing next to a stream or lake.

I usually do the full four elements early on in a workshop. It acts as a gateway to the rest of the day. I find that after doing it people are very stilled and contemplative and so I build on that. There are many activities you can use as a follow-on; two of these follow.

Reflecting on the four elements

Aim: To deepen awareness of the four elements.

Needs: A habitat that has preferably trees and water. Carrier bags or plastic bin bags for people to sit on.

Instructions: In this activity I ask everyone to take a plastic bag to sit on and find a tree to lean against. Make sure they cannot see another person directly in front of them. The instructions are to do a mindfulness breathing activity for 5–10 minutes, then to open their eyes and just sit. Allow thoughts to arise from *The four elements* activity and reflect on your participation in the exchange of elements. You can call them back with a whistle after a suitable length of time.

Walking through the four elements

Aim: To deepen awareness of the four elements.

Need: A mixed habitat of water and woodland.

Instructions: This activity is a group walk. The idea is to have a silent walk with pauses to consider and focus on one element at a time. The intention should be to give the mind something to consider while heightening the senses.

Having explained that it is a silent walk with pauses to attend to each element in turn, you could begin by saying something like: Is a river still a river if you take all the water out? No. The same with us, if you take the nature out of our lives we don't exist. We are in dynamic exchange between our bodies and all that is around us. Can you feel life flowing through you with each step, breath, drink and meal?

Air: you can say something like:

'As you are walking silently and slowly be aware of your breathing. Don't change anything, just pay full attention to air entering your body and leaving it. Clean fresh air. I'm just going to remind you of some things as we walk. You are breathing air that is alive. It all comes from plants and plankton, and will return to plants just as it has been circulating for tens of millions of years. Air flows through you endlessly and effortlessly.'

Continue in this vein.

Earth: hold a spadeful of woodland soil and say something like this:

'This soil is as alive as you or me. In fact there are more living cells in a handful of soil than in the whole of your body. Micro-organisms outnumber all other living things on Earth. If you want to take your shoes and socks off and walk directly on the earth feel free to do so now. Take care.'

Water: go to a stream and do one of the water exercises. Say something like this:

'Watch the motion of water. The same water passes through us all the time and passes through other life forms continuously. It is in clouds, rain, plants, rivers, animals, people.'

Fire: say something like this:

'All life gets its energy from the sun in the sky. The sun warms the earth and us, it also gives light to plants in photosynthesis. When we eat we access that energy and burn oxygen to keep our body a similar temperature to the African savannah in which we evolved. Feel your inner fire, your warmth burning inside, just as a fire does. Feel the sun on you now.

Move forwards, aware that you can experience your body moving intimately as part of nature, in continual exchange.'

THE FOUR ELEMENTS

Fox walking

Aim: To raise awareness of the process of walking.

Need: Nothing.

Instructions: Have you ever watched how a fox or cat walks through snow or long grass while it is hunting? Each limb is tentatively stretched forwards to feel the ground before deliberately committing itself. The weight is held on the other legs until the animal knows it is safe to press the paw down.

I will talk to a group about these actions and suggest a way of walking with attention: by slowing down the process and noticing every part of the movement of walking. I will say something like this:

'I want you to go for a walk and to be as aware as you can of what you are doing. You will need to do this very slowly and carefully, sensing your way along. It helps to keep the bodyweight on the back foot for as long as possible and not to transfer the weight forwards until the foot in front is firmly on the ground. Can you do this without looking down but just by using your body sense and touch through your feet? Can you keep your whole body in your awareness as you move along?'

People realise it is possible to move silently through the woods and to be very sensitive to what is underfoot even with shoes on. Different thicknesses of twigs and roots can be sensed and even the type of leaves.

See: Earth walking, Silent walking

Getting to know another life form

Getting to know an oak tree close up

Partly inspired by *The Box* (Terma 1992).

Aim: Two aims: first to observe nature just as it is, to get to know a plant or creature and maybe engender empathy with another living being; second to see things for what they are without judgement. The activity also has the effect of taking the person out of themselves and their mental chatter.

Need: A5 instruction sheets: one per person. An open area with plenty of space for people to spread out and look at different things around them.

Instructions: I once listened to a BBC journalist on the radio describe how he felt after he had been released from being held hostage in the Middle East. He felt so good doing simple things like walking free down the streets and being able to choose to do whatever he wanted. These were the same things as he had done before capture but now they took on a different meaning. I was intrigued by the journalist's changed way of seeing the previously mundane world.

It is possible to change how we see the world: to change the meaning we give to things even though nothing has really changed. Is it possible for you to look at something for itself, without judgement? Here is an opportunity to experiment.

Take the group to an open place where there is a variety of plants and animal life (including insects). Explain the activity and give out the A5 instruction handout (see the downloadable handout below and online).

You can give verbal instructions something like this:

'I want you to spend some time on your own observing nature just as it is. Find another living plant or creature and get to know it, spend time really looking at it. What shape, colour, size is it? Does it smell? What texture is it? How old is it? Explore how it has grown and adapted to its surroundings. Does it get enough

sunlight, warmth, nutrients and water? What about its surroundings? Where does it live? Who or what does it live with?

Read the first side of the handout and when you have got to know your life form turn over the sheet and follow those instructions. I will wait here; return to me when you have finished or when you hear my whistle.'

Have people share their experiences in pairs or small groups. Before moving off it might be interesting to discuss how everyone responded to the questions on the back of the sheet. Was it possible to be non-judgemental about the life form they looked at? Why is that? Is it therefore possible to view other people, and ourselves, in a non-judgemental way?

Related activities

I often follow up this activity with the *I appreciate…* activity because it turns the perception of self into something positive. You could also do a contemplation activity after doing a physical scan of the body and see how well people can just accept themselves for what they are at this moment.

Getting to know another life form

I want to encourage you to closely observe something living in nature.

NB Read this side of the paper first and only read the other side once you have completed the activity written here.

Take your time and be open to what you experience.

Find another living thing, a plant or creature, and get to know it.

Spend time really looking at this other life form, which is dealing with all the basic processes of life as you are.

What are its colours, textures, smell?

Explore its growth and patterns.

How is it growing or moving?

Can you figure out how it gets what it needs to stay alive: food, water, warmth, etc.?

Any indication how it reproduces?

What about its surroundings? Where does it live, who does it live with?

When you feel you have studied and got to know your other life form turn over this sheet.

When you have taken time to really get to know your unique life form ask yourself the following variations on one theme:

What is wrong with it?

Is it ugly or beautiful?

Is it a bad or a good plant/animal?

Is it badly behaved or good? Is it doing things properly?

Can you see it just for itself?

GETTING TO KNOW ANOTHER LIFE FORM

Gratitude

Adapted from *The Box* (Terma 1992).

Aim: To feel gratitude for something in our lives.

Needs: What you will need depends on the activity. See below for ideas.

Instructions: You can say something like this:

> *'Gratitude is being thankful for something in your life. We are going to stop and ponder for a while something we are grateful for, and then I want you to find a way to express your appreciation for this something which really touches your heart, and make it as an offering.*
>
> *We do not need to make an offering to demand/ask/plead something from God or any supernatural power. This is a simple expression of heartfelt gratitude, appreciation, love for something, given freely.*
>
> *What gives the process of gratitude real power is the feeling within one's body as you make the offering.'*

I like the explanation below from *The Box* (Terma 1992). You may want to read all of it or select examples to illustrate what can be done.

Offerings may be spoken, sung, written or danced.
They can be made, found, or grown.
They can be simple or complex; costly, inexpensive, or free.
They can be an object or an action.
Offerings can be solid as a rock or ephemeral as smoke.
An offering can be a knot tied in a string, an echo bouncing of
*   a cliff wall.*
Perfume, cloth, coloured flags, flowers, incense, candles, fruit,
*   food, water, sweets, smiles, music, dance, song, paintings,*
*   drawings, sculpture.*
Offerings can be visualised - the Sun, the Moon, stars, clouds,
*   jewels and stones, vows or commitments, one's own body,*
*   heart, mind, the things to which one is attached.*
Offerings can be left on the ground or hung on a tree, buried
*   deep in the earth or hidden under a rock.*
They can be traditional, learned from someone else, or original.
They can be placed on an altar, inside a wall, under the floor,
*   on the roof.*
Tossed into a river, left on a mountain top, or given to the wind.
Thrown off a cliff, or sewn in someone's clothes.
Offerings express a sense of reference, gratitude, joy,
*   thanksgiving, affection.*
An offering can be a way of making friends with some thing
*   (someone) you can't see or hear, but know is there.*
An offering is a gift in awe to the Great Mystery of Life.

Hawk and deer

I can't recall where this activity came from. Thanks to Katie Allan for additional ideas.

Aim: To encourage a different way of seeing. The effect can be to take a person away from their internal processes and focus more on their surroundings.

Need: An open area, for example at a woodland edge where people can spread out and see some distance. By a lake is also a good place. An elevated position such as a slight rise overlooking landscape improves the activity.

Instructions: Encourage people to spread out but make sure they can still hear you. Face outwards into an open area. Explain that we are going to alternate our way of seeing the world, moving between two ways.

Say something along the lines of the following:

'First I want you to see with the eyes of a hawk. Scan the surroundings until something catches your eye; focus on it. Stare intently at every detail of a small area. Look at its colour, tone, shape, movement, size. Exclude everything else from your attention.'

After a minute switch to another mode:

'Look with the eyes of a deer. Deer are herbivores who need to keep an eye out for dangerous predators such as hunters, wolves and such like. They don't know where the danger might come from and yet they need to get on with life. Take your attention to your peripheral vision, defocus. Don't pay attention to any particular detail but notice the shape of the broad space in front and to the sides of you. Be sensitive to any movement. Attend with a soft look, heavy lidded and relaxed. Let the light come to you.'

Then after a minute or so change back to the eye of a hawk. Repeat a few times varying the instructions slightly.

To assist in doing the deer part I add something I heard about how hunters train young people. The instructions are as follows:

'I want you to stretch your arms out either side of you at shoulder height. Now slowly move both hands back and forth while twiddling your fingers until you are just aware of both hands. Don't look at the hands directly, look straight ahead and be aware in your peripheral vision of the hand movements alone.'

Discussion

I ask people how they got on with the activity and what they learnt. And then I often refer to the fact that they were controlling their attention. They were all demonstrating to themselves that they could control what they looked at. I point out that it is possible to direct the mind to pay attention to one thing only and to exclude other things. They have just demonstrated this ability. How can we, I ask, direct our mind away from unpleasant thoughts and feelings through conscious effort? I encourage experimentation with this suggestion.

This exercise can be followed by *See with the mind then the heart*. You could also do *Cat's ears* later because it is an activity that heightens listening.

Home in nature

Adapted from an exercise by Ronen Berger which I experienced on a workshop. For more details on how Berger uses it with children see Berger and Lahad (2013).

Aims: To explore what it is a person finds comfortable about being out in nature. It can also be used to explore a person's thinking about their own home situation.

Needs: An open natural area with a range of habitats such as woodland, open meadow, scrub and water - preferably still and moving water. Photocopies of a map showing where you are (not essential: it depends if people could get lost or not).

Instructions: Take the group to the mixed habitat area and if you are using a map give a copy to everyone at the beginning. Talk through the map and check everyone knows where they are on it. If you are not using a map talk through how well people know the area and reassure them that you will stay in one place.

Say something like:

'I want you to go for a walk on your own for up to 20 minutes and come back here when you have finished the exercise. I will wait here. After 20 minutes I will blow the whistle if anyone has not come back by then.

Your task is to find a place that feels like home – not your indoors home but a place here you feel comfortable with. You may want to change or add things to the place. When you have found your special place I want you to stay there a while and reflect on what it is that makes you feel at home. If after searching you can't find your home, look for somewhere you feel more comfortable in compared to other places in the park. You can imagine you are an animal or bird if you like, and seek out a place they would like if that helps. Come back to me when you have finished.'

When everyone has returned discuss how people got on. Then walk to the homes (check that each person is OK about that) continuing the discussion on what makes each place a home for that person.

How to meditate

Meditation is a way of being fully present in the here and now; this attention to one's own awareness is sometimes referred to as mindfulness. Meditation is done by relaxing and attending to whatever is going on in your experience as an interested dispassionate witness.

There are many benefits to regularly meditating:

- a sense of being more in the present, letting go of the past and future concerns, emotional sampling

- feeling relaxed and calmer after the meditation

- a sense of an expanded self, being part of something bigger, a transpersonal feeling.

I suggest to anyone who wants to use meditation in their ecotherapy work that they become competent at doing it themselves first before leading others in to doing it.

When I am on my own in nature and want to meditate I tend to look for a secluded place where I'm not obviously visible to passers-by. I reckon from what I have observed that over 95 per cent of people going for a walk stick to the paths. So you only have to go a few metres from the path to find somewhere secluded. I like to sit between the roots of a tree on a polythene carrier bag – to keep the dampness off – and although I'm not leaning on the trunk I can sense it behind me. With my legs crossed I place my hands on my thighs.

Aim: To learn a method of meditation.

Need: Somewhere comfortable where you will not be disturbed.

Instructions: If I am working in a group I usually get the group to stand in a circle with about an arm's length between us, hands by our sides. We choose somewhere secluded, free of human distraction. I encourage a firm stance, hips, knees and ankles slightly bent with the weight evenly spread between the heel and ball of the foot. Because we stand it means we can comfortably do it in any season or weather condition and it also means that everyone is ready to move off in the same state of mind, maybe to do a silent walk or a walking meditation.

There are lots of ways of meditating; here is one way you can try. These instructions can be adapted as a script for talking a group through the process:

- Commit to doing meditation on a daily basis for a set length of time (initially commit for 10 weeks; begin with 10 minutes and extend as you feel fit to 20, 30, 45 minutes and more. With my regular groups I meditate for about 10 minutes at a time; on workshops I might go for longer.

- Find a quiet place where you won't be disturbed, interrupted or distracted. Sit or stand in a comfortable and alert manner, head upright and level or slightly down. Let the eyes rest softly on a single point a couple of metres away, or you may want to close them.

- Check your emotional state, just notice what is going on for you, don't get involved. Become a silent witness to yourself.

- Check your stance as described above (hips, knees, ankles, foot balance) and settle in an alert posture. Now pay attention to the body. You can begin by going through each part of the body, starting at the feet, and noticing each part: not thinking about it but experiencing it directly. I do this accumulatively, adding each new part of the body as I move up from the feet. Eventually I reach the head and you can experience your whole body as one. When you are comfortably aware of the whole of your body attend to the breath by focusing on counting the out-breath in tens.

- Cultivate a fully experiencing witness state to all that is happening in the present. Observe without engagement all thoughts, emotions and sensations. Put aside all judgements, evaluations and interest. As a thought arises don't shut it out, just notice it. When you have acknowledged it let it go and return to the breathing.

- The mind does not want to be still so when you realise you have been distracted from the present into thoughts let go of the mind's contents (without judgement of yourself) and return to the breathing.

- You are successfully doing meditation just by sitting with the intention of being in the here and now. There is no end goal and if you have a goal let it go; it is an unnecessary distraction (including 'wanting to be more relaxed').

- After a while, and after some practice, you may experience a stillness, a lack of awareness of your body, of an inside/outside distinction, a reduction of thoughts and a heightened awareness of things just happening. This is good.

- It is common to all who meditate to feel emotions welling up unexpectedly at times. Accept it is so, stop using strategies like blame and guilt, just label it, and be with the emotion before letting go. You may also feel fidgety discomfort, sleepiness, boredom and wanting to do something else. Just notice what is happening in your mind and stay with the breathing. If you are someone who tries hard, loosen up and let go of expectations - keep practising doing less. If you are easily distracted return to the discipline of following the breath.

- At the end of the session, stay still for a while and look around, and consider what you want to do next before moving off. See if you can maintain the same awareness and be mindful in what you do.

Some people meditate to relax and others wish to take meditation further by developing it in a transpersonal way to gain insight into the ground of experience. Some join a Buddhist group to share experiences and refine their meditation as well as going on retreats. John Kabat-Zinn has brought mindfulness into the mental health arena; this is a good way to learn to practise mindfulness in a group. Others read books to give meaning to their experiences. Others are content to continue meditating and learn from the experience itself. There are some good CDs of guided meditation to get started but they are not necessary, certainly not when you have nature all around you. (See the section on mindfulness on page 109.)

> The more you talk about it,
> the more you think about it,
> the further from it you go;
> stop talking, stop thinking,
> and there is nothing you will not understand.
>
> *Seng T'san/Jianzhi Sengcan (died 606 CE)*

I appreciate...

Aim: To encourage positive thoughts about a person's current situation.

Need: This activity can be done sitting down in pairs or walking along; no special space is needed.

Instructions: Say something like:

'In this activity you will be working in pairs as we walk along to the next place. I want you to take it in turns to talk.

The first person is the silent witness. You are to just to listen to your partner without comment. You can help encourage your partner and ask for clarification. You can also help your partner keep to the rules below.

The second person is the speaker. The speaker talks about what is going well in their lives. They can be small or big events in your life, including experiences you are having right now.

The speaker must do this by finishing the sentence "I appreciate…"
They must do this ten times at least.
No negative statements or additions are allowed.
There should be no discussion between you until the activity is completed for both.

Take a partner now, someone you feel comfortable with, and walk along. One is listener, the other talks, and after a while you swap over.'

When the activity is over you may want to discuss how it went. Be careful not to undo the positive statements.

I notice

Aim: To increase awareness.

Needs: I like doing this activity in open woodland because it gives a varied view. Plastic bags for each person to sit on.

Instructions: This activity can be done in one place or walking. I would encourage starting with the first variation and allow plenty of time. It can be a very profound experience for some, particularly if it has come after other deepening activities, because it allows time for processing. We live in a time of action and change and we need more time for the pebbles of experience to sink to a deep level before another is thrown in.

Say something like this:

'I want you to walk into the woodland, but not so far that you lose sight of me. Find a tree to sit and lean against where you have a clear and varied view of nature, but you cannot see anyone else in the group.

Relax and lean into the tree, maybe spend a few minutes meditating like we did earlier. Look around you and when something catches your eye just look with real attention as if it is the first time you have seen this thing or event. Notice what it is you are feeling while you look, and remember to return to looking around you and not get too distracted by thoughts.

Make your way back to me when you hear the whistle.'

Variation 1

'On each out-breath complete the sentence to yourself "I notice…"

For example:

I notice…the twigs moving in the wind.

I notice…the clouds drifting and I feel slowed down.

I notice…a bird moving through the trees busy with its own life.

Repeat for five minutes then just sit and watch.'

Variation 2

You can have people do the activity in pairs with the partner offering the question: 'What do you notice?' and the other person replying. Make sure the questioner is out of the field of view of the observer.

Inside/outside me

Aim: To practise controlling awareness and attention. To break undue attention to internal voices and self-talk.

Need: A place with a view, for example a slight rise in the ground with open space.

Instructions: Ask the group to spread out and stand so that no one else is in their field of view; a rough straight line either side of you works well. Talk the group through this activity, which alternates between attending to something a long way away and something near. Say something like:

'I want you to find something to look at in the distance – a tree, cloud, building, a bird. Really look at it, notice all its details, colour, tone, shape, size, how it moves. Look as if the police are going to ask you later on to describe it.'

After 10–15 seconds or thereabouts switch to inside:

'I want you to now switch your attention to inside yourself. Tune in to what is going on inside – it could be a feeling, thought or body sensation. Without getting involved in the content of the thought, feeling or sensation, stand as an interested witness as to what is going on. Just notice without judgement but with affection.'

After 10–15 seconds or thereabouts switch back to outside and repeat something similar to the first instructions. Repeat with the inside attention. You can stop here or repeat the cycle a third time if you wish.

In the debrief ask how people got on doing the activity. Did they learn anything? Was it possible to switch attention? If it was possible there is a lesson for other parts of our life when something seems to be demanding all our attention. It is possible to direct attention between inside and outside self. One of the benefits of ecotherapy is the way nature invites us out and we can lose all the concerns and thoughts going on inside our head for a while.

A variation: Now I'm aware of...

Ask people to work in pairs with someone they feel comfortable with. Instruct them to take it in turns and alternate responses. Remind people to attend to all their senses and to be spontaneous, not thinking too much before saying something.

Each person in turn says what they are aware of as they walk along, responding to the three aspects below. The other person listens but does not make comment.

Complete the statements:

> I am aware outside of my self of...
>
> I am aware inside my body of...
>
> I am aware in my mind of...

After a pause the other person responds with the same statements.
The process is alternated between the two people for a while.

Interview with nature

I was inspired to develop this activity from a similar one I experienced on a workshop by Joseph Cornell.

Aim: To form a closer connection to a specific creature or plant in nature in an imaginative way.

Need: For each participant: an instruction sheet (Interview with nature, see downloadable handout below and online), A4 blank sheets, clipboard and pencil. Maybe a polythene bag to sit on too.

Instructions: Take the group to a varied place in nature with maybe trees, water and grassland. Suggest they get to know another living thing in nature by interviewing it. The instructions handout explains it all.

After the group has returned you can have a discussion on how it went. What did people learn?

See: *A mini-beast's life*

Interview with nature

Instructions

For some people this exercise might seem a bit unusual. If it does seem odd to you I suggest you treat it like an imaginative experiment or fantasy. Assume it is possible and see what comes up. I'm asking you to interview something in the park that isn't a person!

Go for a short exploratory walk near where we are and choose a natural feature, a rock, plant or animal that catches your eye.

Treat your choice as a fellow traveller who like you is living out their life on planet Earth. In your interview try to see the world from this new point of view as you write the answers to your questions. Take your time to get into it.

You can use your imagination to come up with answers, and if you like, you can listen quietly for thoughts that tell you how your fellow traveller might respond. Feel free to adapt and make up your own questions as well. Number the answers on a blank sheet to match the questions.

I won't ask you to read anything out afterwards, this is for you.

Take your time and come back to me when you have finished.

My interview subject is _____

Suggested questions

For natural features, plants and rocks

1. *How old are you?*

2. *Have you always been the size you are now?*

3. *Where did you come from?*

4. *What is it like living in this particular place?*

5. *Who comes to visit you?*

6. *What events have you seen in your life?*

7. *Is there something special you would like to tell me?*

8. *Any other questions you want to ask?*

For animals

1. *Where are you going?*

2. *What are you trying to accomplish?*

3. *Are there any predators you need to look out for?*

4. *What do you eat, and how do you find your food?*

5. *Where do you live? Alone or with others?*

6. *Do you ever travel to other places?*

7. *What would you like to tell others about yourself?*

8. *Any other questions you want to ask?*

INTERVIEW WITH NATURE

The Kawa model

The Kawa model uses the metaphor of the river to examine issues in a person's life. It was developed in Japan by occupational therapists. For Westerners the model can increase a professional's repertoire and be of particular use when working with culturally diverse clients (Iwama 2006; Iwama, Thomson and Macdonald 2009).

The initial discussions by occupational therapists in Japan were motivated by the desire for a model appropriate to their own culture, one less based on Western cultural assumptions.

The Japanese are less individualistic than we are and see themselves as more interdependent. We in the West generally have a tradition of seeing the individual self and the environment as quite separate even if they can be seen to be causally related. Also the client is seen as having a diagnosed condition and the aim of treatment is to deal with the condition and bring the person back to good health. The Eastern Asian view is more systemic and views the individual as being embedded in a multiplicity of interacting elements. The focus is less on the diagnosed illness than on the person's whole life condition, all of which is seen to play a part in illness and recovery. Because each person's circumstances are unique the Kawa model encourages each person to be treated as an individual with unique characteristics, not as an example of a generic label such as an MS patient or a schizophrenic.

As a result of their deliberations the Japanese workers decided that the river was a useful and culturally relevant metaphor for describing a person's life. Life is seen as beginning at the source and flowing along a life course to death when it meets the sea. The river course is not fixed but is in a constant state of change. The flux is as a result of many factors dynamically shifting between health and illness, tracing out various rhythms and cycles. The role of the occupational therapist is to help the client increase the flow of life in the client's metaphorical river.

The elements of the metaphor that a person is asked to identify are as follows:

- Water is the person's life energy or life flow which is strong when a person is healthy, weak when someone is ill. It stops flowing when it meets the sea and the person is dead. The direction, flow rate, depth and clarity of water are significant.

- The walls and bed of the river equate to the environment, both physical and social (family, friends, work colleagues).

- Rocks are life circumstances, problems in life.

- Driftwood are the assets and liabilities a person possesses, explained in more detail below.

- Spaces are where the water can flow between obstacles and life can be enhanced.

Rocks are equivalent to the specific circumstances which make life difficult and are understandably sometimes hard to shift. The size and weight of the rocks are evaluated in the modelling. They may have been there a long time. Others arrive with an illness, and they may be harder to shift if the side walls impede the flow. For example, someone with a physical disability will find life harder if their physical circumstances are in need of change or they have few friends. Each factor in the Kawa model is seen in relation to others at all times. The temptation to see simple causal relationships is to be avoided.

Driftwood, a metaphor for a person's attributes and resources, can include values, character, personality, knowledge and experience, special skills, material assets like money and immaterial ones such as friends and family. Both the last two are very significant in Japanese life. An individual's strong values and beliefs plus a determination to cope with adversity may see them through a difficult time.

The various elements can combine with each other. If the river flow rate decreases then it is easier for driftwood to get stuck between rocks, and things can get even worse from there as the flow rate further decreases.

In the West we might focus on the rocks and on how to shift the problematic ones out of the way. The intention in Japan is to ensure harmony between all the elements in a person's life and circumstances. In the Kawa model the pathology is only part of the person. The task is to be more accepting of the current state while encouraging the positive opportunities for change. This means that the individual's personal meaning and sense of well-being are more important than any external criteria for assessment.

When you consider the behaviour of real rivers, water power can erode banks and shift blockages when there is sufficient pressure. Once the client has mapped out their life river using the Kawa model the focus shifts to examining the existing flow and ways to expand it. The spaces between the rocks, river sides and driftwood are seen as places where progress can come. And what is encouraging about the

Kawa model is that the innate healthy ability of the client is appealed to as a source of energy to shift blockages.

As a relatively new model there seems to be a limited scientific evidence base for its effectiveness at the moment. However, the model has wide acceptance in Japan and to me it has an intuitive sense of being useful.

Aim: Using the metaphor of a river to make sense of one's life.

Needs: Big sheets of paper and various coloured pens, enough for everyone.

Instructions: The instructions below are for working one to one with a client. If you feel your group is capable and has good active listening skills, participants could work in pairs taking it in turns to discuss the personal river drawing they have created.

- The river is drawn on a piece of paper by the client as a watercourse from source to sea and significant life changes are marked along the river.

- A cross-section of the river is also drawn by the client representing this point in time now.

- A list is made of the person's problems and assets and these are drawn in on the cross-section as rocks, driftwood and banks.

- Issues are worked through to see what can be shifted, where opportunities lie for increasing flow rate, all the time taking a systemic perspective.

There is a slide presentation on the Kawa model available online.[9]

Leaning on a tree, a person

An idea developed and adapted from an exercise on a workshop. See also Tufnell and Crickmay (2004).

Aim: To imaginatively explore being in a wood and to experience support and interaction with another person.

Need: Woodland with a lot of trees fairly close together. The trees need to be strong enough for someone to lean their whole weight on them. An area with young trees 20–30cm diameter is good in my experience.

Instructions: Go to the woodland and form a rough circle where you can explain the instructions. Talk through the process very slowly so that people have time to take in what you say. Explain that they are being asked to use their imagination here, including what it is like to be a tree.

Leaning on a tree

Give the following instructions:

'I want you to choose a tree nearby that you can lean on with all your weight and feel as much of your body as possible is in contact with the tree. Make sure you can also see and hear me clearly.'

Wait until everyone has found a tree and is ready, then talk them through the following, allowing time between each statement for the implications to sink in. Allow people more time than this script might imply:

'I now want you to lean against the tree you have chosen. Make sure your feet are firmly planted on the ground and your back is comfortable against the bark… How close can you get with your back against the tree trunk?… Let the tree take your weight… Take your time and check your breathing… Let out a sigh and with each out-breath relax into the tree… Allow the tree to fully support your body… Let go of the need to support yourself… Are you comfortable? Shift your body until you are… How does your body feel?

Now you are comfortable and supported by your tree you can begin to take in your surroundings. Where are you exactly?… What is it like here?…

I want you to use your imagination now…and consider what it is like to become your partner tree… What do you notice?… You could have been here for a hundred years or more, you may be centuries old and you are still fit and healthy…seeing the seasons come and go… Look up and see how close your neighbours are… You have all been here for a long time.

Everything you need to live is here…the sun and rain from above, the earth around your roots, and air all around you… You have no need of anything else…

What is it like being here in one place, unable to move…and to grow and accept where you are?'

Leaning on a person

Give people time for the experience to soak in and then ask participants to stand free of their tree. Ask them to find someone in the group that they feel comfortable with and who is about the same height as them.

Continue with these instructions:

'When you have chosen your partner I want you to stand back to back. Now lean against each other, give each other support. Can you find a balance point that is comfortable for both of you? Can you support another and receive support at the same time?… How does that feel?… Do you feel more comfortable supporting another or receiving support?…

You are safe here…as you breathe out let go a bit more…and relax into the uncertain and unfamiliar experience.

What can you learn about the other person from how you are?… Can you begin to communicate without words to each other?… You have permission to be playful and to explore… Can you both have fun this way?… Can you push each other in different ways?… Surprise the other… Slow down together…

Now see if you can move around together like a crab... Link arms... Keeping together how do you decide where to go and how to move?'

When it seems appropriate ask everyone to stop and discuss with their partner their experience with the tree and with the other person.

Life circle

Inspired by Wild Weaving in *Nature's Playground* (Danks and Schofield 2005).

Aim: A creative activity for celebrating the seasons or habitat.

Needs: Long flexible twigs such as willow; string, thread or wool; scissors or a sharp knife.

Instructions: At the start of a walk have everyone make a life circle to carry with them and decorate. This is something like a dream catcher – a circular hoop criss-crossed with threads which is then decorated with natural materials.

How to make a life circle

Find a flexible twig such as willow and form it into a circle between 10 and 30cm across. Tie the two ends firmly together with string or tough plant material such as lime bark from the twigs or honeysuckle. This bit is fiddly to do on your own: it helps to have another person tie the string while you hold the two ends together. Use wool or more string to criss-cross the circle to create a web. Make sure the thread is wrapped round the twig after each crossing of the circle to hold it in place.

An alternative is to use a Y-shaped twig and to criss-cross the two forks with string and use the long end as a handle.

After everyone has finished making their life circle the instructions are to find interesting objects along the walk which remind them of their time in Nature. There could be a seasonal theme repeated a few times each year or a one-off activity. Found objects can be tied to the rim or tucked between threads.

People could use grass, rush stems, seeds, fruit, feathers, bones, flowers, leaves, cones or snail shells as decoration.

At the end of the walk each person can tie a length of string to the life circle so they can hang it up, either in a tree nearby or at home.

See: *Memory stick*

Listening to silence

Aims: To increase sensitivity to sounds. To direct attention outwards.

Need: Nothing.

Instructions: This can be done at any stage, but after doing a meditation session is a good time. Ask everyone to stand and listen with eyes closed to all the sounds around them. Encourage people by telling them that over time their sense of hearing will become more sensitive. Spend time just listening, allowing sound to arrive at the ears without seeking out particular sounds

You can encourage people to listen to sounds far away: what is the furthest sound? Distant planes? Then suggest people listen to the middle distance, maybe birdsong. Suggest people take in sounds from all directions, gradually bringing attention closer and closer until the challenge is to see what the nearest sound is. Is there a silence between the sounds?

An additional activity is to ask the group to see how many sounds they can hear and in which direction. This can lead to a discussion of how many different birds and insects they can hear.

See: *Cat's ears*, *Sound map*, *Wind in the willows*

Memory stick

Inspired by the Forestry Commission website, which in turn got the idea from Australian native people who use a journey stick to remember where they have been.

Aim: To provide a physical memory aid and record of a walk. This is an obvious activity to use with people experiencing memory problems.

Needs: A stick about 30cm long and a length of wool about 100cm long per person.

Instructions: I suggest, to save time, you collect a set of thick straight twigs of the right length before the activity session. Also bring a ball of wool and cut off 100cm lengths. Ask everyone to tie the wool to one end of the twig. When that has been done the group is ready to begin collecting items.

The idea is for everyone to collect interesting items as they go on the walk and to attach them to the memory stick. This is done by holding the object close to the twig, beginning at the end where the wool is tied on. Spirally wrap the wool thread around the object so that it is held in place. After a while the memory stick will have a collection of items held up its length in the order they were found. Items could include leaves, grass, feathers, bones or flowers.

At the end of the walk the group can recall the journey they have taken by discussing what they found and where they found the items. Why did people choose certain things and what are the similarities and differences between people's collections? If the end of the wool is tied to the end of the twig the memory stick can be taken home and remain a memory of the day's experience.

See: *Nicky's memory cone*

A mini-beast's life

Aim: To look close up at a variety of little creatures found in grassland and to reflect on their ways of living their lives.

Need: Sweep net, lots of stoppered glass or plastic capsules/bottles, at least the same number as there are people taking part. Magnifying glasses.

Instructions: On a warm fine day in July or August go to a meadow with long grass. Use the sweep net (see below for how to make one) to catch various creatures living in the grass. Place one creature per glass container and pass them around the group to look at. A magnifying glass helps here. So does an identification guide with good pictures and text that tells you more about the animals.

When everyone has had a good look at all the creatures ask people to choose a mini-beast and take it in its glass tube. Have people spend some time with their chosen mini-beast, looking at its colours, size, physical make-up and so on. Use the wildlife books to find out more, but this is by no means essential to the enjoyment of seeing the creature close up. Make sure the creature is not kept too hot in bright sunlight but is observed in the shade of the observer's body.

When everyone has had time to appreciate the beauty and complexity of their creature the time has come to release it. Each person is to find their own space in the meadow and gently release their mini-beast. It is best to let the creature go slowly and in a place where it can be observed easily once it has crawled out of the glass container. Encourage people to look at their chosen creature and watch how it lives its life. It may just disappear into the deep grass stems and that is just as telling of its intentions as one that sits still. See if the observers can imagine what it is like to live as this creature.

- Make a sweep net from an old pillowcase and coat hanger by sewing the open end of the pillowcase over a modified coat hanger that is formed into an approximate round shape. Use the straightened-out hook of the hanger as a handle. Drag the net through tall grass.

- Clean out small plastic tubs/herb jars to make observation containers.

- The best identification guide for Britain and the rest of Northern Europe is *Insects of Britain and Western Europe* by Michael Chinery (2012). *Small Woodland Creatures* by Lars-Henrik Olsen, Jakob Sunesen and Bente Vita Pedersen (2001) is also very good.

See: *Interview with nature*

Mirror exercise

Aims: To enable someone to have a new view of natural surroundings. To see the familiar in a different way.

Needs: A set of small mirrors, one per person. I have a collection of mirrors from a variety of sources, such as old compact cases and mirrored bathroom tiles. They have to have smooth edges to avoid anyone cutting themselves. Woodland is the best place to try this activity.

Instructions: The idea is to walk along a woodland path while looking in the mirror. It is held horizontally so that it's possible to see what is above the observer. You can try this with the mirror at waist height or by holding it resting on the end of your nose. Either way you can quickly become skilled at looking in the mirror while keeping an eye out in your peripheral vision to see where you are going. Trust me, it works! Take care not to accidentally look at the sun.

Mirror view of oak tree above

My connection to nature

Aim: To spend time creatively expressing your connection to nature.

Needs: Plenty of time, at least 45 minutes to 1½ hours depending on group size. A whistle. Somewhere where people can find a variety of natural objects.

Instructions: Say something like:

'This is an opportunity to respond to today's events in a creative way. I'm going to suggest that you explore the question: What is my relationship with the rest of nature?

Sit for a while to relax and centre yourself. I suggest a short period of mindfulness. In your own time move off, always keeping in sight of me. Look for somewhere where you can create something that is a response to the question. You can use anything you can find around you. Take your time. When you have finished come back and tell me, I will stay here. If after a long time you don't come back I will blow a whistle sounding like this (demonstrate) and I'd like you to return immediately.

When everyone has returned we will go on a gallery walk and visit what people have made. If you don't want us to see what you have made that is fine, you don't need to show us.'

When everyone has returned explain the next step.

'We will be led by the person showing their piece and follow their instructions on how to approach their work and where to stand. The person can just show their piece or they can talk about it, it's up to them. Others can ask questions to gain understanding or clarification, or they can make a statement, beginning "If it were mine I would want to know…" to avoid interpreting or psychologising someone else.'

There is a reason for the last instruction asking for no interpretation or psychologising. These interventions have the effect of taking us away from what the speaker/client is actually saying. They are abstractions from experience. I am interested in encouraging people to become more aware of what they are experiencing rather than relying on other people interpreting meaning for them. It is a philosophy as well as a style of working with people which I believe is empowering for the speaker.

My special place in nature

Adapted from an activity I did on a Joseph Cornell workshop.

Aim: To allow each individual to select a special place in nature – a place to be mindful and creative.

Needs: For each person an A4-size board (made of card), a pencil, a bin bag to sit on and a copy of the handout below.

Instructions: Give out the handout to everyone and talk the group through it. Allow plenty of time, saying that you will stay in one place and when everyone has had time they are to return to you. If time has run out you will call with your whistle.

When everyone is back you can discuss how things went and what made their place special. If it feels appropriate people can pair up and take one other person to show them their special place.

My special place in nature

Take a short walk from here and wander around until you find a place where you feel comfortable. Find somewhere to sit down and consider these questions.

What are some of the first things you notice about your special place?

How do you feel being here?

Draw a sketch of your special place.

What can you hear? Can you hear at least five sounds? See if you can figure out who or what is making them.

Find something that makes you smile. What is it?

Why is it important to you to spend time in nature? Can you express that in a poetic or persuasive way?

MY SPECIAL PLACE IN NATURE

Nature makes an appearance

Aim: To encourage a relaxed curiosity and permission to stop and take in any situation that arises. You can be a role model for this process, although this is likely to occur spontaneously in the group anyway.

Need: Nothing.

Instructions: As you walk along be alert to activity around you and up ahead. Use any excuse to stop the group and just look. It could be a butterfly on the path, a circling hawk or a feeding rabbit. The mode of being is one of open exploration, not serious searching, and taking time by walking without a goal in mind.

  If the group is moving fast or too deep in conversation with each other it might be appropriate to stop and mentally rest. You can suggest the group stops and does a breathing exercise or stands with their eyes closed listening to sounds around them before continuing the walk in the manner described here.

Nicky's memory cone

The occupational therapist Nicky Tann has a regular ecotherapy group in Dagenham for people with memory difficulties. She came up with a development of the *Memory stick* activity which I really like.

Aim: A way of collecting memories from a walk.

Needs: One big pine cone per person. You will need to keep your eye out in parks and ornamental woodlands for a pine that has shed all its old brown cones. Monterey and maritime pine cones are my favourites for this activity, but most will be of some use.

Instructions: Give everyone a pine cone. You could spend time at the beginning discussing the structure of the cone: how the scales spiral round the cone and get bigger higher up. The pine will have shed all its seeds from high up on the tree, two from beneath each scale.

   The idea is to find interesting things on the walk that can be saved by poking them beneath a scale: things like dead leaves, grass seed heads, flowers and bird feathers will do.

   At the end of the walk each member of the group is invited to talk about their decorated cone. The completed cone can be used to recall where each item was found and why it was chosen. If people want to they can take the cone home with them as a memento from the walk.

See: *Memory stick*

A pine cone decorated with September flowers and fruit

Off the beaten track

Susan Laut told me this activity and I've adapted it from an imaginary to a literal situation.

Aim: To experience how you can raise awareness by doing something different from what you have always done in the past, using the path as a metaphor for a habitual way of being.

Need: A grassy or open area of forest with a path crossing it.

Instructions: Go to a grassy area and walk up and down an existing path that goes through the grass, preferably a path that is surfaced or bare earth. Talk about how the path may have originally become worn by people's repetitive walking along the same way and how we often don't think about where we are going if we go down a familiar path. It becomes a habit.

A change of tack now. Ask the group members to imagine the path is a negative feeling, for example one from childhood when we had less control and awareness of our lives. Talk about how a repetitive feeling from a past event can get us stuck in a particular way of feeling, thinking and behaving. We reinforce the same feeling by going over the same ground, just as this path was created.

Suggest that the group walks off the path into the grass and individuals make a choice not to walk along the path. At this point take people into the long grass or forest. Some may need encouragement to follow you. Lead everyone into the wild areas. Don't go into anywhere unpleasant but wander among long grass or thick bushes.

Ask:

'How does that feel? Unfamiliar, harder work and more conscious?'

Say something along the lines of:

'However, we don't get the same feeling we had on the path and we are more aware of ourselves and the environment around us. We can work at choosing not to feel a particular feeling, such as anger or sadness, if we get away from the situations that trigger it. We may also discover a greater awareness of ourselves and how we are once we are off the beaten track.'

After walking 'off piste' for a while have the group gather round to discuss what it felt like to walk on the path and then off the path. You could discuss the notion that our feelings are not us but something we experience. Nearly all feelings that stay around are old memories we can do without. So what ruts do we get ourselves into emotionally?

You could discuss the risks involved in walking off the path, but also the creative opportunities to have new experiences, some of which may enrich our lives and allow us to get away from the old ways.

You could also discuss other ways of bringing new experiences into our lives that make us re-evaluate negative stuff. Examples can include travel, meeting new people, watching a new TV programme with an open mind, eating new food or listening to a genre of music you are unfamiliar with. Even walking a longer way to the shops or work can be very revealing and helpful in our efforts to change old habits and feelings.

Ask:

'How many of you do the ecotherapy activities you like outside of the session in your own time? Is that about changing a pattern?'

Physical and relaxation warm-ups

Aim: These activities are in the main based on the idea that if you are physically loosened up then your mind will also be more relaxed.

Need: Nothing.

Instructions: For each warm-up use the instructions and demonstrate as follows:

Loosening up

Place your hands on your knees and rotate your knees round; after a while go the other way. Place your hands on your waist and rotate your hips round; after a while go the other way. Rotate the neck very slowly just using the weight of the head to roll round one way and then the other. If there is any sign of stiffness or pain ease off or stop. Stand upright and very slowly flop your head forwards, then down to the upper chest, waist, hips, until with legs still straight your arms are hanging down towards the ground. The idea is not to touch the ground but to relax all the back muscles. Notice, as you hang downwards, how with each breath your body can relax a bit more and your hands go that bit closer to the ground. Now reverse the process very slowly by lifting the hips, then waist and then chest, followed by neck and head. The exercise can be repeated a few times if you want.

Do-in Chinese fist massage

Form the hand into a fist, and using the flat part of the fist formed by the second finger digits and base of the palm firmly tap the body repeatedly. Start with the torso from the shoulders front and back down the chest and round the lower back, then gently tap the soft abdomen and continue round to tap firmly on the buttocks. Then work on each limb in turn; starting from the shoulders work your way down all sides of the other arm. When doing the legs it is possible to use both fists. The whole exercise can be finished off with a gentle finger-tapping massage of the scalp and face which should feel like heavy rain falling on your skin.

Scooping leaves

Bend knees with arms wide out and bring arms in as if to scoop leaves up as you reach the bottom of the crouch. Then rise up with arms crossing on your front, continue by stretching arms above head and down to horizontal. Repeat a few times. This is good for getting the blood circulating because the thigh muscles are asked to do all the work.

Self-massage

Massage the neck and shoulders. You can vigorously tap the scalp with all your fingers before massaging the top of the head. A self face massage is also good to do. Pay particular attention to the sides of the jaw and around the eye sockets.

Bear scratch

I have been told that vigorously brushing or scratching the skin is good for the lymphatic system, which transports cells that play an important part in our immune system. The lymphatic system does not have a pump like the heart and so depends on physical movement to shift cells and fluid around the body. Whatever the explanation, this activity feels good!

Ask everyone in the group to imagine they are a bear or monkey with an itch. Have a good old scratch of your body - all over. Even if you don't have an itch a good scratch can be very satisfying.

See: *Physical relaxation exercises*

Physical relaxation exercises

Aims: To relax people. To put them in touch with their bodies. A stage in getting in touch with nature.

Need: An open space with plenty of room, level clear ground.

Instructions: I say something like this to the group:

> 'These exercises are intended to relax your body but the consequences are many. We know that tension in the mind is held in the body. You only have to look at the language we use to describe many emotions; a person is a "pain in the neck" or someone can't "stomach that". By moving our bodies we can unlock tensions and free up energy to be more alive. These exercises also encourage the blood to circulate more fully. Also, the lymphatic system, which protects us from disease, does not have a heart to pump round its fluid but relies on muscle movement to reach all parts of the body.
>
> The exercises are also a good way to get to know and enjoy our body. Our body is the only one we have and yet so many people believe they do not have

a nice body. They make the mistake of comparing themselves with airbrushed media images which are often stereotypical and uninteresting.

As with sex and dancing, it is not what your body looks like so much as what you can feel and do with your body that is most important. Use this opportunity to get to know your body and enjoy its movement.'

Stance

Give instructions and demonstrate as follows:

'Stand with legs about shoulder width apart, body straight but relaxed, arms hanging loose. Ensure your weight is balanced on both the ball and heel of the foot. Feet should be parallel. Relax the ankle, knee and hip joints to give a springy sense to your stance as if you were about to ski. You should feel a firmer weight on the soles of your feet by standing so. This is the stance adopted by martial arts people to lower their energy and give a better sense of solidity and balance. In other situations it is good to adopt this stance if you are feeling anxious or if you are confronting someone.

It is important with all these exercises that you do the movements in a relaxed way with the minimum of effort, as if you are gently whisking a fly away.

It is also important not to push yourself. Move your body as far as it wants to go. It will stretch over time. If you push muscles while exercising they respond by contracting even more and you could strain yourself. The "no pain no gain" idea is a macho fallacy!

Be aware of stance, look around, notice where you are, let go of time and concerns and give yourself up to the present.'

Limb loosening

Lead the group through the exercise as follows:

'Begin by relaxing the hands and gently shaking them. The hands should be floppy as if you are shaking water off them while you are looking for a towel.

Then bring in the elbows followed by the shoulders so both your arms feel rubbery. If any of the movements hurt ease off or stop doing it.

Work on the shoulders specifically now. Roll them forwards a few times as if you are putting a heavy coat on. You can raise your shoulders up to your ears in a hunch, let go and allow them to drop. Now rotate your shoulders backwards a few times as if you were taking a rucksack off your back.

Now pay attention to the legs. In turn shake each leg much like the way you shook your arms. Begin by shaking the ankle, move up to the knee then hip, and then shake the whole leg in a floppy way.

We can hold a lot of tension in our neck and so it is good to do this exercise but important not to strain the muscles. The intention should be to let go to the direction of movement rather than force anything. Take it slowly. The neck can be turned sideways left and right, down, up and back, and rotated in a floppy manner to trace a circle. Do it slowly with awareness.

Plant the feet firmly on the ground. Stand upright and turn the spine left and right. No other muscles are involved, the arms just move because the spine moves. There should be a carefree attitude to this exercise: you can imagine all your tensions sliding down your relaxed arms and flowing off the end of your fingertips. Take it easy and if there is any sign of pain in the spine ease off the effort of moving.

You should now feel warmer and more relaxed.'

A place, a word, a poem

Aim: To reflect on an experience in nature and to express it in writing.

Needs: For each person: a clipboard, blank paper and a pencil. Polythene carrier bags to sit on.

Instructions: I got the idea from a workshop I attended that was led by Joseph Cornell and then adapted it. It is a good activity for a reflective time when people have moved into a deeper connection to the natural world around them. As people take in what they experience in nature they have an opportunity to connect with what is going on inside themselves as well.

I give out the writing materials and say something like this:

'Choose a place you feel comfortable in, somewhere that attracts you for whatever reason. Sit down and spend a few minutes getting to know the place. Notice the sounds, shapes, colours and movement around you.

If you notice a bird moving about imagine if you can what it must feel like to be moving like the bird. If you see a tree moving in the wind I wonder if you can feel what it must be like to be the tree, in your mind and your emotions.

After a while being in this special place think of a word that captures the place or feeling. Write the letters vertically down the page on the left. You can use each letter to begin each line of your poem.

I wrote this poem in a wood after sitting and looking at an old birch tree.

B *ole twisted and contorted*
I *n lively forms*
R *oots matted out in all directions*
C *alm breeze and birdsong move around*
H *ow at home I feel beneath you*

A *ncient past exposed, beneath*
G *reen showers of myriad leaves*
E *nergy of living forms shared between us.*

Have a go yourself and see what comes up – you may be surprised!
Come back here when you have finished or when I blow the whistle.'

When everyone has returned I have people sit in threes and read out the poems to each other. I then meet as a big group and ask if anyone is willing to read out their poem to the whole group.

Poetry for reflection

Aim: To use the poet's eye to stimulate a thoughtful, reflective approach to being in nature.

Needs: Copies of a selection of poems to do with nature, one set for each person to take home with them. Poems can be chosen for their seasonal relevance, habitat (river or woodland for example) or mood. I also use prose quotes from writers who capture something of the experience of being in nature.

Instructions: I have made a collection on my computer of accessible poems that mean something to me, ones I can read with conviction to a group. I then mix and match them for a particular group and print off a set of sheets for everyone. I have listed a few examples below and there are some quotes on my website.[10]

When the group has been outdoors for some time I find a suitable place for us to read the poems. It is important to read the poems very slowly so that each line can be savoured before the next image or thought comes along. I might read the poem a few times as another way for listeners to take in the meaning.

The first time I did the activity I wasn't sure how it had been received. The group were part of a research project and everyone had been diagnosed as depressed or anxious. Most people said very little. Some people said they found poetry difficult to understand, others were more appreciative. I have persisted and have had the same mixed response from other groups. The week following my first attempt to introduce poetry was a turning point though. A woman came up to me and said she had written a few poems during the week. They were good, not sentimental rhyming couplets, but well constructed. This was the first time she had written poetry in her life. She continued to bring along beautiful pieces which explored what effects being in nature had on her state of mind.

Examples of writing you could use

Mary Oliver, 'Wild geese'

Mary Oliver, 'The sun'

John Clare, 'Wood rides'

Mike Bernhardt, 'My grief lives on in me'

W.H. Davies, 'Leisure'

Ted Hughes, 'River'

---

10   See www.andymcgeeney.com

A question for nature

Aim: To use the metaphorical qualities of the natural world to help resolve a personal question.

Need: Nothing.

Instructions: Gather the group together when you are somewhere outdoors and say something like this:

> 'This activity may work for you or it may not. Give it a try. You may also think I am asking something improbable of you; if that is the case you can pretend it works as an experiment.
>
> I want you to consider a question or a dilemma you have been working on in your mind and don't seem to be able to resolve. Keep it to yourself – I won't ask you to divulge it, unless you want to. I want you to hold the issue in your mind as you go for a walk on your own for the next 10 minutes. Just be open to what is going on around you, don't force or go looking for an answer: it doesn't work that way. If something takes your attention follow it and become absorbed in observing.
>
> At the end of the walk reflect on what you have experienced, and if it has worked the response from nature will come spontaneously. You won't have to think it, it will come to you.'

Scavenger search

Aim: To explore and look intently for things in nature using different senses.

Needs: For each person an A5/A6 printed sheet with a list of things to scavenge and a small brown paper bag (re-used from the greengrocer) to collect things in.

Instructions: Scavenger search lists can be found in lots of books and websites on outdoor activities for children. You can adapt the list to suit your needs, which depend on the age and abilities of the people, the habitat and the particular aims of your session.

I usually get people in pairs because I think it's more fun to share the activity. I give out the Scavenger list sheets and collecting bags and give a few guidelines such as: return when you have collected all the items; don't go to far in the woods or you might get lost; come back to me when you hear my whistle blow three times; don't damage anything living unless it is to take one leaf from a plant.

When everyone has returned you can discuss everyone's finds. Did they get the whole list? What was easiest or hardest to find? Was there any dispute about, for example, 'something perfectly straight'? You can also add interest by talking about the objects: the different textures, smells, shapes and so on. If you know some biological or ecological information share that with the group as well.

The Alternative list contains some more interesting and maybe challenging objects but these can provoke interesting discussions. What is beautiful in nature? Do you get *perfectly* round things in nature? What is of no use in nature? Everything in nature is recycled as food for something.

At the end, if people don't want to take anything home with them, the objects can be returned to where they came from. You can take a bin bag with you to put the litter in if you used that item on your list.

Some additional activities

What do I have?

Ask everyone to look around for something interesting from the forest floor that they can pick up in their hands. Ask them to hide it from others by covering it with their hands, then find a partner and stand back to back. They take it in turns to describe the object they have in their hands to the other person until they guess its identity.

Alternatively they can get the partner to draw what they think it is from the description they give them. This is a good exercise in communication.

What do you have?

Do as the above activity only this time they face their partner who should have their eyes closed. They should have the partner open their hands in front of them. They begin by stroking their hands with the object and ask them what they feel. They then place the object on their hands and ask them to describe what it feels like and guess what they think it is.

Search without collecting

Ask people to go off and find things without a sheet or collecting bag. One way I've done this is to call out contrasting pairs of characteristics, such as rough/smooth, hard/soft, green/red, dead/alive, light/dark. Sometimes the group catches on and other people start calling out pairs of traits.

Scavenger list

An oak leaf

A seed

Something round

Something sharp

Something perfectly straight

A chewed leaf (not by you!)

Something white

Something hollow

Something that makes a noise

Something soft

Something dead

Something that begins with the letter B

A leaf that has hairs on

Additional items which could be added

Feather

One seed dispersed by the wind

Exactly 100 of something

A beech leaf

A thorn

A bone

Three different kinds of seeds

One camouflaged animal or insect

Part of an egg

Something fuzzy

A piece of fur

Five pieces of litter left by people (avoid anything harmful, such as broken glass, sharp metal or needles)

Something beautiful

Something that is of no use in nature

Something important in nature

Something that reminds you of yourself

If you live by the sea you can create a beach version of this activity.

See: *Seaside activities*

Seaside activities

A trip to the seaside offers many new experiences and sensations

Introduction to *Seaside activities*

Doing some mindfulness based activities can make a trip to the seaside even more memorable. I want to thank Sophie Jeffery for creating most of these activities for a great day out in Kent.

Beach mandala

Aim: A creative activity using materials found on the shoreline.

Need: An untidy beach with driftwood and jetsam.

Instructions: The group is asked to make a mandala (a circular plan representing the self or a situation) using driftwood and other found objects. The group can be sent off for 20 minutes to collect interesting things they find on the beach and bring them back to a flat open area. While everyone is off foraging the leader can mark out a circular boundary using stones or driftwood.

Once the mandala has been created you can have interesting discussions on your artwork. What does the mandala say about the place, is it representative or are some things missing? How could this be remedied? What does the mandala say about the group and your interests?

Someone could photograph the mandala from above and if you repeated the activity in different places and seasons some further patterns of activity may arise.

Beach scavenger search

Aim: To explore and look intently for things on the shoreline.

Needs: For each person an A5/A6 printed sheet with a list of things to scavenge and a small brown paper bag (re-used from the greengrocer) to collect things in. You could give out egg boxes for the same purpose.

Instructions: See the activity *Scavenger search* for instructions which can be adapted for a beach.

See: *Stone in my heart* for an activity using pebbles.

Birds' feathers

Aim: To pay attention to birds' feathers found on the beach.

Need: The best time to look for feathers is in July and August when birds moult. They have finished breeding and some are getting ready for migration at this time of year.

Instructions: In July and August ask the group to collect different feathers on the shoreline and see if they can work out which part of the bird they come from and what species they are from. You could do this activity in any other habitat, such as lakes and woodland. The group could make something from the feather collection and leave it on the beach for others to find.

A good book to use if you want to try to identify which bird and which part of the body a feather came from is *Tracks and Signs of the Birds of Britain and Europe* (Brown *et al.* 1992).

Changing tides

Aims: Working with change. To become aware of the changing tides.

Need: A shoreline.

Instructions: Check tide times for your coastal location on the Internet and visit the shoreline at high tide. About six hours later the tide will be at its lowest and another six hours brings it back to high tide again.

If you are doing activities on the beach for a day you could take time out to observe the tide points at their highest and lowest. Consider the passage of time through a single tide. Reflect on the role of the moon (is it in the sky while you are outdoors maybe?) pulling the earth's water towards it. High tides occur when there is a new moon and at the equinoxes. Consider the powerful inevitability of the tides – 'time and tides wait for no man' said Shakespeare. They remind us of the need to work with nature, not be frustrated by it. Many people in the past, such as fishermen, ferrymen and sailors, lived their lives guided by the tides.

Geology of place

Aim: To increase awareness of the environment and of changes in the earth.

Need: A rocky coast, a local/regional geological map and a book on identifying rocks. The British Geological Survey has put maps on the web for free.[11] You can find out about the rocks beneath your feet anywhere in Britain by zooming in to your street or countryside.

Instructions: Suggest the following to the group.

'Find out what types of rocks make up the area where you are standing. Are they made of sandstone, limestone or volcanic rocks? Do you know how old they are and how they were formed? What was living on the earth at that time?'

See: *Visualisation: Our evolutionary story*, which could be read after exploring the rocks.

Message in a bottle

Aim: A fun activity for the group, particularly the discussion on what to write.

Need: Paper and pencil, an old cork stopper or piece of polythene and string, and thin wire or strong nylon string. And you have to have found an abandoned bottle, of course. As a back up you could bring a spare bottle in case one isn't found on the beach.

Instructions: Ask the group members to think about a positive message they would like to give a stranger walking along the beach, and then write it on a piece of

---

11   See www.bgs.ac.uk

paper and put it in a bottle. They should stop up the end with a cork or tie a piece of polythene over the top and launch it into the sea on an outgoing tide.

Who knows where the bottle will end up or who will discover it? There are accounts of coded shrimp net ties drifting on the Gulf Stream from Newfoundland in Canada to Cornwall in England.

There is a section of Woolacombe beach in Devon that receives shells from the Caribbean.

See: *Changes in nature*

Sea rhythms

Aim: Relaxation and mindfulness.

Need: A clean dry beach to lie on. You could use bin liners if people are concerned about getting sand on their clothes.

Instructions: The activity works well on a pebbly beach as the sea makes rhythmic churning sounds over the stones.

Tell the group to lie on the beach, close their eyes and get comfortable. You can then talk them through a relaxation exercise. Encourage a mindful state of being. You could suggest that instead of attending to the breath they follow the rhythms of the sea as it flows back and forth over the pebbles.

Stone tower

Aim: A fun activity.

Need: A pebbly or stony beach.

Instructions: The group are instructed to spread out along the beach and for everyone to make a tower. They can use whatever materials they can find on the beach within a defined period of time, say 30 minutes. You can give more time if needed. Big towers can be made out of large heavy stones or logs and smaller versions can be created from pebbles or shells. If there is an incoming tide the group can watch as the sea devours their work. There is more about natural cairns on page 201.

Stone towers on the beach

See with the mind then the heart

Aim: To learn to shift ways of seeing, between seeing with the mind and with the heart.

Need: An open area, for example at a woodland edge, where people can spread out and see some distance ahead.

Instructions: Encourage people to spread out but make sure they can still hear you. Face outwards into an open area. Explain that we are going to alternate our way of seeing the world, moving between two ways. This exercise can also be done walking slowly.

Say something like:

'First look with the mind. Search for things of interest. Take your eyes to things around you. Notice their qualities - texture, shape, colour and so on. Look ahead and predict where you might be going.

After a minute or so switch to seeing from the heart. Just as the eye is an extension of the brain looking out, imagine you have an open heart to the world in the middle of your chest seeing out. Soften the gaze, defocus a bit and let the world come to you without you having to make any effort. Pay attention to how you feel right now about what you can see. Do your emotions stay the same or shift? How do you feel about what you are seeing? Can you be loving to the natural world around you, accepting all you come across without judgement?'

Go back to seeing with the mind and repeat the instructions above, then see with the heart as instructed.

A discussion can follow to allow people to express their responses to the different modes of being.

Metta – loving kindness in nature

If it seems appropriate with your group you could try a variation on the above activity based a Buddhist practice. I have adapted this activity from Coleman (2006).

Give the following instructions:

'Go on a slow walk and if something attracts your attention, go to it. Pay full attention to it. Become fascinated by it. Use all the senses of sight, touch, smell, sound. Open up your heart to the object in nature. Look as if you are looking onto the face of your beloved.

Notice your responses. How does your body feel? Your heart? What would you say if you were to write a love letter to this object of your attention? Use a Buddhist phrase: "May you be safe, healthy, and happy, and live with ease."

Once you feel complete with doing this with one object try to do it with everything you come across. Do it with people, things you don't like, yourself. If you don't feel any of these feelings just be attentive and accepting as a part of loving. Don't expect or demand anything specific to happen. But be aware, notice what arises in you.'

Note that this activity takes practice.

Silent walking

Aim: To increase awareness. To encourage people to explore their natural surroundings in a group without needing to talk to others.

Need: A quiet undisturbed area. Somewhere open that people can walk across would be ideal.

Instructions: Tell people something like this:

'We are going to go for a silent walk. To take our time experiencing nature around us. I will let you know when you can talk again. We are going in this direction (point to where you want people to go) and I want you to keep behind me and not overtake so that the pace is kept slow.

We spend so much time rushing around in our lives that it is easy to miss the beauty and fascination around us. Move slowly, and give yourself permission to stop at any point to really pay attention to something that catches your eye or ear. Rather than searching for something to look at much like a hunter does when looking for prey, let things come to your attention, be open to the world.

Take your time, enjoy, there is no goal, nothing to achieve today.'

How long you do the walk in silence depends on the group. In my experience if a group has got it they will continue in silence even when you give permission to talk because the experience has been so powerful and profound. You can start by taking a group for 10–20 minutes and see how things develop. It is the sort of thing you can do at any time it seems appropriate.

You may want to allow some time after the walk to process the experience in pairs or as a group. For many people this deceptively simple instruction – to not talk, to be aware – can be very moving. You are giving time and permission to fall in love with the beauty around us.

Smell like a fox

Aim: To increase sensory awareness.

Need: An area in woodland or grassland with fairly dry ground free of nettles, brambles or other possibly irritating plants. Maybe polythene carrier bags for people to kneel on.

Instructions: Say something like:

'Foxes smell really strong and musky so I am not suggesting you give off the scent of a fox! I am suggesting you could smell with your nose to the ground like a fox does. Foxes and dogs have much more sensitive noses than us, but if you get as close to the ground as a fox's nose it's amazing how much you can smell.'

With a group you can't take this activity too seriously. You are going to have to persuade everyone to get down on all fours and sniff the ground like a fox!

Have everyone get down low on hands and knees on a dry area of grassland to start with. Encourage people to put their nose just above the ground. Tell them they are allowed to use their front paws to disturb the ground or crush leaves. Ask them what they can smell.

Tell them to crush leaves, scrape the ground, check out different vegetation and soils, look up occasionally and smell the breeze. Ask:

'What do you notice about your sense of smell? What do you notice about what is going on close to the ground? How would it be if you could smell with your feet?'

Social warm-ups

Social warm-ups are useful for a variety of reasons. Most frequently they are used as icebreakers at the start of a workshop to loosen inhibitions and break away from any serious discussion which might have taken place right at the beginning. They are a leveller, an opportunity to let go of self-presentations, and a chance to be childlike, leading to a state of childlike curiosity and open wonder. I have used the Rainstorm as a physical warm-up when some people have been feeling the cold.

If you enjoy the activities here I suggest you look for books on cooperative games, icebreakers and team building for further inspiration.

Aim: Icebreakers. If you have a group that needs loosening up at the start of a workshop here are a few fun things you can do.

Need: A sense of humour and a willingness to let go yourself. The bigger the group the better it will be.

Instructions: For each warm-up follow the instructions below.

Blind run

Two rows of people form two sides of a narrow funnel. The last pair at the end of the funnel are very close together. Each person holds their arms out in front of them at shoulder height like tentacles. A volunteer runs into the funnel from the wide end, with eyes closed, as fast as they can. The tentacles tell the runner where to go, forwards, backwards, between them and so on, and stop the runner from falling over. Two people stand at the end to stop the runner. This is a slightly scary risk-taking activity that gets the adrenaline going, but fun with the right group.

See: *Ecosystem milling* begins like a warm-up but then takes people much deeper. *The web of life* can also be a warm-up to a session.

Come together

The intention is to get people to be in bodily contact according to your instructions. You can begin with suggesting pairs and add more of a challenge by calling out threes or fours. The leader can join in if there is someone who isn't able to pair up. Between each contact people are asked to mill around in a defined area.

Call out things like:

back to back

head to head

knee to knee

toe to toe

hand to toe

elbow to knee

fingertips.

Human tangle

Ask the group to form a close circle shoulder to shoulder. Each person puts a hand in the middle and holds on to someone else's free hand. Then everyone puts their other hand in and finds another hand to hold. The challenge now is to disentangle the knot and form a big circle!

Rainstorm

This is a good activity if you want to have a bit of fun or if the weather is cold. The sounds created by the following sequence of actions imitate the build-up and passing of a storm.

Ask the group to form a circle. Then say:

'The rule is: do what the person on your right is doing - not what I am doing. Unless I'm the person on your immediate right that is!'

Begin by *rubbing your hands together* to create a sound like the wind coming. The person on your left copies you while you continue to perform the action. Gradually the action spreads round until everyone is doing it. Keep it going until you want to move on to the next action. Do the same process with each action, checking that people are not jumping the gun and starting before the person on their right has begun the action.

The sequence of actions is:

Rubbing your hands together	wind coming
Clicking fingers	first raindrops
Clap hands	heavier rain
Slap thighs	really heavy rain
Stamp on floor and slap thighs	rain and thunder
Slap thighs	really heavy rain
Clap hands	heavier rain
Clicking fingers	last raindrops
Rubbing your hands together	wind dying down

Zest circle

This one is good if the group is flagging a little or is getting a bit cold.

Ask the group to form a circle and hold hands throughout the exercise. Expand the circle to be as wide as possible. Have everyone crouch down slightly and move forwards to the centre. As they move forwards ask them to rise up to full height and even raise their arms high when they reach the centre of the circle. As the group moves to the centre they are to shout, as loudly as possible, the 'stretched out' word 'Zest!' - Zzzzzzzzz eeeeeeee sssssss T! With the final 't' all arms go into the air. Repeat until energised.

Sound map

Adapted from an activity I experienced on a workshop with Joseph Cornell (see Cornell 2015).

Aim: To give people an opportunity to really focus on listening in nature.

Needs: A rich natural environment such as open woodland or coast, preferably with lots of different birdsong. Spring and early summer are best.

A pencil, a sheet of blank paper and a hard surface for each person. You can make a set of hard surfaces from sheets of A4 cardboard cut from boxes. You may need bin bags for people to sit on if the ground is damp.

Instructions: Explain the activity saying something like this:

'The purpose of this activity is to heighten your awareness of the sounds around you.

I want you to find somewhere to sit on your own, but don't go too far. Make sure you can't see anyone else from the direction you are facing. You have at least 10 minutes; I will call you on the whistle when the time is up.

Begin by just sitting on the ground. You could lean against a tree, close your eyes or look down at the ground. When you are settled go into the mindfulness breathing exercise we do for five minutes.

Then continue to relax and be open to all that is going on around you, particularly sounds. Just sit and listen to all the sounds around you, take your time. Then begin to focus your hearing on different sounds around you, both near and far. What do you hear? Where do the sounds come from and what qualities do they have?

Take the pencil and paper and create a sound map using lines, drawings and patterns of your own making to represent each sound. Begin by putting a cross in the centre of the page to represent yourself. Draw or write around the cross.'

When the group reassembles you can discuss how people got on. For some people the experience can be quite profound. I have been told that doing the activity was the first time a person had really listened to natural sounds, and how amazing it was.

See: *Cat's ears, Dawn chorus walk, Listening to silence, Sounds as music, Wind in the willows*

Stone in my heart

I learnt this activity a long time ago from someone whose name I can't remember and then adapted it to suit my needs.

Aim: To raise awareness of negative emotions or thoughts and how they are not us but something we carry around with us in a way that is a limitation. In time we can sometimes choose to let go of these thoughts or emotions.

Needs: This activity works well if you have a beach, exposed riverbed or area of bare gravelly soil along your walk. If that is not possible you could make a collection of pebbles and bring a bag of them to the group.

Instructions: The activity could be carried out with anything natural but I have chosen to use a pebble. At a suitable point on a walk ask everyone to find a small smooth pebble and to clean it up. The pebble is chosen to represent some aspect of themselves they don't like. Encourage people to spend a moment reflecting on what it is they want the pebble to represent: a fear, a personal characteristic or irrational belief. Then they are to put the pebble in their pocket and carry it around with them for a month. The temptation is to get used to it as an object and to forget its symbolic meaning. They are to give the pebble attention whenever they come across it, which means to remember the thought and imagine it embodied in the stone and not truly as part of themselves.

After a month remind everyone about the pebble and invite comments on what happened. Did they do the activity and how did it go? If anyone wants to they could tell everyone what their pebble represented.

You can ask:

'Is anyone ready to let go of the feelings associated with the pebble?'

Can they let go of the emotion or come to accept it as a part of themselves? Ask everyone who wants to reconcile themselves with the feeling or thought to find somewhere to bury the pebble and leave the associations to compost in the ground or be carried away by the waters of the stream to the sea.

A story from today in nature

I developed this activity from experiences in my own life. I adapted it heavily as a result of an activity I did on a Ronen Berger workshop. I subsequently read the ideas behind it in the work of Mooli Lahad and Ronen Berger, which in turn was based on their drama therapy work with children experiencing stress. I like the use of the universal hero's myth structure in the story applied to an individual's life.

Aim: After time in nature people are invited to write a story relating to themselves and to use the structure of a mythic tale as a way of exploring their life.

Needs: Sets of instructions handouts (see the downloadable handout below and online), blank A4 paper, pens, pencils (some coloured), clipboards and carrier bags or similar to sit on if the ground is damp.

Instructions: I use this activity towards the end of a day's workshop as a way for people to respond creatively to their experience of a deeper connection to nature. I suggest you find a place surrounded by trees where people can spread out and lean against a tree and write quietly.

There are three stages to the activity, which can take some time to complete. Stage one is writing the story, two is making a sculpture and the last stage is showing others your creation.

I begin by talking through the instruction sheet with the group, making sure everyone understands what it is they are being asked to do and why. I may say something like this – please adapt to suit your needs and personality:

'What if anything has come up for you today? What has today's time with nature stirred up in you? I want you to weave a story as a response to today's time in nature.

Can you sense something in you that has come up as a person, thing, element, thought, feeling? I want you to spend some time waiting for that something to arise within you. When you have it I want you to weave it into a story. Trust your intuition. This is for you alone. Maybe you can't think anything; that's OK, maybe you only feel it.

When you have a notion of what it is you want to work with I want you to respond to six questions in turn using words, drawings or symbols. See if you can create an imaginative story with your responses, using these questions as prompts. It is for you and no one else to look at. Go with your creative imagination. Take your time to do this.'

Give out the instructions at this point and talk through these questions:

- *Where did she/he/it come from?* Far away/close up, long time ago, recent, now, future, eternal?

- *What does she/he/it want?* Its goal, what is it seeking/asking of you, where is it trying to reach?

- *What helps her/him/it* or the issue on the way?

- *What is the first obstacle,* challenge on the way? What stops him/her/it?

- *How does she/he/it overcome,* cope, deal with the obstacle?

- *What happens then?* How does it end?

Check everyone understands the instructions, then explain the next section which is to be done once they have completed the story:

'When you have finished creating your story I want you to make a sculpture inspired by one element in the story you created. You can use natural materials found around here or use paper. When you have finished your sculpture I'd like you to return to me here so I know you have finished and we can do the last stage. Does everyone understand what I am asking of you? OK, find somewhere among the trees where you can begin.'

Leave the clients/participants alone for a while, but maybe check on anyone who looks puzzled by the instructions. Otherwise just be there for them in one place. Be seen.

When everyone is back in the group explain the last stage. People are asked to get into threes with others they feel comfortable with. They are to walk round and look at each other's sculpture – if a person doesn't want to show others their work that's fine too.

The observers in the trio must not interpret. They can say: 'If this was my creation I would feel, think xxx.' The sculptor gets to hear multiple responses in this way and can take or leave what they hear.

The activity can end there or be added to.

The next stage might be to work with elements in the story, for example get an element to write a letter to the person at home.

Working with a single client it is possible to explore the story in more detail to clarify, challenge and develop aspects of the story.

The individual story is part of a universal story.

A story from your experience in nature today

What has come up for you today? What has today's time in nature stirred up in you? I want you to weave a story as a response to today's time in nature.

Can you sense something in you that has come up: a person, thing, element, thought, feeling? Spend some time waiting for something to arise within you. Trust your intuition. This is for you alone. Maybe you can't *think* anything. That's OK, maybe you only feel it.

I want you to respond to six questions in turn using words, drawings or symbols. See if you can create an imaginative story with your responses, using these questions as prompts. It is for you and no one else to look at. Go with your creative imagination. Don't rush, take your time, enjoy.

- *Where did she/he/it come from?* Far away/close up, long time ago, recent/now, future, eternal.

- *What does she/he/it want?* Its goal, what is it seeking/asking of you, where is it trying to reach?

- *What helps her/him/it* or the issue on the way?

- *What is the first obstacle*, challenge on the way? What stops him/her/it?

- *How does she/he/it overcome*, cope, deal, with the obstacle?

- *What happens then?* And how does it end?

Spend some time *writing down your story* on your own. You can begin on the back of this sheet. If you need more paper ask the leader.

When you have finished writing you can make a sculpture, exploring one aspect of the story. You can use natural materials you find in the wood.

When you have finished let the leader know and come back to the group for the last part of this activity.

A STORY FROM YOUR EXPERIENCE IN NATURE TODAY

Survival for a day

I am indebted to Sophie Jeffery, clinical psychologist, for devising this activity.

Aim: To become aware of our connection to nature by considering how people survived in nature.

Needs: For each team you will need a clipboard, paper and pen. A whistle. A mix of habitats, preferably with water and trees. Identification guides, foraging books and handouts of local edible plants as additional information.

Instructions: Say something like:

> 'We humans have lived in wild nature for 99 per cent of our existence and were adapted to living within the natural world in that time. One way to feel more connected to nature is to imagine how you might live in the semi-natural landscape of this area where you now live. This is bearing in mind that it is heavily degraded and much less rich in resources than it was 8000 years ago after the Ice Ages had ended.'

Divide the group up into small teams of two to five people and give each team a clipboard, paper and pen. You can also give out copies of the Collins small version of *Food for Free* by Richard Mabey (1972) or handouts giving suggested edible plants found in your area.

Ask the teams to see how well they think they could survive as a group out in the wilds for 24 hours. Give them 30 minutes for the task and ask people to come back when they hear your whistle blast. If it is permitted and is safe you could make a fire while the group are off searching.

When the teams return ask each one in turn to report back. Possible aspects to consider are shelter and protection from the weather, food, fire, water, containers, storage, sleeping places.

The ensuing discussion can highlight a range of issues such as the importance of trees to provide fuel, food, shelter, herbs and so on, and also how important it is to have knowledge of what to eat and the skills to make things such as tools, shelters and baskets. The season you do it in makes a difference of course.

You could look at any of Ray Mears's and Richard Mabey's books as background to the activity.

Texture swatch match

Aims: Sensory. To tune in to the sense of touch and increase sensitivity in nature.

Needs: A selection of textured surfaces cut into rectangles to make a set of swatches, with enough sets for a minimum of four groups.

Examples of different materials are: various cloth materials such as silk/rayon, cotton, wool; wood; metal; plastics (various textures); card; leather. Each set can be kept in an envelope or plastic bag.

Instructions: Give out a set of swatches of textured materials to each small group. Ask the groups to go in search of similar textures to the swatches. Ask:

'How close a match can you get?'

An additional activity

Each group could bring back one natural material each, hidden from view, and test it out on other people to see if they can guess what it is when it is put in their hands behind their back.

See: *Scavenger search, Colour chart match, Colour mosaic with leaves*

Thisness

Aims: To increase awareness and attention. To break down the automatisation of seeing.

Need: Nothing.

Instructions: This is a good exercise to do after a meditation and as a silent walk. The intention is to encourage people to really look at things in their environment, to notice the world around them.

Point out that it is commonplace to introduce each person in the group as a unique individual. We accept that.

Explain that you want them to do the same with things they see on a walk. Everything is unique in a way, each fruit or flower is different in some way.

Say something like:

'Walk along slowly and in silence point things out to yourself and give them a name: "this tree", "this leaf", "this path", "this wood". Really look upon each thing as unique, which it is of course.'

Discuss people's observations afterwards.

Visualisations

Introduction to *Visualisations* activities

What is visualisation?

When you imagine your next holiday and what it is you want you are visualising. When we create situations in our imagination as opposed to the real world we are visualising how things could be. The word visualisation emphasises our visual sense because that is our strongest but it is possible to create all the senses in the imaginative mind. We do this when we watch a film or someone tells us a story about a situation they were in.

Visualising is obviously safer than actually doing something. Unconsciously we recognise this and it allows us to feel freer with our imagination.

The effects on a person who is visualising are that they can draw on new thoughts and emotions which can change the way they behave later on. In sports psychology it has been found that if a basketball player imagines putting the ball in the net over and over in their mind then their scoring increases compared to someone who has just sat down and relaxed for the same length of time. It works even better if the visualisations are realistic and the person imagines making a mistake initially or has tough opponents. Likewise relaxation CDs work on the basis that a person is talked into a relaxed state. The listener is asked to imagine a situation, such as lying on a beach, which has positive associations in their mind and which reinforces the feelings of relaxation.

If you are still not convinced visualisation works try this short experiment on yourself now. Imagine going to a bowl of fruit in your house and picking up a lemon, a firm ripe one with that typical waxy and textured feel that lemons have. Now see yourself placing the lemon on a chopping board, getting a sharp knife and carefully cutting it in half. Cut one half again into a wedge and place it in your mouth. Can you experience the sharp citrus taste bursting into your mouth? Isn't it amazing how well and with how many senses you could create that scene? At what point did your mouth start salivating even though I didn't suggest that to you?

Our imagination is such a rich source of playing 'what if...', testing new possibilities and re-imagining known ideas in a novel way.

Some of the visualisations I use are not done to get someone in a relaxed state (although this may be one result) but to get them to experience the world differently. Modern science has given us interpretations of the world that are becoming myths in the original meaning of the word – cultural explanations of how things are. We have our own story of creation in the Big Bang theory of physics. Biology offers us the theories of evolution and natural selection to add to the Big Bang. Genetics offers us its own beautiful iconic emblem, the double helix. Lastly I want to mention the wonderfully interconnected relationships described in ecology. Scientific evidence has high credibility in our society and in this way it gives people permission to think something radical.

I am talking about visualisation as a way of shifting people's thinking and awareness, which, in turn, I hope, will enable them to feel more connected to nature. The mind is given something to contemplate while a person opens up to the natural world around them. It is in this way I offer the visualisations in this book.

How to do a visualisation

Not everyone likes doing a visualisation and some people find it difficult but this minority will at least benefit from the relaxation aspect. I am assuming you are going to be doing this outdoors. I've never tried doing the stories in this book indoors but I imagine it is possible. Most people find listening to recordings of birdsong and sounds of wild places relaxing. You could use them as background sounds if you were to try a visualisation indoors. I will typically take a group out on a day when it is warm enough to keep still for some time and when the ground vegetation is dry. I explain that I am going to give them a visualisation which involves them lying on the ground with their eyes shut while I talk through a scenario. I encourage them to relax and use their imagination. I will usually talk through a simple body relaxation (see *How to meditate*) before going through the visualisation itself. I suggest you use the ones in this book until you have memorised the themes and made up your own. Adapt the words and content to suit the group.

As you talk through the visualisation take your time, speak slowly with long enough pauses to allow people to create images in their mind. Think of a suitable speed of reading and go twice as slowly. Ensure your voice is matching the content and sounds in a relaxed way. Go with the group on their journey while keeping part of your mind on the process, monitoring how the story is unfolding. You may be familiar with the ideas in the story but for some people these will be a revelation and will need time to be absorbed. The listeners can reflect on the ideas later but the telling of the visualisation will be the most powerful effect.

If you are making up your own visualisations it is worth considering how the use of language can make a difference. For example, prefacing a section with permissive phrases allows the listener to feel they are in control of the process and can let go. You can say things like: 'Can you imagine…?' 'You might like to consider…' 'How would it be if…' and even 'You can imagine…or not.' Adding sensory cues like smells and sounds can increase the richness of imagery.

With most of the visualisations presented here the main intention is to add to people's awareness of how the natural world works and consequently it relies on a change in thinking more than sensory awareness. The effect can be very profound.

Honouring our ancestors

Inspired by the work of Joanna Macy from her *Harvesting the Gifts of the Ancestors* (Macy and Young Brown 1998) and Jon Cleland Host (2013).

Aims: To enable people to acknowledge the unbroken connection between themselves and their ancestors and the people they are with today. We would not be here were it not for the skills, knowledge and physical qualities our ancestors passed on to us. The story is also attempting to loosen the prevalent individualistic view and see ourselves interconnected with others through blood.

Needs: A script to get you started. Adapt and create your own as I have done. Bin bags for people to lie on.

Instructions: Find a place where people can sit or lie down in a group while you guide them through the visualisation. You can use the text below as a script before you develop your own version, perhaps incorporating regional history. Earlier versions of this process that I have come across are Eurocentric; this needs to be avoided for obvious reasons. We all have ancestors in Africa – some are more recent than others.

I think it helps to explain what you are going to do at the beginning because the process, although not difficult, may well be new to listeners. It is important to take the story particularly slowly at the beginning of the visualisation journey when people are using their memory to recall events. I'd also advise going very slowly at the beginning of the return phase in the second half as people begin to tune in to a slightly different process.

Script (about 10–15 minutes reading time)
Introduction

'We are going to do a visualisation, using your imagination to go back in time to the first humans and to return again to the present day. Whatever comes up for you is right. Feel free to creatively use your imagination as we travel back in time…

Before we begin the visualisation proper I want to explain a few things you may not have heard or thought about.

The only reason we are alive today is because of an unbroken chain of ancestors that go back to the first people and beyond. All of our ancestors must have done many things well for the generations to have continued down to the present day. It may have been because they used a quality they were born with; they may have used their inventiveness, for example. Today we are going to acknowledge the gifts they applied and in many cases passed on to the next generation.

DNA research has shown that everyone in Europe, Asia, Australasia and America is so alike that we could have descended from one group of people who began dispersing from Africa 100,000 years ago... All of humanity goes back to a single woman (Mitochondrial Eve) only 200,000 years ago in East Africa...

Considering the scientific statement above we are all related to each other by blood. However, our ancestry is not a straight line. Our ancestors continually intermarried distant relatives without knowing it. You could, for instance, be partnered with someone who is related to you genetically but this happened ten generations back. This is not a biological problem, we are all the result of this process. It is an acknowledgement that our ancestors are closer than we might think. Genetically the differences between us all here today are fractions of a percentage.

We all have four grandparents, eight great grandparents and so on, doubling each generation. After only a few centuries the number of ancestors is greater than the world population at that time, which sounds impossible. What this shows is that we all share common ancestors if we go back a few centuries.

Settle yourselves for a journey into the past and back. Let your imagination work for you and don't be too concerned about details; go with the process.'

Visualisation journey

'We are here today in the month of XXXXXX in the year 20XX resting outdoors. Can you recall something from earlier today? If so, your memory and imagination are working well...'

(Go slower in the next paragraph.)

'I wonder if you can slip backwards into last week – can you recall something which happened then...? Last month, is there something you remember?... How about last year?... Keep going back in time at your own pace, accelerating and pausing at different times of your choosing... Can you recall the you of your adolescence...and childhood?... Go back through your birth into your mother's womb. Keep going back past your own existence...into your parents before they conceived you...

Move a bit faster now through their lives and on to your grandparents. Pick one grandparent, it doesn't matter who for the journey, and go through their lives in the twentieth century, surviving a world war, as well as experiencing many exciting times... Maybe you have inherited some qualities from them, a physical feature like nose shape, perhaps a way of being that still lives on in you. Acknowledge it and move on backwards.

Back through the generations...great grandparents in Victorian times, prosperous or poor, who knows... Further back to generations whose names are unknown to you... Feel the great migrations of people across the world – Jews from Russia, evicted Scots and slaves from Africa.

The Black Death killed half of all Europeans 700 years ago, your ancestors may have been among the survivors... What lives did they live? Farming families or craftspeople, landowners or fisher folk?... Maybe they carved one of the great cathedrals or beat metal jewellery for one of the princes of India. Did they cast the gold figures of Benin in West Africa? I wonder what skills they had in their hands and minds that they passed on to future generations...

Go back to a time when there were no cities, no towns...only scattered villages of men and women farmers.

Keep moving back further and further in time, through hundreds of generations. Become a member of the small bands of people, the hunter-gatherers who migrated across Africa in search of new possibilities...

Some stayed, some left Africa and over generations travelled through Europe, Asia and down to what we now call South America and Australia. One of your ancestors may have been on the first boats to land on a Pacific island after travelling for days by the stars. People have been migrating for millennia searching for a better life.

Go back...much further back...before the Ice Ages to a time when the Sahara was forest and hippos swam in the rivers there... Go and join a circle around the fire at night where people are talking... Maybe discussing the future, making plans, hoping for a family. They saw with your eyes and felt the reassuring touch of a friend as you do...

At this point in our journey we choose to stop; we could go back through the animals, other primates, back to our evolutionary origins in the sea... But today we are in touch with our human ancestors...

We are alive on a fine morning in Africa. An ancestor of ours wakes up by some trees, looking out over the wide savannah and contemplating the day ahead. Though they don't know it they are one of the first of our species of humans 500,000 years ago. That is less than 20,000 generations of ancestors. Take a moment now to be that ancestor, with limbs like yours and your enquiring mind...'

(Go slower in the next paragraph.)

'Now we begin the journey forwards in time... Take your time...for we have an important task to do on our return journey. As you pass through each generation open your arms to the gifts of the ancestors... Feel the mother's love wishing you well in life and hoping goodness for the future. What is it you take up in your arms now?

A strong back maybe...a sense of humour...the creative mind of the cave painter, the deep connection to nature from the hunter, and the ability to empathise with the struggles of others in life? ... Keep moving forwards receiving the gifts freely from all sides of the family of humanity... Ninety-nine per cent of our time for tens of millennia we lived as hunter-gatherers... What skills do you bring forwards? ... Keep moving forwards...

Until you come to the Agricultural Revolution...the discovery of farming and a settled life in one place...and then to the Industrial Revolution when many moved to cities and factories... And finally we arrive in modern times at the twenty-first century...to the world we live in today and the ever-moving arrow at the edge of time...

What will you make of all the gifts of the ancestors you have inherited? What is it in you?... Your unique mix that calls out to make the world a better place, so that we may all continue the journey?

Spend a while resting with these thoughts; you have been on a long journey today. And when it feels right open your eyes in your own time. (Leave time for people to sit in silence.)

Eventually you can find three other people to talk to about your experience, or if you want to remain on your own, that's OK.

What did you learn?

What are these many gifts?

How do you want to use them?'

Inheritance of the wild

Aim: To bring into awareness how much we are animals and have inherited our characteristics through evolution. A reminder of how much we are a part of nature.

Need: The script below. Bin bags if people are to lie down.

Instructions: You can run this activity with the whole group standing and continually pairing up or with the group lying down listening to you.

I usually begin by talking about some of the family characteristics I have inherited: facial features, height, the sound of my voice and so on. I then remind people that we have more basic characteristics which we have inherited from our earlier ancestors: primates, other mammals, right back through the Tree of Life to fishes, worms and single-cell organisms. Many single-celled creatures need oxygen to live, just as we do, for example.

Instruct people either to lie down and listen to you or mill around as a group in a defined area. The standing group are asked to stop every so often and pair up (if there is an odd number do a threesome). When they stop they are to face their partner and follow your instructions for each item and then move on again to another partner. If you have asked the group to lie down and listen to you the script needs to be adapted slightly. Begin by encouraging a sense of curiosity and amazement with each activity. Instead of examining another person ask them to touch their own body, for example taking their own pulse. After the activities individuals can form small groups to discuss their experience.

Script

Say something along the lines of:

> 'Take it in turns with each activity. Change partners after each one. As you face each other I will give a characteristic and you are to be aware of the other person and the fact that they have this quality. Have a sense of amazement or fascination that this person has inherited such an incredible quality. These are qualities we tend to think of as solely human but which in fact are inherited from our ancestors.'

The bloodstream:

> 'Can you feel the pulse in your partner's wrist? Blood is a characteristic of all multi-cellular organisms that need to transport food and oxygen to all parts of their body. This characteristic goes back to our ancestor, the sea worm. In time a muscular pump, the heart, was evolved. The first vertebrates, ancestors of fish, had red blood. Later on our mammal ancestors gave us warm blood and hair which enable us to keep active even when it is cold.'

Spinal column:

> 'If your partner gives permission, feel the bones of the neck and upper back. The separate vertebrae are held in place by strong ligaments which are flexible, supportive and protective of the spinal column. You inherited your spine from fish who needed it to swim fast and we now need it to stand upright.'

Limbic system:

> 'Lean head to head so that you touch foreheads. Deep inside the skull is a system in the brain inherited from our reptile ancestors that allows us to feel emotions: fear, attraction, pleasure and anger. What makes us emotional beings rather than machines is in part due to the involvement of the limbic system in our consciousness. Notice if you have any emotional feelings at the moment.'

Binocular vision:

> 'Look into each others' eyes and hold your gaze. Our eyes are no longer on the sides of our head like they are in deer and mice but in front. Our tree-climbing ancestors, the primates, needed eyes that could judge distances very well as they climbed and jumped through trees. They also gave us our particular colour vision with a preference for reds and yellows, the colour of ripe fruit.'

Hand:

> 'Take it in turns to hold your partner's hand. See how the hand curls over, look at the space between fingers and thumb – just the right size to grasp a branch. Notice the absence of claws; the fingers now have nails made of the same stuff and they allow the sensitive fingertips to pick up small objects and touch another human. Our ancestors the monkeys developed this ability.'

Speech:

> *'We are talking and understanding each other. Speech enables us to live together and collaborate on big projects like building a house or raising children for many years. We can hurt each other with words and also pass on our wisdom. Our close ancestors, other species of humans, worked to develop this ability we now inherit.*
>
> *Stay with your last partner, or form small groups of six, and find somewhere to talk together. Be aware of how useful speech is as you discuss with your partner your thoughts and feelings regarding this activity.'*

See: *The ecological body*

Our evolutionary story

Adapted from a workshop activity I experienced run by Joanna Macy. See her *Cosmic Journey* (Macy and Young Brown 1998).

Aim: To raise awareness of our ancestry with the rest of nature.

Needs: The script below. Bin bags for people to lie on.

Instructions: Invite people to lie down on the ground, maybe under a tree, and to get comfortable. You can suggest they close their eyes while you tell them a story. Encourage them to be open with their imagination as the story unfolds and to be aware of their feelings as well.

    The visualisation takes approximately 30 minutes in all: 20 to read and 10 minimum to discuss.

Script

> *'You are in a natural area now surrounded by other living plants and animals, all living together on planet Earth. I am going to tell you the story of our evolution and our relationship with life around us.*
>
> *I want you to begin by lying on the ground, getting yourself comfortable and closing your eyes... Can you feel your body resting on the ground, allowing you to relax fully into the earth? Take a deep breath and let go so that you can fully listen to the story I am about to tell you.*
>
> *Cultures around the world all have a creation story of how we came into being. Since the theory of evolution was put forward science has been able to create a new story of how we came to be here and how we are connected to all life on Earth. It is as beautiful and as complex as any story that came before it.*
>
> *Paradoxically we are destroying the natural world through overuse at a time when we are also understanding anew how much we are a part of life on Earth. With this new recognition from science and our personal experience many are seeking ways to let go of the illusion of an individualised self.*

This is our creation story, the evolution of life, which we share with all that is living around us...

Let us go back to a very brief time that happened a long time ago. In billionths of a second and 14.7 billion years ago the Big Bang happened and all the universe was exploding energy. We were there at the beginning and so was everything else – all the atoms and energy that make you up right now were there in the Big Bang.

Energy attracted energy and formed atoms spinning through space and time, working at the speed of light over millennia, creating billions of galaxies. There was light and heat in unimaginable abundance as there is today. One of those galaxies was our Milky Way and halfway along one of its spiral arms, five billion years ago, an eddy of energy balled into becoming our sun, source of all our light and energy today. As other stars exploded they sent great swirls of gas towards our sun star. You were there too, do you remember? The gravitational laws of attraction pulled atoms of stardust together and around the sun the planets coalesced. One of these planets, where it was not too hot and not too cold, was to become our home.

To help our human mind grasp the cosmic times we are dealing with, that is to say 4.6 billion years of Earth's existence, imagine Earth as a woman of 46 years of age today and let us call her Gaia. We will use her life, which is cosmically ours as well, to trace Earth's story. She was born as a fiery mass of molten iron and other metals spinning yearly around the sun. She developed a crust over her molten metallic body and later comets curved into the solar system and provided water for the blue planet. And water is the basis of all life.

Fairly early on in her life deep in the ocean's volcanic vents the first molecules of life were formed. In time they grouped to form the first cell with its strands of DNA. Every single plant and animal can trace its ancestry back to that first cell, which means we are all related to each other; we were there at the beginning and have been ever since. Can you feel yourself dividing into two and going your own ways?

Some cells were able to photosynthesise light and became algae. The byproduct was oxygen. Over billennia a blanket of ozone was formed which protected life near the surface of the earth from the sun's harmful UV rays. Animals began to use the oxygen as fuel to move around so that by the age of eight Gaia's bacteria were established. These were the ancestors of bacteria in our gut and of ourselves for we all share a common parentage.

In this salty oceanic womb of life natural selection continued to bring forth new life forms: multicellular corals, crabs, jellyfish, worms and eventually fish with backbones. We have in our bodies today the inheritance of our ancestors as they survived and bred. Do you remember developing a spine? Our backbone, nervous system, heart and gut come from our fishy ancestors. Can you recall wriggling through the sea? Can you flex your spine now? The salt from the sea still flows in our tears and sweat. Even as an embryo in the womb we had gills and a tail.

Can you recall using your fins to haul up onto the beach for the first time? Gaia waited till she was 42 years old before living on land. Plants began to move onto land and turn rock dust into soil. Amphibians which need to return to water to breed and insects followed soon after.

In places where the climate changed and became hot and dry reptiles evolved to seal their eggs in a watertight shell and grow a skin that could prevent them drying up. Some developed into dinosaurs, only two years ago in Gaia's life, and at around the same time the first mammals and later birds came into being.

As mammals we can keep our blood warm internally and don't have to rely on the sun to get going. By changing our limbs and lifting our belly off the ground we can move faster. We suckle our young and grow hair.

Life evolves as the survivors live to be old enough to produce the next generation, all the rest fall by the wayside and do not pass on their characteristics. We and all the living life forms today are descendants of those that did survive and succeed in life.

Do you remember being a shrew scurrying around at night, nose twitching for interesting scents and going back to look after your babies in a nest? Needing a home to call your own goes back that far, 200 million years.

The first monkeys could move fast by swinging through the trees in search of fruit and insects. We developed hands and an opposable thumb to grip branches and our eyes moved forwards for stereo vision to make sure we didn't miss a hold. Our eyes also acquired colour vision with a preference for reds and yellows, the colours of ripe fruit. Our fingertips became sensitive now that we had nails instead of claws and we could squeeze fruit and groom our friends. We formed social groups for protection and to make it easier to bring up our babies together.

Only three months ago in Gaia's life we became great apes and began to use tools and think ahead, continually developing our intelligence and social skills. We are more closely related to chimpanzees (98% same DNA) than horses are to donkeys. Three weeks ago we split off from the other primates as the climate changed and the forests of Africa began to shrink.

Ten days ago the first hominids walked on two feet, hunted game animals, and dealt with the heat by losing hair and sweating. What does it feel like to stand up and look out over the grasslands of the savannah? Are there trees nearby you can run to if a predator comes along? We are living in groups of up to 250 people maximum who wander around as the seasons change. We think creatively, use fire, make art, music. We have the power of speech to form friendships and pass on to the next generation all we have learnt. At one time there were five different species of humans on the planet, all with different strategies for living. Neanderthals lived much longer than we have so far. They had culture. They buried their dead in the foetal position aligned east-west like the path of the sun. They left flowers in the grave for the deceased.

Our species arrived two days ago and modern people are only a day old in Gaian time. We have lived in nature as hunter-gatherers for 99 per cent of our time on Earth, owning only what could be carried in the hands and believing we are part of the land. Hunter-gatherers spend a minority of time finding food and building homes, the rest of the time is for pleasure. What is it like to have all your needs within easy reach and to be surrounded by a community you were born into?

Since the last Ice Age we learnt how to farm - that's an hour ago in Gaia's life of 46 years. And in the last 60 seconds of that hour we have gone through the Industrial Revolution. We invented machines to do so much - cars, factories, planes - and the digital revolution has just begun. Half of humanity lives in the city and the human population is increasing by four people a second. We are now the biggest consumer of natural resources on the earth.

Life on Earth is unstoppable but the human systems we have for living today no longer work for our long-term survival. In all of us, even if it is deeply buried, there is a recognition that we cannot carry on this way. We are at the point Joanna Macy calls the Great Turning when we have to do something different if we want to continue to be part of life on Earth. It is the only known place in the universe with consciousness, which took 4.6 billion years to evolve...

Take your time to reflect on your story. There is no need to get up immediately. When you want to, open your eyes and sit up. After you have done that find someone else and take it in turns to talk about your experience of our evolutionary journey. You may want to remain by yourself reflecting and that is fine too.'

The web of life

Inspired by a workshop of Joanna Macy's that I took part in. See also a similar script in Macy and Young Brown (1998).

Aims: To visualise the place of the ecological self. To plant thoughts in people's minds of how interconnected we are with the rest of life, and how good it is to know it: how right that is.

Needs: The script below and bin bags for people to lie on, one per person. Find a place outside where people can lie down on soft grass or dry leaves and relax undisturbed.

Instructions: The script can take 15–20 minutes.

Introduction and relaxation

Explain first what you will do: a relaxation exercise and the telling of a story for them to listen to called the 'web of life'. Invite everyone to participate by using their imagination. Suggest people lie down and settle comfortably. Talk through a process of body relaxation. Remind people to let go and just listen to your voice. Suggest they feel the weight of their body being supported by the soft grass and ground. They can let go now. No effort is required to lie down. Then begin the visualisation. Speak slowly and with pauses to allow the thoughts and images to sink down into their minds.

Script

'This is the web of life. In the next 15 minutes you may want to use your imagination to experience in your mind the web of life that holds you and will continue to hold you all your life...

Imagine now a vast web, like a soft luxurious hammock in which you are comfortably supported, just as the ground supports you now... See the thick threads of the web go off in all directions across the landscape and in different coloured strands...

We will begin our awareness of the strands of life with the air... Let a deep breath out and feel the air return on its own...easy... It is just happening in you, you are being breathed, life is breathing into you... With every breath, your blood draws fresh oxygen to every part of your body, every cell...and fires each cell with power and energy... Extend your imagination deep within to feel this energy burning and keeping you warm at the temperature you are...

And now imagine the carbon dioxide gas gently streaming out of you on the out-breath, mixing with the wind and flowing off to be breathed in by the trees and grass around you and beyond...

See this vast continuous network of exchanges between us and plants as threads in the web of life that sustains us both...the Great Interbreathing... as if we were one... Plants and us, us and plants, back and forth...'

People:

'The web also stretches in other ways through the people we are fond of... relationships created through smiles, encounters, conversations, hugs and tears... See the strands in your mind's eye...all those good connections...They could include close friends, or a stranger who shared a smile, or someone you were able to help in some small way... Your experience of life so far may have been mixed so right now you can pay attention to the positive people you know and hope to meet soon...

It is said we are only seven relationships away from everyone on the planet... seven steps to someone in Argentina or Japan... Experience in your mind's eye now the great network of possible interconnected strands with others... There may be pain that comes along the strands of the web... a close friend in distress... reports of an oil spill...a Syrian mother (adapt to the current conflicts) weeping for her lost children...do not shut them out...be open to these sorrows, breathe them in... Feel the caring and love that flows from you, through you... To feel everything, pain and happiness, is to be more fully alive as a human being...'

Body:

'The web sustaining you is made of stuff too...your bones and muscles, blood and skin are connected with such incredible complexity... Consider this, you are formed entirely out of the food you've eaten...and what is eliminated from your body becomes purified by bacteria and taken back into growing things... Consider your nourishment through the web of life...grains and vegetables and fruit and meat... Consider for a moment the grass and munching jaws of a cow

in a far-off place as she makes her milk, for butter, for cheese, for you... See the rich soil that held and fed and yielded the grain for your bread, the boughs of the tree that bore the orange for your juice... Consider also the hands of others that ploughed and sowed and reaped...and processed... All these food strands feed into you, and you are now them... You could not be here without them. They are a part of you...'

Ancestors:

'The web of life extends far far back in time... We all have a biological mother and father, grandparents and great grandmothers and great grandfathers... They gave us our features and colouring...maybe we can even hear them in our voice and gestures.

The web extends back through countless generations... Through the numberless ancestors we all eventually share... All the way back to our brothers and sisters who lived in Africa in small bands at the dawn of humanity... We are the living descendants of an unbroken lineage that goes back to those same people...so we all share the same ancestors... The family of humanity... And before them was the apes...and creatures with tails and gills and wings...going right back to the first cells of life 3.8 billion years ago...for we are all made of the same stuff...created in evolutionary diversity...and organised by the same DNA just in different mixes...

In your mind's eye can you stand at the birth of the first cell of life and see a vast web of different life forms, descendants, stretching through millennia of time before you to today... If this is so then we are all related by blood to all living things around us...how does that seem to you?'

Ending:

'You can open up to the pulsing web of life... It is powerful enough to hold the whole world and is indestructible and everlasting...we are like knots on the net of life...held by the rest of life...in dynamic exchange...interdependent... It is said we humans are the universe knowing itself... Be open to it all, unafraid, relaxed, alert knowing it is so...

To all our fellow travellers in life we are now open to them... We can rest with the knowledge that we arose like a wave from the darkness and will one day return into that gentle darkness... Right now we are sustained within the vast great web of life, our home...and we can draw strength from it...accepted, cradled...held, like our breath, without effort or intention...

Stay resting on the ground and spend a while now reflecting on your place in the web of life... (Give a few minutes for reflection.)

Still sensing these connections you can stretch now, and in your own time open our eyes, slowly move to rise... when you are ready turn to someone else and discuss how you feel now. If you would prefer to stay silent that is fine too, indicate this by staying seated.'

See: Indra's net, Network of life, Web of life game

Watching water

Introduction to *Watching water* activities

Research has shown that when people are asked to select the most attractive landscape they would like to be in one of the most important elements is the presence of water.

The aquatic ape hypothesis proposes that humans had a stage in their evolution where they spent a lot of time in water. It has been pointed out that we have many physical features that seem to be adaptations to a water environment. This is not the place to discuss the pros and cons of this fascinating and controversial hypothesis but our attachment to water is almost self-evident. As a species that evolved in hot savannah Africa we would have sought out freshwater supplies first of all when moving to a new area. Today when we take a holiday most of us choose to be by water and would pay more for a hotel room with a view of water.

The Chinese ancient philosophy of Taoism assumed that humans were part of nature and subject to the same principles. Consequently they believed that by studying nature they could learn about themselves. Two fundamentals of Taoist thinking are the contrasts between mountains and rivers. They asked the question: what do mountains and rivers do well that we could learn from? They observed that mountains are solid, firm, immovable, unyielding. How could the body be like a mountain? In the Chinese martial arts there are ways of sinking your body mass so that your opponent finds it very difficult to shift you. Likewise the early Taoists observed the flow of water down mountain rivers and saw a different quality that they could emulate. When water meets an obstacle in the river it finds the easiest path and flows around the blockage. Over time it even wears mountains down through steady persistence. Likewise in martial arts you can respond to your opponent's force by relaxing and deflecting their energy away from you rather than meeting it head on. In these few examples you can see not only a different way of thinking to Western thought but a methodology based on observation of nature and suggestions for understanding human behaviour and attitudes. It is with this in mind that I developed a series of activities which encourage people to get to know the properties of water and to consider how they can learn from water to their advantage.

Moving water watching

Aim: To familiarise people with a river's qualities and to consider what they can learn about themselves in the process.

Need: A river.

Instructions: When you have spoken for a short while about the properties of water, maybe using some of the information above, you can ask people to watch the river. They can sit or stand, making sure they find a place that is safe and not where the bank could collapse into the river – that would be taking the connection to water a stage too far!

You can say something like this:

'I want you to spread out along the river bank and find a safe place to watch the river flow. Make sure you can still hear my voice. (If the river is noisy you can walk up and down giving repeated instructions.)

What can you know of the depths from watching the surface? Notice the speed, movement and patterns the water makes. Why do you think the river flows that way? When you have watched the way the river flows for a while ask yourself: what can you learn about yourself from watching free water flow?

Try this activity. Look at one portion of the river and follow the flow of current repeatedly with your eyes, downstream and back up again.

When you have done this a few times and noticed how you feel I want you to change your way of looking. This time put your gaze on one point in the river and let the current flow through your visual field, don't follow the current downstream. How does that feel, what are your thoughts?

Move along the river now and find a stretch that has a different current and compare a fast-flowing area with a slow part of the river.

Listen to the water music: how many sounds can you hear? What does the river tell you?'

Watching the river flow

Standing by the river/ going with the flow

Aim: To continue to familiarise people with water's qualities.

Need: A river.

Instructions: I may take a group down to a river and begin by talking about some of the qualities of water before suggesting people go off and look for themselves. I am feeding their minds with possibilities for when their senses take in the experience. You can find your own words to talk about these thoughts:

- Water flows through you at a slow pace and it never stops; you take a drink of water or eat fruit and before long the water is peed out of you. The water in you will have flowed through many rivers. The river will have contained water that has passed through many humans and animals and plants since its origins in the creation of the earth. We are up to 70 per cent water and we cannot survive for more than a few of days without it.

- Water interconnects us to all life. Imagine water flowing round the Earth in vast hydrological cycles, through clouds and rivers, seas and all living things, and over many millennia. It is universal, all life has it and it continuously interchanges with elements of the world and is purified. Consider, water on Earth is 4.6 billion years old. Nature continually refreshes it anew.

- The land is created by water. Look around you, the hills, the mountains, the valleys, the soil, the plain, all were created by the action of water. The moon has no water and has not changed in billions of years since it was impacted by meteors. Earth, the watery planet, is continually being changed by the actions of water.

- Consider where the water in the river has travelled. The river water you see travelled from upstream a few days ago after trickling through soil. Before that it landed as rain from a cloud in the sky. One rain cloud carries on average eight million tons of water. Our weather systems are created from the spiralling of warm air laden with moisture from the Caribbean and cold Arctic air flowing from the north. As they mix we get rain. Consider this: the water you drank today was not long ago steamy tropical water in the Caribbean Sea. When you next go for a pee (which is over 95% water) it won't be long before it will be part of the North Sea and the Atlantic Ocean.

- Where is the river going? A bit of research, by looking at a local OS map, will help you find out where the water in your river has come from and how it flows to the sea. If you are with a group you can talk to them about the river catchment area and the story of the river as it flows down to the sea. You can use local landmarks people will be familiar with as markers of its journey. You can remind them that the seas around Britain are all connected by the Gulf Stream cycle to the Caribbean Sea.

Step out of the river
of thought

Aim: This activity aims to raise awareness and quieten the mind.

Need: A river or stream of moving water.

Instructions: I suggest you stand by the river with the group and talk through the ideas and instructions below in your own words.

'When we are fully aware, our senses (touch, sight, hearing, smell, taste etc.) enable us to directly experience the world as it is. For most of us, much of the time, our monkey mind is chattering away inside, commenting on what we experience and pulling out memory, thoughts and emotions from who knows where, all the time making experience more like a real-time video than the real thing, with the result that we don't experience the world with full awareness.

When we fully experience the world in the present we can let go of our irrational fears and concerns.

Look at the river as it flows along, rushing to the sea. Now close your eyes and imagine your mind as a river constantly flowing, as it chatters and worries its way along through time… You can see yourself standing in the river with the water flowing fast all around you… You are not the river and you are not your mind chatter.

Continuing with your eyes closed imagine you can do something different about your situation… Instead of standing in the river step out of it onto the bank and watch it flow past you… Spend time witnessing your mind, your thought processes, in a kindly yet detached way. Don't attempt to change the thoughts, just let them float downstream… (Allow people time to experiment with these new ways of looking at themselves.)

If the thoughts become strong and seek to drag you back into the river try this process. When a thought occurs, for example if you feel an anxious thought, notice it and say to yourself: "I experience anxiety but I am not my anxiety."

Another method is to get in touch with your body through your inner awareness. Go through your whole body noticing each part of it until you can feel your whole body on the inside. Go back to this state in order to stand firm on the bank when the river gets too strong.'

Still water watching

Aim: To familiarise people with the qualities of still water.

Need: Water, ideally a puddle or a pond, if not a large dark bowl of water.

Instructions: Either take the group to a puddle or pond or bring along a big dark bowl that can be filled with water and placed on the ground. Some observations you could encourage people to consider are:

Look at the water. What qualities do you see in water?

See how mobile and restless it is after any disturbance and how it returns to stillness.

Look into the depths, what do you see? Sometimes it is not possible to see into deep water and all we are aware of is the surface skin of water.

What can you see reflected in the water? Can you see the sky, clouds moving past? In Buddhism the clear mind is sometimes talked of as being like a water surface: effortlessly reflecting the world without needing to judge or evaluate. We must clearly distinguish between what is in our mind and what is being perceived. They are not the same.

After looking at still water it is interesting to do the activity *Moving water watching*.

What does the river teach us of life?

Aim: To consider what we can learn about life from watching flowing water.

Need: A river or flowing stream.

Instructions:

Part 1: Sensory and motion

Ask the group to spread out and walk along the river bank exploring how the river flows. Encourage people to enjoy and notice how water runs to the sea. How does the river behave when it is wide, narrow, shallow, deep? How is it when it is fast or slow? How does it deal with barriers and obstacles in the riverbed?

Meet as a group and discuss what you have learned.

Part 2: River as a metaphor of life

Give the following instructions to the group:

'Find a leaf, short twig or piece of wood, throw it in the river and watch how the river carries it downstream. Imagine you are watching someone's life flow down the river. What do you notice and what can you learn about life from watching how the river behaves?'

Meet as a group and discuss what we have learned.

See: *The Kawa model, Weather you like it or not, Getting to know another life form* (the last two can be modified to look at a river or stream and ask the same questions).

Weather you like it or not

Aim: To explore how we respond to the weather. To consider acceptance of 'bad' weather and then acceptance of other parts of our lives.

Need: Pick a day when people express feelings of dissatisfaction with the weather – so almost any day in Britain then!

Instructions: I'm going to assume it is raining on the day you take a group out. Gather the group round, maybe under the shelter of a big tree, and find your own words to talk through the following passage:

'The intention of this activity is to notice how we respond to the weather. There are many things in life which we cannot control and we can get frustrated and angry about this. So what do we do – carry on the same way? Or are there other ways of dealing with the feelings that arise?

The weather is something we have absolutely no control over and yet it affects us – we can get cold or wet or thirsty under some conditions. Our response to weather is a good thing to work with if we want to understand more about how to cope with things we have no control over. Because weather is not a result of human actions it can have less emotional charge compared with the behaviour of other people.

Let us pay attention to the weather now. What do you sense?… What we are sensing is how things really are right now, not our memories or automatic responses. Take a few moments to really sense your weather environment in all sensory dimensions and to use all your senses in turn – sight, hearing, smell, taste, touch, temperature…

The next step is to notice our feelings and thoughts about the situation. These are the things our mind adds to the situation and over which we have more influence. Is there disappointment, a withdrawal from being outdoors, or maybe irritation? Notice these feelings and thoughts, label them as to the kind of thought they are. Accept them in a kindly way. Then put them to one side as you return to the sensations of the weather itself.

Can you accept the weather as it is today right now, without evaluation? Say to yourself, "This is how things are right now, so why fight it? There is nothing I can do to change the weather."

The weather exercise is a good way to learn about and practise acceptance. Are there other areas of your life over which you feel you have little or no control? If so can you accept these situations? This does not mean using rose-tinted spectacles to say everything's fine. It means starting by being fully aware of how you experience the situation without judgement and settling into that. Then see what happens when all the anger and resentment or fear are laid to one side. Your actions to change things will be a better quality once the emotional charge has been left behind.'

Additional things to do in the rain

Walk in the rain and get your hands wet – how does it feel? What thoughts come up?

What do you notice about the smells that come up when it's raining? See 'Smell and autobiographical memory' in Chapter 7.

Lick things such as leaves that are covered in rain. What do they taste of? Rain or what?

Where has the rain come from and where is it going?

See: *Watching water*

What to do in winter

This activity has a slightly different format to the rest. It is a collection of various activities that lend themselves to winter time. I have written it to reassure and encourage people that there are plenty of enjoyable things to do at this time of year.

There is further discussion of wintertime activities in Chapter 3 under Winter Activities in Ecotherapy.

Rose hips or haw sweets: In early winter before the birds have eaten them it is possible to make delicious food from rose hips and haws. It is important to know what you are picking of course, rose and hawthorn bushes are very common and the thorns and fallen leaves should help you identify them. I had a go at making Turkish Delight from haws that a group collected with me. Here is the recipe I adapted.

We collected about 2kg of red berries and I washed and boiled them with water for about an hour until it was a pulp. I poured the pulp into a muslin bag and left it overnight to drip into a glass bowl. The strained juice came to about 1kg. I returned this to the saucepan, added 700g of sugar and left it to simmer until it became a sticky mass. At some point I added a teaspoon of rosewater (bought from a middle-eastern shop) for authenticity. I tested its thickness by taking small samples out with a teaspoon, cooling it and seeing if it was congealed enough to make a stiff jelly. I lined a metal baking tray with icing sugar (rice paper might have been easier) and poured in the jelly. I filled two rectangular baking trays with a thin layer of jelly and left them to cool by an open window before cutting them up into squares. I placed the squares, heavily dusted with icing sugar, into little pots. Some I put in the freezer and others I decorated as presents for friends.

The boiled jelly (before adding sugar to make sweets) can be used to thicken sauces; it is very rich in pectin. Recipes for ketchup can be adapted for haws.

Hawthorn is good for the heart and circulation, it reduce blood pressure and lowers cholesterol. It is also high in vitamin C and several B vitamins although I'm not sure how much survives prolonged boiling.

Rose hips can be used in the same way to make a sauce, using more water and less sugar. After collecting the rose hips wash them, cut them open and scrape out the itchy seeds and hairs. Boil up the hips with a little water until you have a pulp that you can strain as described for the haw berries.

Sloe spirit is an adaptation of sloe gin. I use vodka, which I now prefer, because it gives prominence to the plummy flavours of the sloes. In early winter collect the sloes from the hedgerows, wash them and slit each fruit with a sharp knife before putting them in a plastic bag and leaving them in the freezer for a week. This last process simulates winter frost. If you leave the sloes until after the first frost many will have been eaten by birds. Take a big airtight jar such as a Kilner jar and fill it two-thirds with sloes and then cover the sloes with cheap vodka, right up to the top. Leave the jar in a dark place and shake it around for the first week before leaving for three months. After three months the fruit juice will have been absorbed by the alcohol and can be strained off and bottled for drinking. Add sugar to taste. The leftover berries can be destoned and made into a nice chutney, or dipped in chocolate to make liqueur sweets.

Baretree: In winter look at the shape of *bare trees*, the texture and colour of different barks, the different types of fallen leaves below them, and the colour and texture of the buds. The Woodland Trust have a twig identification sheet on their website under children's activities.

Scavenger games: See the activity *Scavenger search,* adding seeds, nuts, bones and shells to the list.

Measure the *girth of trees and estimate their age*. See the activity *The age of a tree*.

Look at *fungi* and the different gill patterns. If a fungus cap is placed on grey paper, gills face down, overnight, in the morning there will be a beautiful radiating pattern of spores that have fallen from the gills. This can be protected with sticky-back transparent paper.

Watch birds with binoculars and a field guide. Many birds come over from the continent to feed over here in the winter; mudflats and lakes are the best places to see them.

Feed the ducks: Take old wholemeal bread to the ducks and geese on a local lake. All sorts of interesting conversations have come out of observing the behaviour of the birds at feeding time. Topics such as: how birds let go of conflict once it is over – no apparent held resentment or revenge; participants looking after the weaker birds such as moorhens, in the face of a flotilla of Canada geese; or how individual birds can be distinguished over time.

Conservation work is most often carried out in winter when it is possible to cut down trees and bushes without disturbing breeding birds and animals. A visit to a conservation group may encourage people to join on a regular basis. There is firm evidence that the combination of exercise, companionship and engagement with nature makes conservation work very therapeutic. Local wildlife trusts, local authorities and national bodies like the Woodland Trust and RSPB all run conservation sessions.

Have a look at all the activities in this book; you will find many that lend themselves to winter time.

See: *Being with trees, Death and life in winter, Scavenger search, Weather you like it or not*

Wild food for ecotherapy

Aim: To use the experience of eating to consider our intimate ecological participation in wild nature.

Needs: Polythene collecting bags, sharp knife (a small penknife is legal to carry around), identification guides to plants.

Instructions: I sometimes read a poem called *Standing by Frazier Creek Falls* (1993) by Gary Snyder and talk about how our interdependence is fundamental to us. You could read this poem or another poem that you find.

One key aspect of our intimate belonging in wild nature is that we as a species have spent 99 per cent of our time living in nature. The fact that urban people alive today haven't lived as hunter-gatherers makes the thought seem strange and maybe even impossible to imagine, but all our ancestors prior to 6000BCE did. A significant question then is: how did we find shelter, drink and eat? The answer is not a hand-to-mouth, semi-starving scrabble for survival (which city dwellers would experience if they were left outdoors for long enough). Life as a hunter-gatherer would have been much better than camping. We would have lived in warm heated accommodation with friends and family around us and abundant fresh, locally sourced and organic food!

Fresh water would have come from streams and lakes. What about food though, what would people have eaten? They would have eaten the wild originals of the food we eat today. We have all gone for a walk in the countryside in August and idly eaten delicious blackberries. Carrots and lettuce still grow wild in our hedgerows. The human population is too big today but it would be possible to live by eating the landscape if numbers were much lower.

Why encourage people to eat wild food on an ecotherapy walk? The answer is because it provides another way of connecting to nature in an enjoyable sensory way. It is also a reminder of our direct ecological participation in nature. All our food ultimately comes from the living world.

On walks with groups I often stop and talk about a plant before offering a sample for others to taste. For many this is an opportunity to have a new experience. Some caution is expressed by most people in taking this new step. Is the plant poisonous or covered in germs? Will it have grubs in it or taste strange? But having chewed peppermint leaves on a hot day or put garlic mustard leaves in their sandwich, the idea of eating wild food becomes more and more attractive.

You can learn about which plants to eat by reading books or checking websites on bushcraft and wild food. You do need to be able to identify the edible and similar inedible plants in the same habitat, of course. Local wildlife trusts often run workshops and courses on plant identification. I am presenting a few examples here of abundant and easily identifiable wild food sources you can begin with. I have not given the identification features; you need to check these from a reliable source.

Begin by nibbling a small amount until the flavour kicks in. If you don't like it don't continue: spit it out, simple as that. If you do like it then consider putting green leaves in a salad bulked up with lettuce (which has its wild ancestor living near you). Here are a few examples to get you started.

Spring greens

Hawthorn: When hawthorn buds have just broken and the baby leaves are fresh out of the bud cases this is the time to nibble them. Many plants have bitter chemicals such as tannin in their leaves to deter animals from eating them. However, in early spring the plant is keen to grow as fast as possible to begin the process of photosynthesis and so delays adding the bitter flavours for a short while. At this point we find the leaves edible. Some of the plants which subsequently produce bitter leaves we use as herbs or teas. After a harsh winter new hawthorn leaves were a good source of fresh greens for the poorest of poor people in the past who would go searching the hedgerows for nutritious free food in spring.

Nettle tops make a good tea and an excellent soup with potatoes as thickener.

Garlic mustard is well named because you can taste the two flavours in its leaves. If you can find *wild garlic* in damp woodland then the leaves make an excellent addition to a sandwich.

Rocket has made the transition from wild food to supermarket in recent years but it is only one of many edible plants that are abundant in urban wasteland.

Sorrel: The leaves have a sharp astringent almost lemon tartness about them. This is because they contain the same sour chemical as rhubarb, oxalic acid. The French have traditionally made soup out of the leaves.

Fat hen can be cooked like spinach. Young plants are best between April and May. Our stone-age ancestors ate a lot of fat hen and its relatives. The leaves are rich in vitamins and iron.

Blossom eating in spring

Flowers look attractive in salads and the nectar gives a sweet flavour to the whole bloom. Here are the results of one group's walk, tasting flowers in April:

Blackthorn tastes sweet and almond flavoured.

Cherry is sweet and a bit almondy.

Red nettle is earthy and we didn't like the taste.

Maple is sweet and tasty.

Sallow/pussy willow catkin's pollen is pleasant to suck.

Gorse: A mug of tea can be made from two tablespoons of flowers mashed for 7-10 minutes in boiled water.

Elderflower heads with the stalks on can be coated in batter and deep fried. Serve hot dipped in sugar.

Autumn fruit

Blackberries are the obvious fruit to demonstrate our connection to nature. They are abundant in hedgerows as you walk along and they make delicious pies cooked with apples.

In a hundred metres a person can eat a juicy apple and then throw away the slightly woody core. The seeds are carefully designed not to be eaten; they are very slippery and if the brown outer case is punctured the taste of the cyanide inside puts animals off.

Some fruits go a stage further in their adaptation and exploitation of animals and birds. They add a laxative! This makes sure the seeds don't go too far away from the favourable habitat the parent plant is living in. And the seeds get a nice deposit of dung fertiliser surrounding them.

Further resources

Harding, P., Lyon, T. and Tomblin, G. (1996) *How to Identify Edible Mushrooms*. London: Collins.

Irving, M. (2009) *The Forager Handbook*. London: Ebury Press. The best up-to-date book on eating wild food. You will need good identification books as well as this cookbook.

Mabey, R. (1972) *Food for Free*. Glasgow Fontana/Collins. The first and one of the best. New edition 2001. The Collins Gem (2012) edition is small and easily fits in the pocket.

Mears, R. and Hillman, G. (2007) *Wild Food*. London: Hodder and Stoughton. Makes the connection between our ancestors and the food they ate and what we can still find in our countryside. The book reads like work in progress unfortunately, with a lot of unfinished threads.

Phillips, R. (2014) *Wild Food: A Complete Guide for Foragers*. London: Macmillan.

Rose, F. (2006) *The Wild Flower Key*, revised edn. London: Warne/Penguin. The best wildflower identification book for Britain.

The Free Range Activism Website: This is a good starting place for thinking about wild food harvesting *www.fraw.org.uk*

Fruity city: Where to find fruit trees in London *http://fruitcity.co.uk*

Hedgerow Harvest: London and South East Counties project linked to Tree Council *www.hedgerowharvest.org.uk*

See: *Awareness and contemplation, Eating with eyes closed*

Wildlife watching

When I am out with a group on an ecotherapy walk we often spot things of interest. It might be a plant gall, a stripy caterpillar or a bird behaving strangely. I use these opportunities to encourage people to really pay attention with all their senses to whatever it is we are observing. I invite close attention and encourage questions: 'Look at the strange shape'; 'What is it doing now?'; 'Why do you think it is coloured that way?'

Because of my knowledge and experience of wildlife I can often expand people's awareness and understanding of various life forms. I often do this in the form of questions or I might tell an ecological story. The information may give a greater understanding of the creature's ecology, celebrate its sensory capabilities or make the group stand back in amazement at a creature's capacity to survive so well in a tough environment. When we do this we are looking at the almost unbelievable diversity of creative outpourings from natural selection. I offer a few examples below to get you started. The Internet can be a great source if you know what you are looking for.

I suggest reading the section on wildlife knowledge in Chapter 3 (pages 54-7) in relation to this activity.

A sample of wildlife notes

Swifts

They leave the nest and don't land for two to four years. A First World War French pilot's engine cut out at 10,000ft and he went through a flock of birds. When he landed he found dead swifts stuck to the fuselage. Radar confirms this. Swifts can sleep for five seconds at a time. Night vision is poor so they sometimes don't know where they are going. They glide down maybe 50 miles from where they started. They can keep going at 25 miles per hour and fly 500 miles in a day. Over a lifetime a swift will fly two million miles which is four times to the moon and back. A swift feeds its young with a ball of 300-500 insects collected in its mouth. The young can go torpid and last three days without food. They visit Britain for just three months of the year, arriving here from Africa in May and leaving at the end of July. A swift lives for a long time: 15 years. The oldest recorded is 21 years old in Switzerland (2012) and is estimated to have flown three million miles. The swift is the fastest bird for its size, clocking 137 miles per hour.

Jay

In autumn jays come out of hiding in the woods and can be seen collecting acorns and other nuts to store for the winter. A close relative in the USA called Clark's nutcracker, which specialises in pine nuts, has been extensively studied and been found to have a remarkable memory. It can store 30,000 pine nuts in the autumn for the winter. The nuts are stored up to 15 miles away covering an area of 100 square miles. The nuts are stored in tens and the stash is covered by a stone. The birds recover 70 per cent of the stashes months later, sometimes under deep snow.

Fairy rings

Circles of darker green grass on lawns are created by fungi, which form a mutually beneficial relationship with the grass. The circle begins as a spot where the fungal spore landed and each year the fungus grows and expands outwards, dying in the middle of the circle. The rate of growth is 99-350mm per annum (4"-14"). Scientists have estimated that some rings are 600-700 years old. The main part of the fungus grows below ground as white interconnected threads, the toadstool being a bit like the fruit. The grass can photosynthesise and make sugar which the fungus can't do, and in turn the fungus can extract minerals the grass can't easily access. The fungus and grass do a swap and this explains why the grass is greener in the circle; it is healthier than the surrounding grass.

Mini-beasts

Mini-beast is the term invented to cover all very small creatures including insects, spiders, worms and snails. Most people tend to ignore or actively dislike creepy crawlys or slimy things for quite irrational reasons, even though they are on the whole harmless to us. They don't conform to conventional ideas of beauty and are hard to identify with, but they are essential to our existence. Perhaps an occasional pause to contemplate the place of mini-beasts in the living world might be a good thing for us all to do. Consider the following pieces of information:

Two-thirds of all species on the planet are mini-beasts and there are almost 50,000 species in Britain.

Greenfly are a type of aphid, which are insects. In a rich, balanced community there could be as many as five billion aphids per hectare living on leaves, roots, flowers and bark. Gardeners and farmers see them as pests but in the wider ecosystem they are essential. Ants feed on the sugar aphids excrete while the aphids suck out the sap from plants. The ladybird's main diet is aphids. A lot of woodland songbirds feed on aphids. Aphids can breed very fast and can produce ten babies a day; each baby is born with embryos already developing inside it.

Without worms we would not eat because the farmers could not grow crops without soil that has been worked on by worms. Charles Darwin studied earthworms and found that one hectare of grassland has seven and a half million worms which turn over 10 tonnes of soil a year. Worms aerate, drain and neutralise the acid/alkali balance. They digest dead and decaying matter, pulling goodness back into life systems and in turn providing food for many birds and mammals.

See: *A mini-beast's life*

Wind in the willows

Aim: To have a sensory experience of the wind.

Need: A windy day and some trees; tall young ones you can lean on are best. Willows are good because they are very flexible. You will get a lot less 'give' in an old oak bole.

Instructions: Go to a wood or any group of trees on a windy day and have each person find a young tree they can lean against. Make sure they are near enough to hear you over the noise of the wind. Obviously trees exposed to the wind are going to be more fun but it is surprising how the tree tops in the middle of a wood catch the wind if it is strong enough.

I suggest you talk about the windy trees in this way:

'Begin by touching your tree and feeling its bark and solidity; is it warm or cold, dry or damp? What does it smell of? What colours can you see? Is anything growing on it?

Now look up at the trees – what can you see, leaves, branches? Look how the trees relate to each other and share out the sky space. The trees have grown so they don't touch each other when they are still. See how much the tops of the trees move. Have you noticed how sheltered we are by the trees in the wood? The trees take the energy of the wind and bend flexibly to absorb it. A lot more is going on in the tree tops than down here.

When a gust of strong wind comes along lean against the tree and feel the tree yield to the pressure of the wind. You may have to press your back and shoulders onto the tree or push your hands against it firmly to feel the movement of the tree trunk.

Can you tell the different sounds the wind makes with different trees? Maybe you haven't thought about this before.'

Here are two naturalist writers describing their experiences. You can read these extracts to the group.

> *The trees as the wind rises find their voices, and the wood is full of strange tongues. From each green thing touched by its fingers the breeze draws a different note; the bennets on the hillside go 'sish, sish'; the oak in the copse roars and groans; in the firs there is a deep sighing; the aspen rustles. In winter the bare branches sing a shrill 'sir-r-r-r'. (Jefferies (2011 [1879])*

> *But the Silver Pines were now the most impressively beautiful of all. Colossal spires 200 feet in height waved like supple goldenrods changing and bowing low as if in worship, while the whole mass of their long, tremulous foliage was kindled into one continuous blaze of white sun-fire. The force of the gale was such that the most steadfast monarch of them all rocked down to its roots with a motion plainly perceptible when one leaned against it. Nature was holding high festival, and every fibre of the most rigid giants thrilled with glad excitement.*

I drifted through the midst of this passionate music and motion, across many a glen, from ridge to ridge, often halting in the lee of a rock for shelter, or to gaze and listen. Even when the grand anthem had swelled to its highest pitch, I could distinctly hear the varying tones of individual trees - Spruce, and Fir, and Pine, and leafless Oak - even the infinitely gentle rustle of the withered grasses at my feet. Each was expressing in its own way - singing its own song, making its own peculiar gestures - manifesting a richness of variety to be found in no other forest I have yet seen. (Muir 2015)

See: *Being with trees, Dawn chorus walk, Listening to silence*

Witnessing

Adapted from a Chan Buddhist meditation method.

Aim: To learn how to observe events in full awareness without feeling the need to respond with automatic thoughts and emotional triggers.

Need: Nothing.

Instructions: In your own words talk the group through the following:

What is witnessing?

'Witnessing is an active process like active listening. It means observing what is going on. You can be a witness to yourself. It sounds simple and it is. It also takes practice to get it right.

It means being fully aware and open to all experience without necessarily responding or doing anything about the experience. It is possible for me to witness my own anger or irritation without doing anything about it, without expressing it and without stopping the feeling either. We are not our thoughts and feelings any more than we are the rain we feel falling on our skin. They can, however, be part of our experience. Just noticing.

In practising witnessing we can give ourselves more choice about when to express a feeling or respond to a thought. It makes us less a victim of what can feel like driven impulses.'

Witnessing using the breath

'Stand now with your eyes closed and take a moment to settle into yourself and become aware of your breathing without changing anything. With each breath witness what is going on for you.

Breathe in and then out naturally. As you expel air and wait for the breath to return spontaneously in your body, be open to whatever comes up. It can be a sensation, thought, emotion, or whatever – who knows what it will be, wait in open anticipation.

If it helps in the early stages, say these same words to yourself with each out-breath: I am aware of...and say what comes up for you. For example with a sensation it could be: I am aware of my feet on the ground. With a thought it could be: I am aware of wondering if I'm doing this right. An emotion could come up such as: I am aware of feeling irritated, followed on the next breath with: I can feel my shoulders are tense, then: I am angry about something, and then: I can just feel my anger as anger I don't need to do anything.'

After doing this activity for a while stop and discuss with the group how they got on. Was everyone able to understand the instructions and become a witness to themselves? What did they learn?

See: *How to meditate*

Useful Resources

Joseph Cornell's Flow Learning Model

Flow Learning is Joseph Cornell's model of teaching.

1. *Awaken enthusiasm:* Children are emotionally engaged, motivated, having fun. Enthusiasm is generated to take them to the next step.

2. *Focus attention:* Students are encouraged to concentrate and pay attention. The effect is calming and it increases observational skills.

3. *Direct experience:* Students are taken deeper in their understanding and appreciation at an emotional level.

4. *Share inspiration:* A time for reflection, sharing of experiences, and creative expression.

Adapted from Cornell (2015)

Wildlife resources

Increasingly people are using apps and websites on their phones and tablets to identify wildlife. It is possible to download audio and video clips with these media and they are usually lighter to carry than a book. However, books continue to be used so I include some recommendations below.

Identifying wildlife - books

There are many field guides on the market to help put a name to a bird, animal or plant. Many are excellent (e.g. Collins, British Wildlife Publishing) but for a beginner they can be overwhelming. They will show every species possible including a lot of rare ones, and they include anything seen across the whole of Europe. The beginner needs common species found in Britain to begin with. The RSPB do some good British birds guides and the Woodland Trust website has lots of resources to help identify trees and leaves. Some of the materials are aimed at children but that needn't be a problem. My favourites with walking groups are the Usborne Spotters Guides (covering birds, mini-beasts, pond life, wild flowers, trees and more). Usborne Books do books and sets of cards for around £5, and they are easy to use and fit in the pocket.

See *Wildlife watching* in the Activities section. It describes how to use wildlife identification as a group activity in which everyone can discuss what they are looking at. You don't need to know yourself; everyone can join in.

The FSC (Field Studies Council) not only run courses which can help you learn more about wildlife and ecology but they produce a series of laminated waterproof cards to help identification. See www.field-studies-council.org/publications/fold-out-charts.aspx

FSC AIDGAP guides are light, laminated and waterproof with good colour illustrations. See www.field-studies-council.org

The *Woodland Trust Leaf Identification Swatch Book* is small, laminated, waterproof, leaf shaped in colour and very good for putting in your pocket. It illustrates the leaf, seed and bare twig in winter. The back of each swatch gives a description, interesting facts and where the tree is likely to be found. See www.woodlandtrust.org.uk

Birdsong

The RSPB has audio clips of birds singing: *www.rspb.org.uk/wildlife/birdidentifier*

British Garden Birds had birdsong tutorials: *www.garden-birds.co.uk/information/tutorials*

The British Dragonfly Society has an app for identifying dragonflies: *www.british-dragonflies.org.uk*

The BBC also have a selection of bird calls with hints on how to identify them: *www.bbc.co.uk/radio4/science/birdsong.shtml*

Morning Earth, a North American resources website, has lots of ideas to use in the classroom, some of which can be adapted for adults: *www.morning-earth.org/LearningContents.htm*

Equipment

Binoculars: I would recommend the Pentax Papillio 8.5x21. They focus closer than any other binoculars down to 50cm (18") and are amazing for watching butterflies without disturbing them. They are light at 290g and fit in the pocket. Taking a pair on a walk means that people get to see the intricate beauty of an insect or flower. They are good for looking at birds as well.

Nets, pond dipping equipment and so on are also available from NHBS: www.nhbs.com/equipment

A x10 *hand lens* or magnifying glass is worth taking with you to look at insects, leaves and flowers.

Further Reading

Allan, S. (1997) *The Way of Water and Sprouts of Virtue*. New York: SUNY Press.

Bateson, B. (1997) *Steps Towards an Ecology of Mind*. New York: Ballantine.

Berry, B. (1988) *The Dream of the Earth*. San Francisco, CA: Sierra Club Books.

Bohm, D. and Edwards, E. (1991) *Changing Consciousness, A Dialogue in Words and Images*. New York: Harper Collins.

Brazier, D. (1995) *Zen Therapy*. London. Constable.

Chalquist, C. (2009) 'A look at the ecotherapy research evidence.' *Ecopsychology 1*, 64–74.

Fisher, C.H. (2013) *Meditation in the Wild: Buddhism's Origin in the Heart of Nature*. Winchester: Change Makers Books.

Mabey, R. (2006) *Nature Cure*. London: Pimlico.

Macy, J. (1983) *Despair and Personal Power in the Nuclear Age*. Philadelphia: New Society Publishers.

Maitland, S. (2008) *A Book of Silence*. London: Granta.

Miyazaki, Y. and Motohashi, Y. (1995) 'Forest Environment and Physical Response.' In Y. Agishi and Y. Ohtsuka (eds) *Recent Progress in Medical Balneology and Climatology*. Hokkaido: Hokkaido University.

Suzuki, S. (1999) *The Sacred Balance*. London: Bantham.

Thoreau, H.D. (1995) *Walden, or, Life in the Woods*. Dover Thrift Edition. Dover Publications. (Original work published 1854.)

Watts, W. (1992) *Tao, The Watercourse Way*. London: Arkana Books London.

Useful websites

Caught by the river: Interesting mix of writing, arts, nature and other things *http://caughtbytheriver.net*

Ecopsychology UK: A good site to keep up to date with what's going on in the UK *http://ecopsychologyuk.ning.com*

Going wild: Good UK site for kids and nature activities *www.goingwild.net*

Green exercise: Promoting research into green exercise, based at University of Essex *www.greenexercise.org*

Joanna Macy: An inspirational site describing her work and resources. Check out the interviews *www.joannamacy.net*

Nature Therapi: Danish site on ecotherapy *www.naturterapi.dk/english.html*

Nature Therapy Center: The work of Ronen Berger in Israel. His ideas and practice of nature therapy *www.naturetherapy.org*

NHS forest: Making a direct link between health and green space in the UK *www.NHSforest.org*

Open Space: University of Edinburgh research group doing interesting work *www.openspace.eca.ac.uk*

Psychology in the real world: Community-based mental health in UK. Encourages Walk and Talk, created by Guy Holmes *www.psychologyintherealworld.co.uk*

Walking for Health: Find out where your local healthy walking scheme has sessions *www.walkingforhealth. org.uk*

European Journal of Ecopsychology *http://eje.wyrdwise.com*

Wilderness Foundation: Takes people into wilderness *www.wildernessfoundation.org.uk*

Walking for Health: Find out where your local healthy walking scheme has session *www.walkingforhealth. org.uk*

References

Akhter, A., Fiedorowicz, J.G., Zhang, T., Potash, J.B. *et al.* (2013) 'Seasonal variation of manic and depressive symptoms in bipolar disorder.' *Bipolar Disorders* doi:10.1111/bdi.12072. Available at www.ncbi.nlm.nih.gov/pmc/articles/PMC3731411, accessed on 2 December 2015.

Alvarsson, J.J., Wiens, S. and Nilsson, M.E. (2010) 'Stress recovery during exposure to nature sound and environmental noise.' *International Journal of Environmental Research and Public Health 7*, 1036–1046.

Ambrose-Oji, B. (2013) *Mindfulness Practice in Woods and Forests: An Evidence Review.* Research Report for the Mersey Forest, Forest Research. Farnham: Alice Holt Lodge.

Annerstedt, M.I., Jönsson, P., Wallergård, M., Johansson, G. *et al.* (2013) 'Inducing physiological stress recovery with sounds of nature in a virtual reality forest – results from a pilot study.' *Physiology & Behavior 118*, 240–250. doi: 10.1016/j.physbeh.2013.05.023. Epub 18 May 2013. Abstract available at www.ncbi.nlm.nih.gov/pubmed/23688947, accessed on 20 September 2015.

Ashley, A., Bartlett, S., Lamb, M. and Steel, M. (1999) *Evaluation of the Thames Valley Health Walks Scheme. Participants Feedback Survey.* Oxford Brooks University Report no 9. Oxford: Oxford Brooks University.

Baines, C. (2003) *Broadleaf* No 60, Spring. Woodland Trust.

Baker, R., Holloway, J., Holtkamp, C.C.M., Larsson, A. et al. (2003) 'Effects of multi-sensory stimulation for people with dementia.' *Journal of Advanced Nursing 43*, 5, 465–477. Available at www.rima.org/web/medline_pdf/JAdvNurs_465-77.pdf, accessed on 2 February 2016.

Barton, J., Griffin, M. and Pretty, J. (2011) 'Exercise, nature and socially interactive based initiatives improve mood and self-esteem in the clinical population.' *Perspectives in Public Health.* doi: 10.1177/1757913910393862

Barton, J., Hine, R. and Pretty, J. (2009) 'The health benefits of walking in green space of high natural and heritage value.' *Journal of Integrated Environmental Sciences 6*, 4, 1–18.

Barton, J. and Pretty, J. (2010) 'What is the best dose of nature and green exercise for improving mental health? A multi-study analysis.' *Environmental Science and Technology 44*, 3947–3955.

Beethoven, L.,van (1972) *Beethoven Letters with Explanatory Notes by Dr. AC Kalisher.* New York. Dover Publications.

Bell, S.L., Phoenix, C., Lovell, R. and Wheeler, B.W. (2015) 'Seeking everyday wellbeing: the coast as a therapeutic landscape.' *Social Science and Medicine.* doi: 10.1016/j.socscimed.2015.08.011

Berger, R. (2009) *Nature Therapy Selected Articles.* Kibbutz Snir. The Nature Therapy Center. Available at www.naturetherapy.org, accessed on 26 November 2015.

Berger, R. and Lahad, M. (2013) *The Healing Forest in Post-Crisis Work with Children.* London: Jessica Kingsley Publishers.

Berger, R. and McLeod, J. (2006) 'Incorporating nature into therapy: a framework for practice.' *Journal of Systemic Therapies 25*, 2, 80–94.

Berman, M.G., Jonides, J. and Kaplan, S. (2008) 'The cognitive benefits of interacting with nature.' *Psychological Science 19*, 12,1207–1212.

Bird, W. (2007) *Natural Thinking.* Sandy: RSPB.

Bird, W. and Adams, F. (2001) 'Sonning Common health walks: a four year review.' Paper presented at Australia: Walking the 21st Century, An International Walking Conference. Perth: Western Australia. 20–22 February 2001.

Blue Mind (n.d.) www.wallacejnichols.org/467/bluemind-research.html, accessed on 30 November 2015.

Bischoff-Ferrari, H.A., Willett, W.C., Wong, J.B., Stuck, A.E. et al. (2009) 'Prevention of nonvertebral fractures with oral vitamin D and dose dependency: a meta-analysis of randomized controlled trials.' *Archives of Internal Medicine*, 169(6): 551–61.

Blyth, R.H. (1942) *Zen in English Literature and Oriental Classics*. Tokyo: Hokuseido Press.

Bossen, A. (2010) 'The importance of getting back to nature for people with dementia.' *Journal of Gerontological Nursing 36*, 2, 17–22.

Bragg, R. amd Atkins, G. (2016) *A review of nature-based interventions for mental health care*. Natural England Commissioned Reports, Number 204. London: Natural England.

Bragg, R., Wood, C. and Barton, J. (2013) *Ecominds Effects on Mental Wellbeing: An Evaluation for Mind*. London: Mind. Available at www.mind.org.uk/news-campaigns/campaigns/ecotherapy-works/, accessed on 26 November 2015.

Brewerton, T.D. (1989) 'Seasonal variation of serotonin function in humans: research and clinical implications.' *Annals of Clinical Psychiatry 1*, 3, 153–164.

Bridges, F.S, Yip, P.S.F. and Yang, K.C.T. (2005) 'Seasonal changes in suicide in the United States, 1971 to 2000.' *Perceptual and Motor Skills 100*, 920–924.

Brown, R., Ferguson, J., Laurence, M. and Lees, D. (1992) *Tracks and Signs of the Birds of Britain and Europe*. London: Christopher Helm.

Buchanan, H.C., Bird, W., Kinch, R.F.T. and Ramsbottom, R. (2000) 'The metabolic and physiological demands of brisk walking in older men and women.' Health Walks Research and Development Unit Symposium, Oxford Brookes University.

Burns, G.W. (1998) *Nature Guided Therapy Brief Integrative Strategies for Health and Well-being*. London: Taylor & Francis.

Buzzell, L. and Chalquist, C. (2009) *Ecotherapy: Healing with Nature in Mind*. San Francisco, CA: Sierra Club Books.

Capra, F. (1997) *The Web of Life*. London: Flamingo.

Carpe Diem Gardens (n.d.) Available at www.carpe-diem-gardens.co.uk, accessed on 19 November 2015.

Castree, N. (2014) *Making Sense of Nature*. Oxford: Routledge.

Centre for Mental Health (2011) *The Economic and Social Costs of Mental Health Problems in 2009/10*. London: Centre for Mental Health.

Chalfont, G. (2008) *Design for Nature in Dementia Care*. London: Jessica Kingsley Publishers.

Chief Medical Officer (2013) *Annual Report of the Chief Medical Officer 2013. Public Mental Health Priorities: Investing in the Evidence*. London: Department of Health. Available at www.gov.uk/government/uploads/system/uploads/attachment_data/file/413196/CMO_web_doc.pdf, accessed on 26 November 2015.

Chinery, M. (2012) *Insects of Britain and Western Europe*. London: Domino Guides.

Chokor, B.A. and Mene, S.A. (1992) 'An assessment of preference for landscapes in the developing world: case study of Warri, Nigeria, and environs.' *Journal of Environmental Management 34*, 237–256.

Cleland Host, J. (2013) *Meditation on Ancestors*. Available at http://humanisticpaganism.com, accessed on 5 October 2015.

Coleman, M. (2006) *Awake in the Wild: Mindfulness in Nature as a Path of Self Discovery*. Novato, CA: New World Library.

Cooper-Marcus, C. and Barnes, M. (1995) *Gardens in Healthcare Facilities: Uses, Therapeutic Benefits, and Design Recommendations.* Martinez, CA: The Center for Health Design.

Cornell, J. (2015) *Sharing Nature: Nature Awareness Activities for All Ages.* Nevada City, CA: Crystal Clarity.

Coss, R.G. (1990) 'Picture perception and patient stress: A study of anxiety reduction and postoperative stability.' Unpublished paper. Davis, CA: University of California, Davis.

Costello, C.G. (1982) 'Fears and phobias in women: a community study.' *Journal of Abnormal Psychology 91,* 280–286.

Countryside Commission (1997) *Public Attitudes to the Countryside,* CCP 481. London: Countryside Commission.

Danks, F. and Shofield, J. (2005) *Nature's Playground.* London: Frances Lincoln.

Danks, F. and Shofield, J. (2012) *The Stick Book.* London: Frances Lincoln.

Davidson, R.J., Kabat-Zinn, J., Schumacher, J., Rosenkranz, M. *et al.* (2003) 'Alterations in brain and immune function produced by mindfulness meditation.' *Psychosomatic Medicine 65,* 564–570.

Detweiler, M.B., Murphy, P.F., Myers, L.C. and Kim, K.Y. (2008) 'Does a wander garden influence inappropriate behaviors in dementia residents?' *American Journal of Alzheimer's Disease and Other Dementias 23,* 31–45.

Deudney, D. (1995) 'In Search of Gaian Politics.' In B. Taylor (ed.) *Ecological Resistance Movements: The Global Emergence of Radical and Popular Environmentalism.* Albany, NY: SUNY Press.

Devall, B. (1990) *Simple in Means Rich in Ends: Practicing Deep Ecology.* London: Green Print.

Devall, B. and Sessions, G. (1985) *Deep Ecology: Living as if Nature Mattered.* Salt Lake City, UT: Gibb Smith.

de Vries, S., Verheij, R.A., Groenewegen, P.P. and Spreeuwenberg, P. (2003) 'Natural environments – healthy environments? An exploratory analysis of the relationship between green space and health.' *Environment and Planning 35,* 1717–1731.

Donovan, G.H., Butry, D.T., Michael, Y.L., Prestemon, J.P. *et al.* (2013) 'The relationship between trees and human health: evidence from the spread of the emerald ash borer.' *American Journal of Preventive Medicine 44,* 139–145.

Drury, C. (n.d.) Available at www.chrisdrury.co.uk, accessed on 30 November 2015.

Drury, C. (1998) *Silent Spaces.* London: Thames & Hudson.

Earth First! (n.d.) Available at www.earthfirst.org.uk, accessed on 30 November 2015.

Eliot, T.S. (1968 [1942]) 'Little Gidding'. *Four Quartets.* Boston, MA: Houghton Mifflin Harcourt.

Fabrigoule, C., Letenneur, L., Dartigues, J., Zarrouk, M., Commenges, D. and Barberger-Gateau, P. (1995) 'Social and leisure activities and risk of dementia: a prospective longitudinal study.' *Journal of American Geriatrics Society 43,* 485–490.

Faculty of Public Health (2010) *The Great Outdoors: How Our Natural Health Service Uses Green Space to Improve Wellbeing. Briefing Statement.* London: Faculty of Public Health.

Faculty of Public Health and Natural England (2010) *Great Outdoors: How Our Natural Health Service Uses Green Space To Improve Wellbeing.* London: Faculty of Public Health. Available at www.fph.org.uk/uploads/bs_great_outdoors.pdf, accessed on 27 November 2015.

Flory, R., Ametepe, J. and Bowers, B. (2010) 'A randomized, placebo-controlled trial of bright light and high-density negative air ions for treatment of Seasonal Affective Disorder.' *Psychiatry Research 177,* 1–2, 101–108. Available at www.ncbi.nlm.nih.gov/pubmed/20381162, accessed on 27 November 2015.

Forestry Commission (n.d.) Available at www.forestry.gov.uk, accessed on 30 November 2015.

Francis, C. and Cooper-Marcus, C. (1991) 'Places People Take Their Problems.' In J. Urbina-Soria, P. Ortega-Andeane and R. Bechel (eds) *Proceedings of the 22nd Annual Conference of the Environmental Design Research Association.* Oklahoma City, OK: EDRA.

Fuller, R.A., Irvine, K.N., Devine-Wright, P., Warren, P.H. and Gaston, K.J. (2007) 'Psychological benefits of green space increase with biodiversity.' *Biological Letters 3*, 390–394. Available at http://depts.washington.edu/hhwb/Thm_Mental.html, accessed on 27 November 2015.

Gardens for Patients with Alzheimer's Disease (n.d.) Available at http://alzheimer-architecture.nl/wp-content/uploads/2012/04/Gardens-for-Patients-with-Alzheimer.pdf, accessed on 2 February 2016.

Gill, T. (2011) *Children and Nature: A Quasi-systemic Review of the Empirical Evidence.* London: London Sustainable Development Commission (LSDC), Greater London Authority. Available at www.londonsdc.org/documents/Children%20and%20Nature%20-%20Literature%20Review.pdf, accessed on 27 November 2015.

Gladwell, V.F., Brown, D.K., Wood, C., Sandercock, G.R. and Barton, J.L. (2013) 'The great outdoors: how a green exercise environment can benefit all.' *Extreme Physiology and Medicine 2*, 3. Available at www.extremephysiolmed.com/content/2/1/3, accessed on 1 February 2016.

Goel, N. and Etwaroo, G.R. (2006) 'Bright light, negative air ions and auditory stimuli produce rapid mood changes in a student population: a placebo-controlled study.' *Psychological Medicine 36*, 1253–1263.

Golden, R.N., Gaynes, B.N., Ekstrom, D.R., Hamer, R.M. *et al.* (2005) 'The efficacy of light therapy in the treatment of mood disorders: a review and meta-analysis of the evidence.' *American Journal of Psychiatry 162*, 656–662.

Goldsworthy, A. (n.d.) Available at www.goldsworthy.cc.gla.ac.uk and http://beta.photobucket.com/images/andy%20goldsworthy, accessed on 30 November 2015.

Goldsworthy, A. (1988) *Parkland.* Wakefield: Yorkshire Sculpture Park.

Goldsworthy, A. and Friedman, T. (1993) *Hand to Earth: Andy Goldsworthy Sculpture, 1976–1990.* New York: N.Y.H.N. Abrams.

Government Office for Science (2008) *Foresight Mental Capital and Wellbeing Project. Final Project Report – Executive Summary.* London: GoS. Available at www.gov.uk/government/uploads/system/uploads/attachment_data/file/292453/mental-capital-wellbeing-summary.pdf, accessed on 27 November 2015.

Greenspace (2011) *Blue Sky Green Space: Understanding the Contribution Parks and Green Spaces Can Make to Improving People's Lives.* London. Greenspace. www.greenflagaward.org/media/51265/green_space.pdf, accessed on 1 February 2016.

Grossman, P., Niemann, L., Schmidt, S. and Walach, H. (2004) 'Mindfulness-based stress reduction and health benefits.' *Journal of Psychosomatic Research 57*, 35–43.

Hartig, T., Evans, G.W., Jamner, L.D., Davis, D.S. and Garling, T. (2003) 'Tracking restoration in natural and urban field settings.' *Journal of Environmental Psychology 23*, 109–123.

Hartig, T., Mang, M. and Evans, G.W. (1991) 'Restorative effects of natural environment experience.' *Environment and Behaviour 23*, 3–26.

Hartig, T., Mitchell, R., de Vries, S. and Frumkin, H. (2014) 'Nature and health.' *Annual Review of Public Health 35*, 207–228. Available at www.annualreviews.org/doi/abs/10.1146/annurev-publhealth-032013-182443?journalCode=publhealth

Harvard Medical School (2012) 'Blue Light has a Dark Side.' Harvard Health Publications. Available at www.health.harvard.edu/newsletters/Harvard_Health_Letter/2012/May/blue-light-has-a-dark-side, accessed on 27 November 2015.

Heerwagen, J.H. (1990) 'The Psychological Aspects of Windows and Window Design.' In K.H. Anthony, J. Choi and B. Orland (eds) *Proceedings of the 22nd Annual Conference of the Environmental Design Research Association.* Oklahoma City, OK: EDRA.

Hine, R. (2008) 'Care farming: bringing together agriculture and health.' *ECOS 29*, 2, 42–51.

Hofmann, S.G., Sawyer, A.T., Witt, A.A. and Oh, D. (2010) 'The effect of mindfulness-based therapy on anxiety and depression: a meta-analytic review.' *Journal of Consulting and Clinical Psychology 78*, 169–183.

Holmes, G. and Evans, N. (2011) 'Walk and Talk.' Paper presented at the First International Conference on Multidimensional Aspects of Well-being, University of Central England. www.psychologyintherealworld.co.uk/resources/Holmes_and_Evans_paper_Wellbeing_conference.pdf, accessed on 1 February 2016.

Hudson W.H. *Nature in Downland* (1923) London: JM Dent & Sons.

Hughes, T. (1976) *Seasons Songs*. London: Faber.

Humpel, N., Owen, N. and Leslie, E. (2002) 'Environmental factors associated with adults' participation in physical activity: a review.' *American Journal of Preventive Medicine 22*, 188–199.

Huxley, A. (2009 [1962]) *The Island*. New York: Harper Perennial Modern Classics.

INFOM (International Society of Nature and Forest Medicine) (n.d.) Available at http://infom.org, accessed on 30 November 2015.

Isen, A.M. (1985) 'The asymmetry of happiness and sadness in effects on memory in normal college students.' *Journal of Experimental Psychology: General 114*, 388–391.

Iwama, M. (2006) *The Kawa Model: Culturally Relevant Occupational Therapy*. Edinburgh: Churchill Livingstone.

Iwama, M., Thomson, N.A. and Macdonald, R.A. (2009) 'The Kawa model: the power of culturally responsive occupational therapy.' *Disability and Rehabilitation 31*, 14, 1125–1135.

Jahncke, H., Hygge, S., Halin, N., Green, A.M. and Dimberg, K. (2011) 'Open-plan office noise: cognitive performance and restoration.' *Journal of Environmental Psychology 31*, 373–382.

Jefferies R. (1883) The Story of My Heart: *My Autobiography*. Cambridge: Green Books.

Jefferies, R. (2011[1879]) *Wild Life in a Southern County*. Wimborne Minster: Little Toller Books.

Jordan, M. (2015) *Nature and Therapy: Understanding Counselling and Psychotherapy in Outdoor Spaces*. London: Routledge.

Kabat-Zinn, J. (1994) *Whereever You Go, There You Are: Mindfulness Meditation in Everyday Life*. New York: Hyperion.

Kaczynski, A.T. and Henderson, K.A. (2007) 'Environmental correlates of physical activity: a review of evidence about parks and recreation.' *Leisure Sciences 29*, 315–354.

Kaplan, R. and Kaplan, S. (1989) *The Experience of Nature: A Psychological Perspective*. Cambridge: Cambridge University Press.

Kellert, S.R. and Wilson, E.O. (eds) (1993) *The Biophilia Hypothesis*. Washington, DC: Island Press.

Khoury, B., Lecomte, T., Fortin, G., Masse, M. *et al.* (2013) 'Mindfulness-based therapy: a comprehensive meta-analysis.' *Clinical Psychology Review 33*, 6, 763–771.

Kight, C.R. and Swaddle, J.P. (2010) 'How and why environmental noise impacts on animals and humans: an integrative and mechanistic review.' *Ecology Letters 1*–10. Available at http://jpswad.people.wm.edu/Kight%20and%20Swaddle%202011%20ELE%20proofs.pdf, accessed on 1 February 2016.

Kjellberg, A., Muhr, P. and Skoldstrom, B. (1998) 'Fatigue after work in noise: an epidemiological survey and three quasi-experimental field studies.' *Noise and Health 1*, 1.

Klatte, M., Bergstrom, K. and Lachmann, T. (2013) 'Does noise affect learning? A short review on noise effects on cognitive performance in children.' *Fronters in Psychology 4*, 578. Available at www.ncbi.nlm.nih.gov/pmc/articles/PMC3757288, accessed on 27 November 2015.

Klein, N. (2015) *This Changes Everything: Capitalism vs the Climate*. New York: Simon & Schuster.

Krauss, B. (2012) *The Great Animal Orchestra*. Boston, MA: Little, Brown Company.

Krogh, J., Nordentoft, M., Sterne, J.A. and Lawlor, D.A. (2011) 'The effect of exercise in clinically depressed adults: systematic review and meta-analysis of randomized controlled trials.' *Journal of Clinical Psychiatry 72*, 4, 529–538.

Kuo, F.E., Sullivan, W.C., Coley, R.L. and Brunson, L. (1998) 'Fertile ground for community: inner-city neighbourhood common spaces.' *American Journal of Community Psychology 26*, 823–851.

LaChapelle, D. (1988) *Sacred Land, Sacred Sex: Rapture of the Deep*. Durango, CO: Kivaki Press.

Leakey, M. (1980) 'Early Man, Environment and Tools.' In L.-K. Königsson (ed.) *Current Argument on Early Man*. New York: Pergamon Press.

Learning Through Landscapes (2003) Available at www.ltl.org.uk, accessed on 30 November 2015.

Lessons from Berlin (2011) *Lessons from Berlin's School Playgrounds*. Alloa, Scotland: Grounds for Learning. Available at www.ltl.org.uk/pdf/lessons-from-Berlin1300362288.pdf, accessed on 27 November 2015.

Li, Q., Morimoto, K., Nakadai, A., Inagaki, H. *et al.* (2007) 'Forest bathing enhances human natural killer activity and expression of anti-cancer proteins.' *International Journal of Immunopathology and Pharmacology 20*, 2 (Suppl 2), 3–8. Available at www.ncbi.nlm.nih.gov/pubmed/17903349, accessed on 2 December 2015.

Li, Q., Otsuka, T., Kobayashi, M., Wakayama, Y. *et al.* (2011) 'Acute effects of walking in forest environments on cardiovascular and metabolic parameters.' *European Journal of Applied Physiology 111*, 2845–2853.

Listening Earth (n.d.) Available at www.listeningearth.com, accessed 30 November 2015.

Lohr, V.I., Pearson-Mims, C.H. and Goodwin, G.K. (1996) 'Interior plants may improve worker productivity and reduce stress in a windowless environment.' *Journal of Environmental Horticulture 14*, 97–100. Available at www.hriresearch.org/docs/publications/JEH/JEH_1996/JEH_1996_14_2/JEH%2014-2-97-100.pdf, accessed on 2 February 2016.

Louv, R. (2005) *Last Child in the Woods: Saving Our Children from Nature-Deficit Disorder*. Chapel Hill, NC: Algonquin Books.

Lundén, O. and Ulrich, R. (1990) 'Effects of nature and abstract pictures on patients recovering from open heart surgery.' Paper presented at the International Congress of Behavioural Medicine, 27–30 June, Uppsala, Sweden.

Mabey, R. (1972) *Food for Free*. Glasgow: Fontana/Collins.

Macfarlane, R. (2007) *The Wild Places*. London: Granta Books.

Macy, J. (1983) *Despair and Personal Power in the Nuclear Age*. Philadelphia, PA: New Society Publishers.

Macy, J. (1991) *World as Lover, World as Self*. Berkley, CA: Parallax Press.

Macy, J. and Young Brown, M. (1988) *Coming Back to Life*. Gabriola Island, Canada: New Society Publishers.

Maller, C., Townsend, M., St Leger, L., Henderson-Wilson, C., Pryor, A., Prosser, L. and Moore, M. (2008) *Healthy Parks Healthy People: The Health Benefits of Contact with Nature in a Park Context*, 2nd edn. Melbourne: Deakin University. Available at www.academia.edu/1782291/Healthy_Parks_Healthy_People_The_health_benefits_of_contact_with_nature_in_a_park_context, accessed on 1 February 2016.

Martsolf, D.S. and Mickley, J.R. (1998) The concept of spirituality in nursing theories: differing world-views and extent of focus. *Journal of Advanced Nursing 27*, 2, 294–303.

Marvell, A. (1621–1678) *The Garden*.

McGeeney, A. (n.d.) Available at www.andymcgeeney.com, accessed on 30 November 2015.

McGeeney, A. and Jeffery, S. (2011) 'The perceived multiple benefits of ecotherapy for mental health service users.' Research paper by Andy McGeeney and Dr Sophie Jeffery. Available at www.andymcgeeney.com/read-more-by-andy, accessed on 1 February 2016.

McNair, D. (2012) 'Sunlight and Daylight' In J, Gilliard and M. Marshall (eds) *Transforming the Quality of Life for People with Dementia Through Contact with the Natural World: Fresh Air on My Face.* London: Jessica Kingsley Publishers.

McNair, D., Cunningham, C., Pollock, R. and McGuire, B. (2010) *Light and Lighting Design for People with Dementia.* Stirling: The Dementia Services Development Centre, University of Sterling.

McNally, R.J. (1987) 'Preparedness and phobias, a review.' *Psychological Bulletin 101*, 283–303.

Mellersh, H.E.L. (1995) *Chronology of World History, Compact Edition.* Oxford: Oxford University Press.

Mental Health Foundation (n.d.) Available at www.mentalhealth.org.uk/help-information/mental-health-statistics, accessed on 30 November 2015.

Mental Health Foundation (2009) *Moving On Up.* London: Mental Health Foundation.

Mersch, P.P.A., Middendorp, H.M., Bouhuys, A.L., Beersma, D.G.M. and van den Hoofdakker, R.H. (1999) 'Seasonal affective disorder and latitude: a review of the literature.' *Journal of Affective Disorders*, 53: 35–48.

Midgley, M.B. (1979/2002) *Beast and Man: The Roots of Human Nature.* London: Routledge.

Mind (n.d.a) Available at www.mind.org.uk, accessed on 30 November 2015.

Mind (n.d.b) Available at www.mind.org.uk/news-campaigns/campaigns/time-to-change, accessed on 30 November 2015.

Mind (2007) *Ecotherapy: The Green Agenda for Mental Health.* London: Mind. Available at www.mind.org.uk/media/273470/ecotherapy.pdf, accessed 27 November 2015.

Mitchell, R. and Popham, F. (2008) 'Effect of exposure to natural environment on health inequalities: an observational population study.' *The Lancet 372*, 9650, 1665–1660.

Moncrieff, J. and Kirsch, I. (2005) 'Efficacy of antidepressants in adults.' *British Medical Journal 331*, 155–159.

Mooney, P. and Nicell, P.L. (1992) 'The importance of exterior environment for Alzheimer's residents: effective care and risk management.' *Health Care Management Forum 5*, 2, 23–29.

Morita, E., Fukuda, S., Nagano, J., Hamajima, N. *et al.* (2007) 'Psychological effects of forest environments on healthy adults: Shinrin-yoku (forest-air bathing, walking) as a possible method of stress reduction.' *Public Health 121*, 54–63.

Moss, S. (2013) *Natural Childhood.* Rotherham: National Trust. Available at www.nationaltrust.org.uk/documents/download-the-natural-childhood-report.pdf, accessed on 27 November 2015.

Muir, J. (2001 [1938]) 'John of the Mountains.' In M.L.Wolfe and E.W. Teale (eds) *The Wilderness World of John Muir.* Boston, MA: Houghton Mifflin.

Muir, M. (2015[1894]) *The Mountains of California.* Charleston, SC: Bibliolife.

Naess, A. (1973) 'The shallow and the deep: long-range ecology movement.' *Inquiry 16*, 95–100.

Naess A. (2008) T*he Ecology of Wisdom: Writings by Arnie Naess*, edited by A. Drengson and B. Devall. Berkeley, CA: Counterpoint.

Nakamura, R. and Fujii, E. (1990) 'Studies of the characteristics of the electroencephalogram when observing potted plants: *Pelargonium hortorum* "Sprinter Red" and *Begonia evansiana*.' *Technical Bulletin of the Faculty of Horticulture of Chiba University 43*, 177–183. (In Japanese with English summary.)

Natural England (2009) *Our Natural Health Service: The Role of the Natural Environment in Maintaining Healthy Lives.* London: Natural England.

New Economics Foundation (2008) Available at www.neweconomics.org, accessed on 30 November 2015.

NEF (New Economics Foundation) (2008) *Five Ways to Wellbeing: A Report Presented to the Foresight Project on Communicating the Evidence Base for Improving People's Wellbeing.* London: NEF.

NEF (2013) Available at www.neweconomics.org/projects/five-ways-well-being.nef, accessed on 30 November 2015.

NHS (1999) *A National Service Framework for Mental Health.* London: NHS. Available at www.gov.uk/government/uploads/system/uploads/attachment_data/file/198051/National_Service_Framework_for_Mental_Health.pdf, accessed on 27 November 2015.

NHS (2011) *No Health without Mental Health: A Cross-government Outcomes Strategy* London: NHS. Available at www.gov.uk/government/uploads/system/uploads/attachment_data/file/138253/dh_124058.pdf, accessed on 27 November 2015.

NICE (National Institute for Clinical Excellence) (2008) *NICE Guidance on Physical Activity and the Environment.* Available at www.nice.org.uk/guidance/index.jsp?action=byID&o=11917, accessed on 27 November 2015.

NICE (2010) *Depression in Adults: Full Guidance.* NICE Guidelines CG90. Available at www.nice.org.uk/guidance/CG90, accessed on 27 November 2015.

O'Brien, E.A. and Murray, R. (2006) *A Marvellous Opportunity for Children to Learn: A Participatory Evaluation of Forest School in England and Wales.* Alice Holt Lodge, Farnham: Forest Research.

Olsen, L.-H., Sunesen, J. and Pedersen, B.V. (2001) *Small Woodland Creatures.* Oxford: Oxford University Press.

Orians, G.H. (1980) 'Habitat selection: general theory and applications to human behaviour.' In J.S. Lockard (ed.) *The Evolution of Human Social Behaviour.* New York: Elsevier North-Holland.

Orians, G.H. (1986) ' Ecological and Evolutionary Approach to Landscape Aesthetics.' In E.C. Penning-Rowsell and D. Lowenthal (eds) *Meanings and Values in Landscape.* London: Allen & Unwin.

Owen, J. (2010) *Wildlife of a Garden: A Thirty-Year Study.* Wisley: RHS.

Oyane, N.M., Bjelland, I., Pallesen, S., Holsten, F. and Bjorvatn, B. (2008) 'Seasonality is associated with anxiety and depression: the Hordaland health study.' *Journal of Affective Disorders 105*, 147–155. Available at www.ncbi.nlm.nih.gov/pubmed/17573120, accessed on 2 December 2015.

Park, B.-J., Furuya, K., Kasetani, T., Takayama, N., Kagawa, T. and Miyazaki, Y.M. (2011) 'Relationship between psychological responses and physical environments in forest settings.' *Landscape and Urban Planning 102*, 1, 24–32.

Patrick, R.P. and Ames, B.N. (2014) 'Vitamin D hormone regulates serotonin synthesis. Part 1: relevance for autism.' *FASEB Journal* 10.1096/fj.13-246546 *fj.13-246546.*

Pendse, B., Westrin, A. and Engström, G. (1999) 'Temperament traits in seasonal affective disorder, suicide attempters with non-seasonal major depression and healthy controls.' *Journal of Affective Disorders 54*, 55–65.

Perez, V., Alexander, D.D. and Bailey, W.H. (2013) 'Air ions and mood outcomes: a review and meta-analysis.' *BMC Psychiatry 13*, 29. doi: 10.1186/1471-244X-13-29. Available at http://bmcpsychiatry.biomedcentral.com/articles/10.1186/1471-244X-13-29, accessed on 1 February 2016.

Polak, E.H. and Provasi, J. (1992) 'Odor sensitivity to geosmin enantiomers'. *Chemical Senses 17*, 23. doi:10.1093/chemse/17.1.23.

Potkin, S.G., Zetin, M., Stamenkovic, V., Kripke, D. and Bunney, W.E. (1986) 'Seasonal affective disorder: prevalence varies with latitude climate.' *Clinical Neuropharmacol*, 9: 181–3.

Pretty, J., Angus, C., Bain, M., Barton, J. *et al.* (2009) *Nature, Childhood, Health and Life Pathways.* Interdisciplinary Centre for Environment and Society Occasional Paper 2009-02. Colchester: University of Essex.

Pretty, J., Griffin, M. and Sellens, M. (2003a) 'Is nature good for you?' *ECOS 24*, 3/4, 2–9.

Pretty, J., Griffin, M., Sellens, M. and Pretty, C. (2003b) *Green Exercise: Complementary Roles of Nature, Exercise and Diet in Physical and Emotional Well being and Implications for Public Health Policy.* Colchester: University of Essex.

Pretty, J., Hine, R. and Peacock, J. (2006) 'Green exercise: the benefits of activities in green places.' *Biologist 53*, 143–148.

Pretty, J., Peacock, J., Sellens, M. and Griffin, M. (2005) 'The mental and physical outcomes of green exercise.' *International Journal of Environmental Health Research 15*, 5, 319–337.

Prow, T. (1999) *The Power of Trees*. Available at http://lhhl.illinois.edu/media/thepoweroftrees.htm, accessed on 27 November 2015.

Quiller-Couch A. (1971) *The Oxford Book of Victorian Verse*. Oxford: Clarendon Press.

Rappe, E. and Topo, P. (2007) 'Contact with Outdoors Greenery can Support Competence among People with Dementia.' In S. Rodiek and B. Schwartz (eds) *Outdoor Environments for People with Dementia*. London: Routledge.

Ratcliffe, E., Gatersleben, B. and Sowden, P.T. (2013) 'Bird sounds and their contributions to perceived attention restoration and stress recovery.' *Journal of Environmental Psychology 36*, 221e228.

Robertson, R., Robertson, A.R., Jepson, R. and Maxwell, M. (2012) 'Walking for depression or depressive symptoms: a systematic review and meta-analysis.' *Mental Health and Physical Activity 5*, 1, 66–75.

Roe, J. and Aspinall, P. (2011) 'The restorative benefits of walking in urban and rural settings in adults with good and poor mental health.' *Health and Place 17*, 103–113.

Rohde D.L.T., Olson S. and Chang J.T. (2004) *Modelling the recent common ancestry of all living humans.* Nature 431, 562–566. doi:10.1038/nature02842

Rootless Garden (n.d.) Available at www.rootlessgarden.org, accessed on 30 November 2015.

Rosenthal, N.E., Sack, D.A., Gillin, J.C., Lewy, A.J. *et al.* (1984) 'Seasonal affective disorder: a description of the syndrome and preliminary findings with light therapy.' *Archives of General Psychiatry 41*, 72–80.

Roszak, T., Gomes, M.E. and Kanner, A.D. (1995) *Ecopsychology: Restoring the Earth and Healing the Mind.* San Francisco, CA: Sierra Club Books.

Royal Society of Chemistry (n.d.) 'Chemistry in its element: compounds – Geosmin.' Available at www.rsc.org/chemistryworld/podcast/CIIEcompounds/transcripts/geosmin.asp, accessed on 30 November 2015.

Ryan, R.M., Weinstein, N., Bernstein, J., Warren Brown, K., Mistretta, L. and Gagne, M. (2010) 'Vitalizing effects of being outdoors and in nature.' *Journal of Environmental Psychology 30*, 159–168.

Sansone, R.A. and Sansone, L.A. (2013) 'Sunshine, serotonin, and skin: a partial explanation for seasonal patterns in psychopathology?' *Innovative Clinical Neuroscience 10*, 7–8, 20–24.

Schroeder, H.W. (1986) 'Psychological Value of Urban Trees: Measurement, Meaning, and Imagination.' In *Proceedings of the Third National Urban Forest Conference*. Washington: American Forestry Association.

Seed, J., Macy, J., Fleming, P. and Naess, A. (1988) *Thinking Like a Mountain*. Philadelphia, PA: New Society Publishers.

Sempik, J., Aldridge, J. and Becker, S. (2005) *Health, Well-being & Social Inclusion: Therapeutic Horticulture in the UK*. Bristol: Policy Press.

Shackell, A. and Walter, R. (2012) *Greenspace Design for Health and Well-being*. Forestry Commission Practice Guide. Edinburgh: Forestry Commission.

Shepard, P. (1998) *Coming Home to the Pleistocene*. Washington, DC: Island Press.

Shepard, P. and McKinley, D. (eds) (1969) *Subversive Science: Essays Towards an Ecology of Man.* Boston, MA: Houghton Mifflin.

Shilling, R. Available at www.richardshilling.co.uk and www.landartforkids.com

Shin, W.S. (2007) 'The influence of forest view through a window on job satisfaction and job stress.' *Scandinavian Journal of Forest Research 22*, 3, 248–253.

Shin, Y.-K., Kim, D.J., Jung-Choi, K., Son, Y.-J. *et al.* (2013) 'Differences of psychological effects between meditative and athletic walking in a forest and gymnasium.' *Scandinavian Journal of Forest Research 28*, 64–72.

Shonin, E., Van Gordon, W. and Griffiths, M.D. (2015) 'Mindfulness in psychology – breath of fresh air?' *The Psychologist 28*, 1, 28–31.

Siddons-Hegginworth, I. (2009) *Environmental Arts Therapy and the Tree of Life.* Exeter: Spirit's Rest.

Silkin, L. (1949) *Hansard, Column 1493. 2nd Reading of the National Parks and Access to the Countryside Bill.* London: HMSO.

Society of Forest Medicine (2014) Available at http://forest-medicine.com/page11.html, accessed on 30 November 2015.

Snyder, G. (1990) *The Practice of the Wild: Essays by Gary Snyder.* New York: HarperCollins.

Snyder, G. (1993) *Turtle Island.* Boston, MA: Shambhala.

Suda, R., Yamaguchi, M., Hatakeyama, E., Kikuchi, T., Miyazaki, Y. and Sato, M. (2001) 'Effect of visual stimulation (I): in the case of good correlation between sensory evaluation and physiological response.' *Journal of Physiological Anthropology and Applied Human Science 20*, 303.

Swinton, J. (2001) *Spirituality and Mental Health Care: Rediscovering a 'Forgotten' Dimension.* London: Jessica Kingsley Publishers.

Tabbush, P. and O'Brien, L. (2003) *Health and Well being: Trees, Woodlands and Natural Aspects.* Bristol: Forest Research, Forestry Commission.

Takano, T., Nakamura, K. and Watanabe, M. (2002) 'Urban residential environments and senior citizens' longevity in megacity areas: the importance of walkable green spaces.' *Journal of Epidemiology and Community Health 56*, 913–918.

Taylor, B. (ed.) (1995) *Ecological Resistance Movements: The Global Emergence of Radical and Popular Environmentalism.* Albany, NY: SUNY Press.

Taylor, B. (2000) 'Deep Ecology and its Social Philosophy: A Critique.' In E. Katz, A. Light and D. Rothenberg (eds) *Beneath the Surface: Critical Essays in the Philosophy of Deep Ecology.* Cambridge: MIT Press.

Terma (1992) *The Box: Remebering the Gift.* Santa Fe: Terma Foundation.

Thoreau, H.D. (1991) in R.W. Emerson R.W. and H.D. Thoreau, *Nature and Walking.* Boston, MA: Beacon Press. (Original work published 1862)

Thrive (n.d.) Available at www.thrive.org.uk, accessed on 30 November 2015.

Tsunetsugu, Y., Park, B.J. and Miyazaki, Y. (2010) 'Trends in research related to "Shinrin-yoku" (taking in the forest atmosphere or forest bathing) in Japan.' *Environmental Health Preventive Medicine 15*, 27–37. Available at www.ncbi.nlm.nih.gov/pmc/articles/PMC2793347, accessed on 27 November 2015.

Tufnell, M. and Crickmay, C. (2004) *A Widening Field: Journeys in Body and Imagination.* Alton: Dance Books.

Udo, N. (n.d.) Available at www.morning-earth.org/ARTISTNATURALISTS/AN_Nils_Udo.html, accessed on 30 November 2015.

Ulrich, R.S. (1981) 'Natural versus urban scenes: some physiological effects.' *Environment and Behaviour 13*, 523–556.

Ulrich, R.S. (1984) 'View through a window may influence recovery from surgery.' *Science 224*, 420–421.

Ulrich, R.S. (1986) *Effects of Hospital Environments on Patient Well-Being.* Research Report 9(55). Trondheim: Department of Psychiatry and Behavioural Medicine, University of Trondheim.

Ulrich, R S. (1991) 'Effects of health facility interior design on wellness: theory and recent scientific research.' *Journal of Health Care Design 3,* 97 109.

Ulrich, R.S. (1993) 'Biophilia, Biophobia and Natural Landscapes.' In S.R. Kellert and E.O. Wilson (eds) *The Biophilia Hypothesis.* Washington, DC: Island Press.

Ulrich, R.S. (1999) 'Effects of Gardens on Health Outcomes: Theory and Research.' In C. Cooper-Marcus and M. Barnes (eds) *Healing Gardens: Therapeutic Benefits and Design Recommendations.* New York: John Wiley.

Ulrich, R.S. (2002) 'Health Benefits of Gardens in Hospitals.' Paper for conference, Plants for People. International Exhibition Floriade 2002.

Ulrich, R.S. and Addoms, D. (1981) 'Psychological and recreational benefits of a neighbouring park.' *Journal of Leisure Research 13,* 42–65.

Ulrich, R.S., Simon, R.F., Losito, B.D., Fiorito, E., Miles, M.A. and Zelson, M. (1992) 'Stress recovery during exposure to natural and urban environments.' *Journal of Environmental Psychology 11,* 201–230.

van den Berg, A.E., Hartig, T. and Staats, H. (2007) 'Preference for nature in urbanized societies: stress, restoration, and the pursuit of sustainability.' *Journal of Social Issues 63,* 79–96.

Vardakoulias, O. (2013) *The Economic Benefits of Ecominds: A Case Study Approach.* London: NEF Consulting.

Viola, A.U., James, L.M., Schlangen, L.J. and Dijk, D.J. (2008) 'Blue-enriched white light in the workplace improves self-reported alertness, performance and sleep quality.' *Scandinavian Journal of Work, Environment and Health 34,* 4, 297–306.

Wallin, N.L. (1991) *Biomusicology: Neurophysiological, Neuropsychological and Evolutionary Perspectives on the Origins and Purposes of Music.* Stuyvesant, NY: Pendragon Press.

Wheeler, B.W., White, M., Stahl-Timmins, W. and Depledge, M.H. (2012) 'Does living by the coast improve health and wellbeing?' *Health and Place 18,* 5, 1198–1201.

White, M.P., Pahl, S., Ashbullby, K., Herbert, S. and Depledge, M.H. (2013a) 'Feelings of restoration from recent nature visits.' *Journal of Environmental Psychology 35,* 40–51.

White, M.P., Alcock, A., Wheeler, B.W. and Depledge, M.H. (2013b) 'Coastal proximity, health and well-being: results from a longitudinal panel survey.' *Health and Place 23,* 97–103.

WHO (World Health Organization) (2011) *Burden of Disease from Environmental Noise.* Copenhagen: WHO Regional Office for Europe.

Wilderness Foundation (n.d.) Available at www.wildernessfoundation.org.uk, accessed on 30 November 2015.

Williams, F. (2012) Available at www.outsideonline.com/fitness/wellness/Take-Two-Hours-of-Pine-Forest-and-Call-Me-in-the-Morning.html, accessed on 30 November 2015.

Wilson, N.W., Ross, M.K., Lafferty, K. and Jones, R. (2008) 'A review of ecotherapy as an adjunct form of treatment for those who use mental health services.' *Journal of Public Mental Health 7,* 23–35.

Wordsworth, W. (1959 [1798]) 'Composed a Few Miles above Tintern Abbey.' In T. Hutchinson (ed.) *The Poetical Works of Wordsworth.* London: Oxford University Press.

Wordsworth, W. (1959 [1807]) 'Sonnet XXXIII.' In T. Hutchinson (ed.) *The Poetical Works of Wordsworth.* London: Oxford University Press.

Yerrell, P. (2008) *National Evaluation of BTCV's Green Gym.* Oxford: Oxford Brooks University.

Zeisel, J. (2005) 'Treatment Effects of Healing Gardens for Alzheimers: A Difficult Thing to Prove.' Edinburgh Garden Paper. University of Salford. Available at www.healinglandscapes.org/pdf-library/Zeisel%20Treatment%20Effects.pdf, accessed on 27 November 2015.

Subject Index

Author Index